MAKING
TAROT
MAGIC

MAKING TAROT MAGIC

Rituals and Remedies to Transform Readings into Action

BRIANA SAUSSY

Foreword by Theresa Reed

Weiser Books

This edition first published in 2025 by Weiser Books, an imprint of
Red Wheel/Weiser, LLC
With offices at:
65 Parker Street, Suite 7
Newburyport, MA 01950
www.redwheelweiser.com

ISBN: 978-1-57863-876-5
Library of Congress Cataloging-in-Publication Data
Names: Saussy, Briana author | Reed, Theresa (Tarot reader) writer of foreword
Title: Making tarot magic : rituals and remedies to transform readings into action / Briana Saussy ; foreword by Theresa Reed.
Description: Newburyport, MA : Weiser Books, 2025. | Summary: "Many times, people walk away from a tarot reading thinking, "Now what? Is this it?" What can they do to improve their situation? This book provides the answers. In various traditions around the world, divination is not a stopping point. It's the beginning. Tarot has been used for centuries not only as a divination tool but also as a magical tool. This book teaches you how to tune in, interpret an issue, and find the remedy"—Provided by publisher.
Identifiers: LCCN 2025024021 | ISBN 9781578638765 trade paperback | ISBN 9781633413689 ebook
Subjects: LCSH: Tarot | Magic | BISAC: BODY, MIND & SPIRIT / Divination / Tarot | BODY, MIND & SPIRIT / Occultism
Classification: LCC BF1879.T2 S335 2025 | DDC 133.3/2424—dc23/eng/20250916
LC record available at https://lccn.loc.gov/2025024021

Cover design by Sky Peck Design
Interior tarot card images from *The Weiser Tarot*
© Red Wheel/Weiser. All rights reserved
Interior by Michele Quinn
Typeset in Adobe Jenson Pro

Printed in the United States of America
IBI
10 9 8 7 6 5 4 3 2 1

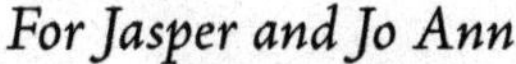

For Jasper and Jo Ann

Contents

Foreword

I'll never forget the first time I got a tarot reading that scared me a little. At the time, I was in a vulnerable position and confused about my next big move. The reader didn't mince words: she said I was about to make an epic mistake. When I inquired about how to avoid this, she shrugged. I left feeling disempowered. Worse yet, shortly after that reading, I made a stupid decision which caused me a lot of unnecessary drama. The reader was right . . . and my life felt like it was a series of wrong turns.

Many years later, I received another reading during a tumultuous time. (Isn't that always when we seek a tarot reading?) This reader was different. She suggested I use a little magic to protect my energy until the situation died down. I had been practicing magic for a long time but never thought about using it in tandem with a tarot reading. I took her advice, and sure enough, the trouble was minimized!

That reader was Briana Saussy.

One of the things you'll often hear me say is that tarot is not a passive act. A reading can reveal the future, but it's never set in stone. Instead, the future is malleable—subject to change based on decisions or actions taken.

Even so, many people view it as a passive experience. "Tell me my future," they'll say, hoping you'll see the outcome they desire. But sometimes, the cards do not present a rosy picture. In those situations, the querent may feel stuck with the prediction. That leads to helplessness and, in some cases, creates a victim mentality.

Tarot should empower, not entrap.

A good reading pinpoints the issue and provides pertinent information so the querent understands the problem they are facing. A great reader, however, finds ways to help the querent take the wheel. This might come through commonsense guidance, additional tarot spreads for clarification, or magic.

Magic is a means to shift energy and create real change. After all, *everything* is made of energy. So why not stack the odds in your favor or lessen the chances of disaster? Rituals can help harness your power so you're no longer at the mercy of fate but squarely in the driver's seat.

Ancient practitioners understood this. In many traditions around the world, diviners tossed coins, bones, shells, or cards to diagnose the issues and prescribe magical treatments. Sometimes that involved complicated ceremonies. Other times, the "prescription" might be simple practices the querent could do at home. These rituals are still practiced around the world.

Unfortunately, many folks in the Western world have forgotten these practices—or, like me, were never given these tools. *Making Tarot Magic: Rituals and Remedies to Transform Readings into Action* is a practical, accessible guide for anyone who wants to divine their future and transform it. Briana knows how to *bend* the future rather than just accept whatever fate dishes out.

In the years I've known her, I've had the privilege to work side by side on many projects. She has taught me a lot about magic, and that knowledge has helped me through dark times. Recently, I leaned on her again when a situation seemed to be spinning out of control. Briana pulled a few cards, spotted the problem, and gave me a honey jar recipe. Once again, the universe seemed to offer me a gentle way out.

Briana Saussy is wise beyond her years. She is a seer, scholar, diviner, trusted friend, and skilled magician—an enlightened sage with ancient knowledge for modern times.

Making Tarot Magic goes beyond tarot basics. It bridges divination with action, offering magical ways to work with whatever the cards reveal. Instead of feeling like life is happening *to* you, this book helps you make life happen *for* you.

This book is divided into sections based on typical issues that might come up in a tarot reading—love, money, healing, and more. What's going on in your life? Go to that chapter, lay out your cards, interpret the meanings . . . and apply the suggested magical techniques. That might mean invocations, sachets, spiritual baths, or sacred vessels. Briana breaks it down so even newbie practitioners can easily follow the instructions.

Seasoned tarot readers and Sacred Artists will find much to love here as well. Instead of letting your clients walk away with that feeling of "now what?" you can share magical practices to help them take command of their lives.

Whether you're a longtime tarot reader and magician or just mystically curious, *Making Tarot Magic* is for anyone who wants to work with tarot in a deeper, proactive way.

Remember: tarot and magic are not about "fixing" the future. They're about cocreating it, about shaping your own destiny. Let Briana's warm guidance light the way as you turn the pages and start your journey.

The tarot cards tell the story, but magic can help you find your happy ending.

—Theresa Reed, *The Cards You're Dealt: How to Deal When Life Gets Real: A Tarot Guidebook*

Introduction

Is It Going to Be OK?

THERE IS SIGHT AND THERE is vision, and they are not the same thing. Perhaps this is why the greatest seers were physically blind. Lack of physical sight requires a necessary shift in perspective, what those who have normal vision assume to be simple and straightforward is not so for the individual who is blind. Those lacking physical sight are required to open to their surroundings and work with their other senses in a deep way. They must bring their full attention to whatever it is that they are doing no matter how simple or easy it may seem. Assumptions can be the difference between safety and harm, and nothing can be taken for granted. Those who practice the Sacred Art of divination would do well to learn at the feet of those ancient blind seers, for many of those qualities also apply to divining for ourselves or others: avoiding assumptions, refusing to take things for granted, paying full attention, and calling upon all our senses in order to truly understand whatever it is we are reading on. It's employing not just our sight, but our vision.

Typically, when people seek out divination, be it a tarot reading, astrological analysis, rune or bone throwing, scrying, or what have you, they have tried the more "normal" approaches first. They have spoken with teachers and mentors, lawyers and financial advisors, doctors and therapists. In many cases those specialists have assisted the individual in their own ways, but there is still something missing—a lingering question—and that is what brings them to my door. Diviners like me are the last, not first, line of help, support, and service. Often by the time someone gets to a session with me, they are worried, anxious, afraid, and have one spoken and one unspoken question.

The spoken question is: *Will it, will I, be OK?*

The unspoken question is: *How? How will it be OK? How will I be OK?*

Divination, when performed sincerely and ethically, is concerned with answering both. Divination is a Sacred Art, and like the best art, one of its primary gifts is to give us perspective, to shift us from a place of sight into a place of vision, to help us see possibilities and choices that were obscured only moments before. Where before there was only fate, after a good reading there should be freedom.

An honest reader knows that in some cases we cannot answer the first question—*will it, will I, be OK?*—until we answer the second. This is why divination, practical actions, and magic have gone hand in hand throughout time and culture. Whatever divination method you work with, fundamentally you are telling a story: the stories may be written in cards or numbers or bones or crystals ... it doesn't matter. The divination is the *telling* of a story and embedded in that story is the answer to how. *How does it get better? How do I gain success? How do I find safety? How?* By taking smart action. By transforming the things that are hard into the things that are sacred. By making magic.

Once upon a time, diviners knew this. Magic and divination were Sacred Arts that went hand in hand. A tarot reading told you a story ... *and* told you what you needed to do to change the story, to give it a better ending, to create more spice, adventure, and depth. As time progressed, the Sacred Arts became the scandalous and superstitious arts, and our traditions were fractured, fragmented, lost ... for a little while. But nothing that powerful can remain lost long, and this book is a small effort in restoring this aspect of divination, calling back the magic into these practices. *How will it be OK? What do I need to do?* Let's look at the cards, the bones, the stones ... they will tell us. All it requires is some basic knowledge and, of course, your own unique, one-of-a-kind vision.

◆ *Chapter One* ◆

Tarot and Magic Basics

Welcome!

Welcome to a new/old way of engaging with the tarot that can change your life for the better. *Making Tarot Magic* is an approach to tarot reading designed to teach you how to give or receive a tarot reading and then be able to answer the question *Now what?* After you've read the cards for your client, friend, or family member, what can they actually do to improve their situation? Or now that you have had your cards read or read them for yourself, what can you do to improve your situation? Answering those questions inspired this entire book!

Making Tarot Magic focuses on the eight most common life situations—or *conditions*, to use some folk magic parlance—I encounter when I read for my clients. They are:

1. Love, marriage, romance, and reconciliation
2. Personal prosperity, wealth, and abundance
3. Business prosperity and career success
4. Healing
5. Legal issues and court case success
6. Fertility, pregnancy, and the work of manifesting
7. Baneful work
8. Safeguarding vital energy and opening to divine empowerment and blessing

The Format

You will find that each chapter is dedicated to a single magical condition. I have broken up the chapters dealing with money and prosperity into personal and professional because they call for somewhat different approaches. In each chapter every tarot card, from the Fool to the Ten of Coins, has an interpretation through the lens of and with respect to these magical conditions.

In the case of the Major Arcana and Court cards these interpretations are followed by two subheadings: *Magical Techniques* and *Intentions*. Magical techniques are just that: what types of magical work would be best suited to a given the card's presence and meaning in a reading. Intentions provide guidelines for what attitude or spirit you may want to infuse your work with in order to produce the best result. Once we get into the pip cards, all magical techniques may be appropriate, depending on the elemental association of the numbered card.

Because the tarot cards will be referenced frequently throughout each section of the book, we're provided all tarot imagery up front for easy reference. On pages 6–7 you'll find the twenty-two Major Arcana images; on pages 8–11 you'll find pips one through 10 for each suit; and on page 12 you'll find the court cards (Pages, Knights, Queens, Kings) for each suit. You'll want to bookmark these pages since you'll no doubt be visiting them often to visualize the tarot imagery each magical working deals with.

Tarot Basics

Working the Cards

A tarot deck is not an oracle deck or a playing card deck. The word *taro* is short for the Italian word *tarocco*. Tarot cards were first documented in the fourteenth-century Italy, where the evidence suggests they were used in games and *not* for divination purposes. Of course, there are those who believe that the tarot is much, much older and has been primarily worked with as a system for spiritual enlightenment as well as prophecy. There is also one theory that suggests that because games of chance already dealt with themes like fate and destiny, it was a short and easy step to begin employing tarot cards to tackle questions with those themes.

Structure of the Tarot

A tarot deck consists of seventy-eight cards. These cards may be divided into two or three categories, which are: the Major Arcana and the Minor Arcana *or* the Major Arcana, Court/Face cards, and the pips or numbered cards.

The **Major Arcana** includes well-known cards like the Moon, the Sun, and the Lovers. These cards represent large, universal, archetypal themes in someone's life. There are twenty-two cards in the Major Arcana starting with card 0—The Fool—and ending with card 21—The World. The word *arcana* means "teaching" so the Major Arcana are the cards that deliver big, universal lessons for each of us.

The **Minor Arcana** refers to the rest of the cards in a tarot deck, which can be further divided into Face/Court cards and pip or number cards:

The **Court/Face** cards take their name from the oldest decks wherein they, along with the Major Arcana, were the only cards with actual human figures on them. The Kings, Queens, Knights, and Pages of each suit fall into this category. In some decks the Knights are referred to as Sons and the Pages are referred to as Daughters.

The **pip** cards are the numbered cards 1 (Ace) through 10.

In today's market there are many, many different types of tarot decks, but the industry standard is the Rider-Waite-Smith (RWS) deck. This deck was published between 1909 and 1910 by the Rider Game publishing company. The design of the deck was engineered by Arthur Waite and executed by Pamela Colman Smith. There is much to say about the RWS, but whatever your personal feelings about the deck may be, it set a powerful and new standard because, before the RWS, all of the pip cards were simply stylized with their object (Wands, Cups, Coins, or Swords) in the appropriate number.

For instance, in older decks like the Tarot de Marseille the Ten of Wands is simply a bundle of ten wooden staffs. When illustrating the RWS deck, Smith crafted an image for every single one of the seventy-eight cards, and this forever changed the world of tarot—so much so that almost all decks that have been created after the RWS take their inspiration (and in large part interpretation) from that deck.

As mentioned, there are four suits in the tarot, and they correspond with the following four classical elements:

Coins/Disks/Pentacles—Resonant with the element of Earth, the suit of Coins/Disks/Pentacles (the cards can be labeled as any one of these depending on the deck/reader) deals with issues around security, finances, cash flow, and practical concerns about money and foundations. Coins can give us information about our careers, practical resources, as well as issues like inheritance.

Swords—Attuned to the element of Air, the suit of Swords deals with both right and wrong speech as well as right and wrong thought. These cards also indicate intellectual concerns, scholastic endeavors, and mental acuity. They also often refer to some white-collar professions like law and medicine. Strategizing, planning for the future, and understanding our enemies are also lessons found in this suit.

Wands—Representing the element of Fire, the suit of Wands deals with creativity, sexuality, passion, and self-expression as well as our physical energy/vitality and the "hotter" emotions like passion or lust. Wands oversee artistic and creative expression, competition of all kinds, and can also give us information about embracing magic and transformation.

Cups—Affiliated with the element of Water and matters of the heart, the suit of Cups deals with our emotions, feelings, fears, and loves as well as magical interest and psychic abilities. Cups speak to our romantic relationships, deep friendships, and spiritual and emotional health. Cups can also let us know when it is time to engage in some spiritual cleansing.

The classical elements of Earth, Air, Fire, and Water date back to at least the ancient Greeks, and evidence suggests that they were actually worked with in ancient Persia by the Magi, temple priests and priestesses serving in the Zoroastrian tradition. These four classic elements form the basis not only of many forms of Western esoteric divinatory systems but also magic and ritual. There are two more elements that are sometimes referred to in tarot and often referred to in Sacred Arts work: they are **Above and Below**, also sometimes conceived of as Stellar and Terrestrial.

Understanding the general principles of how number works in the pip cards in the tarot will also be useful as we move forward:

Aces/Ones: a fresh start or new beginning

Twos: important decisions need to be made—take your time and do not rush into anything.

Threes: fertility, manifesting celebration, support, and accomplishment

Fours: stability, structure, appropriate placement, and integrity

Fives: chaos, change, difficulty, conflict—both inner and outer

Sixes: reconciliation, harmony, balance, and give-and-take

Sevens: struggle, challenge, entrapment, illusion, and delusion

Eights: achievement, success, mastery, and a project near its zenith

Nines: endings, closure, final challenges, departures or arrivals

Tens: new beginning, big picture, bird's-eye view, and the sum total of a given experience

0
THE FOOL.

I
THE MAGICIAN.

II
B
J
HIGH PRIESTESS.

III
THE EMPRESS.

IV
THE EMPEROR.

V
THE HIEROPHANT.

VI
THE LOVERS.

VII
THE CHARIOT.

VIII
STRENGTH.

IX
THE HERMIT.

X
WHEEL OF FORTUNE.

XI
ל JUSTICE. ♎

XII
מ THE HANGED ONE. ♆

XIII
נ DEATH. ♏

XIV
ס TEMPERANCE. ♐

XV
ע THE DEVIL. ♑

XVI
פ THE TOWER. ♂

XVII
צ THE STAR. ♒

XVIII
ק THE MOON. ♓

XIX
ר THE SUN. ☉

XX
ש JUDGEMENT. ♇

XXI
ת THE WORLD. ♄

ACE OF PENTACLES.

II

IV

VI

VII

VIII

IX

X

ACE OF SWORDS.

II

III

IV

V

VI

VII

VIII

IX
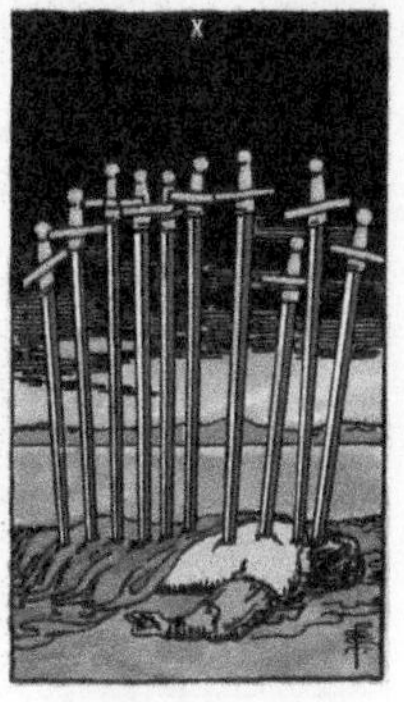
X

ACE OF WANDS.

II

III

IV

V

VI

VII
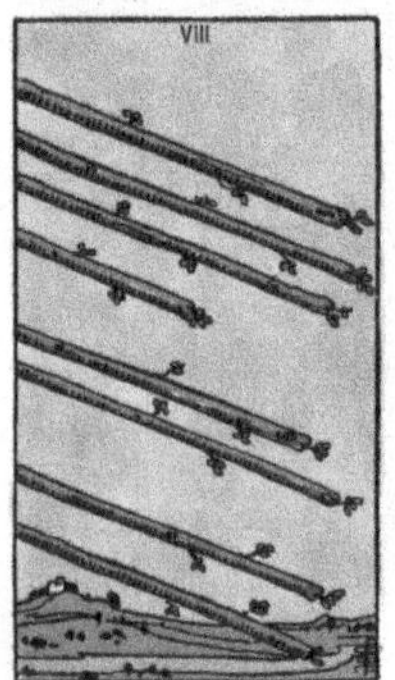
VIII

IX

X

ACE OF CUPS.

II

III

IV

V

VI

VII

VIII

IX

X

PAGE OF PENTACLES.

KNIGHT OF PENTACLES.

QUEEN OF PENTACLES.

KING OF PENTACLES.

PAGE OF SWORDS.

KNIGHT OF SWORDS.

QUEEN OF SWORDS.

KING OF SWORDS.

PAGE OF WANDS.

KNIGHT OF WANDS.

QUEEN OF WANDS.

KING OF WANDS.

PAGE OF CUPS.

KNIGHT OF CUPS.

QUEEN OF CUPS.

KING OF CUPS.

How Do We Read Tarot Cards with an Eye to Magic?

Different tarot readers have vastly different approaches to the way they read, and this book is not about teaching reading techniques or various spreads. However, there are a couple of considerations we need to be clear on before proceeding in our tarot work. First, as the title of the book should give away, the goal here is to learn to work with the tarot in a *magical fashion*. When considering magical work for yourself or for someone else you are reading for, there are two questions that you must ask of the cards in some form if the reading is going to be truly magical. After cutting your cards and laying out whatever spread you are going to work with, make the following queries:

1. *Can magical methods support the most beneficial resolution to this current situation?* This is a yes/no question—so if you work with a pendulum or a specific way of obtaining a yes/no answer, then feel free to employ that instead of, or alongside of, pulling a tarot card. The longer you read cards, the more aware you will become that some cards carry an affirmative or *yes* aspect to their interpretation while others carry the opposite. If, by whatever method, the answer to this question is unclear, then I recommend you take that as a sign from your Holy Helpers that the answer is not yet ready to be given and *do not* proceed with magical work or recommendations.

2. Assuming you receive a yes for question number one, you may then ask: *What magical technique is best suited to bring beneficial resolution to this current situation?* It is here that the information you will encounter in this book will be most useful to you. Each tarot card holds special clues about what types of magical work are most appropriate for a given situation, and that is what I'll teach you to discover.

Understanding Magic and Sacred Arts Work

Magic is a way of asking the universe for help.
—Caroline Casey, *Making the Gods Work for You*

If you can understand the basic tenet expressed in the above quote, you are well on your way to creating and working potent magic. Historically, magic has been with us longer than tarot, but magic and divination are sisters stretching their sacred roots back into time before time. In ancient texts and modern indigenous societies alike, the process of working with these two systems is simple: whenever a situation arises that an individual feels they cannot appropriately deal with on their own, they seek out magical assistance. First, a divination of some sort is performed, and then a magical ritual, ceremony, charm, and/or preparation inspired by or recommended during the divination is given by the magic-maker to the person in need.

The intention-setting, petition-crafting, and magic-making involved in this process are perhaps best thought of as forms of prayer. In fact, I have had more than one teacher refer to spell craft as "prayer with props." This begs the question: who or what are we talking to when we set our intention, read our cards, and make our magic?

Without going on a journey that could take us far afield, I do have some suggestions for how to approach answering this. First of all, consider your current understanding of what is holy and sacred. What is your sense of the sacred right now? Second, consider your upbringing and background. Many soulful seekers drawn to the Sacred Arts are recovering from wounds they received as children or young adults at the hands of various religious traditions. At the same time my experience has taught me that, for many, there *are* aspects of your childhood/early experiences that still resonate with your adult self. It could be a hymn, a specific feast or holy day, an image, a scent. . . . Note what, if anything, resonates for you when you feel into what is most sacred—that will give you a powerful place to begin. Finally, think about the tools you are working with. In our case we are focused on the tarot, and while its origins may be murky to some extent, we know that the tarot has been worked with both as a tool for gaming and for divination for hundreds of years by Europeans who identified as Pagan, Christian, Jewish, or a mixture of all. As a result, our tarot decks call heavily on Christian, Jewish, and Middle Eastern magic and storylines, and it is useful to be at least passingly familiar with those when you sit down to read for yourself or someone else.

Crafting Your Magical Approach

All magic is rooted in a strong and sure intention. The setting of intention is not merely a way to pay lip service to the work about to be performed; it is an opportunity for each individual to come into fast and sure alignment with themselves so that their words reflect their thoughts and their actions reflect their words. In that spirit, let's set down the intention for this book:

> ***My intention is that each of you will learn to work with the tarot as a tool that points the way to appropriate magical creation and transformation.***

After reading this book and putting the recommendations into practice, you should be able to pull cards on a situation and see not only the likeliest paths for it to unfold on, but also what magical recommendations you might make for yourself or a querent, friend, or family member. After working through this first chapter, it may be a good idea for you to state your own intention in reading this book and record it in your journal for future reference.

Throughout these pages I will write about doing work with an intention of clarity/wisdom, healing, or attraction—just to name a few. And you might rightly ask: *how do I align a given magical working with a specific purpose or desire?*

For instance, the intention of getting clarity/wisdom in deciding about whether or not to move out of state for a new job might be very different than the intention for the kind of clarity/wisdom we might seek out in assessing old wounds or destructive patterns we are ready to release once and for all. So the question naturally arises: how do I make modifications to my magical intentions so that they reflect the current situation I face with accuracy? This takes us into the deep work of not only crafting magic but creating *appropriate magic.*

The creation of appropriate magic may be thought of as a layer cake. First there is the baker's **intention:** what kind of cake are we making? Here is a list of the most common magical intentions:

- **Attraction:** We can intend to attract all manner of things: the right partner, opportunity, situation, career, support person, specific object, as well as things like more money or better health.
- **Banishing:** This can be baneful or positive magic depending on the context, but it is very specific. To banish something is to take a step deeper into loss and absence, as banishing implies permanent removal.
- **Beginning:** You will find as you go through the cards that some speak to starting things, initiation, and nascence. This is powerful energy to recognize and work with in certain cases.
- **Blessing:** This is perhaps the most widely sought-out intention because it speaks to so many different areas of our lives. Think of any life area and tell me it wouldn't be improved by being blessed. And remember: blessing the lovely, positive elements of life is easy; blessing the hard stuff—including enemies—is the difficult yet still essential work.
- **Clarity/wisdom:** You will find that clarity/wisdom is perhaps the most popular intention along with blessing. This is because infusing almost

all work with more clarity/wisdom brings nothing but benefit to both the magic-maker and the person on whose behalf magic is being made.

- **Cleansing:** Cleansing along with blessing is perhaps the most important intention. Ritual cleansing has been performed throughout time and culture, before, during, and after significant magical and ceremonial undertakings. We can cleanse to remove, cleanse to call in, and cleanse to reset ourselves and/or a situation.
- **Cursing/reversing:** There is an entire chapter in this book dedicated to baneful work, or cursing and reversing. Baneful is an umbrella term that covers the harsher side of magic including cursing, crossing, jinxing, revenge, and reversing magic.
- **Ending:** The equal and opposite of beginning, some magic is also concerned with ending, conclusions, and tying off loose ends. Endings that are not honored are as problematic as beginnings that are not recognized.
- **Gain/increase:** There is the intention to attract, and then there is the intention to build up and multiply. That is where gain/increase come into play.
- **Healing:** The intention of healing speaks to multiple levels: physical, emotional, mental, and spiritual. It is worthwhile to remember that while people need healing, other things do as well—including places and creatures.
- **Loss/removal:** An entire world of magic, usually baneful in nature, deals with removing, taking away, and losing. Sometimes this can be positive, as in losing a bad relationship or excess weight, but other times it is painful, even when necessary.
- **Mental/psychic/dream influence:** An entire family of magic is all about influencing targets on a mental/psychic level, which often involves sending specific dreams to a person. This magic can again be put to positive or negative use. One of my favorite ways to work with this magic is influencing those clients with mental disequilibrium to experience serenity, stability, and peace.
- **Protection:** Protection is one of the oldest magical intentions, and much magic that we find today has to do with conferring protection on people

or a place. Sometimes people think that you only need protection if you are under spiritual attack, but Sacred Artists know that protection is something that should be both ongoing and changed up season to season.

- **Road opening:** Some of the oldest magical intentions deal with opening the road and clearing the way. In many cultures before any ceremony is begun, the road flowing between the magic-maker and their Holy Helpers is opened. In Mexican folk magic we call this work Abre Camino, and the idea is that no matter how much goodness the querent may have coming to them, if the road is full of obstacles they will never experience it—therefore, we need a clear road.
- **Stability:** The intention of stabilization is not one that you hear about often, but it is something I work with quite a bit because many of my clients are fundamentally happy with where they are (usually after a lot of hard work!) and want to keep things good.
- **Success/mastery:** These intentions go together because success often implies a level of mastery and mastery most often results in success. This intention can be held for goals you or your querent have set and also applied to situations of competition, especially when combined with the next intention.
- **Victory:** This intention implies a contest or competition (even if it's with yourself) where you come out a winner. It is often combined with success/mastery as well as attraction.

Next comes the **condition** that the magic-maker seeks to address. Is this a concern of employment, romance, marriage, fertility, or something else entirely? The following list offers a comprehensive view of all the different conditions that magic can address:

- Love, romance, sex, and passion
- Money and abundance (both personal prosperity and business success)
- Healing and blessing
- Pregnancy and fertility
- Cleansing and clearing
- Baneful work (cursing/hexing)

- Legal issues
- Protection

Then, there is the family of **magical techniques** that may be worked with to create rituals, spells, and ceremonies. These include things like candles on an altar, sacred vessel workings, or working with an object like a lodestone. While the conditions that magical enchantments can address are not affiliated with any one specific element, the magical techniques employed do usually have an elemental association. Some of the most popular magical techniques that we run into again and again include:

- **Candles/oil lamps:** Working with candles or oil lamps to achieve a desired outcome resonates with the element of Fire.
- **Lodestones:** Nature's magnets! Lodestones are magnetized iron ore that are worked with to draw and attract all the good things in life. Lodestones are considered living beings in most folk magic traditions. Working with them properly includes naming them, feeding them with magnetic sand or iron filings, and writing a petition indicating what you want them to draw and attract to you. Lodestones resonate with the elements of Earth and Fire.
- **Magical words/prayers/petitions:** Working with spoken or written words, sounds, prayers, and thought to influence a specific situation is attuned to the element of Air.
- **Physical manipulation:** This involves moving objects to certain areas, toward specific objects, and/or away from other objects or physically blessing an object. Doll babies and poppets are one example of working with physical items to achieve a transformation. Other examples include moving candle spells, sacred smoke offerings made in a specific direction, and working with objects like a crystal skull to mentally influence or mentally heal someone.
- **Sacred vessels:** Medicine bags, mojo hands, doll babies, and sacred vessels like honey jars or witch bottles all resonate with the element of Earth.
- **Spirit work:** Working with Holy Helpers in the form of saints, spirits, angels, ancestors, and deities to accomplish a desire resonated to the sixth classic element: the element of Above.

- **Spraying/washing/spitting/asperging:** This is working with special washes, waters, oils, and alcoholic libations for a variety of outcomes. It includes potions and philters, some of which may be safely consumed while others cannot. Spraying can include spraying a space, laundry, an object, or an individual. Spitting is usually done when baneful magic is being worked or as an offering to certain Holy Helpers. Asperging traditionally involves taking a bundle of fresh, leafy plants, dipping them in whatever liquid you wish to work with, and then shaking them over a space, object, or individual. All of these are associated with the element of Water.
- **Textile magic:** Knot and sewing spells and embroidery charms are all quite ancient forms of magic. Working with specific kinds of cloth, colors, and patterns of cloth to cover, protect, reveal, or bundle up also falls under this aegis. These are all associated with the fifth classic element: the element of Below.

Finally, the icing on the cake so to speak, are the **ingredients** selected to tweak one's magical work in this or that specific direction. These ingredients also resonate with specific elements. The ingredients that we work with carry their own energetic and magical signature. In many cases a specific ingredient has been worked with for centuries for the same ends, and these raw ingredients can and are worked with to make more refined materia magica as well. Let's take a quick tour.

- **Candles** are perhaps the most widely utilized magical ingredient available today. They come in countless shapes, colors, sizes, and materials, from paraffin to beeswax with many choices in between. I recommend beeswax candles to my querents and colleagues because even though the price of beeswax is high, candles made from this precious material have a host of benefits beyond their role in any given working. Oil lamps actually predate candles and are worked with in a similar fashion. Candles and oil lamps are of course associated with the element of Fire.
- **Herbs, roots, and zoological curios** are often called for in magical work, especially in older recipes. Along with their specific use in various types of magic, roots and herbs are of course worked with in the crafting of magical anointing oils, magical baths, incense, sacred waters and special sprays, and magical sachet powders. Zoological curios are often incorporated into box or bottle workings as well as into some talismans. All

herbs, roots, and zoological talismans have their own unique resonances, but they are foundationally affiliated with the element of Earth.

- **Incense** has been worked with since ancient times as an aromatic offering to the Divine and to cover up the smell of sacrifice in temples. It is now often worked with as a magical accessory, meaning that the burning of incense is not typically the "main event" of a ritual or spell, but is often worked with to open up magical space and also to close out magical space. However, don't be too hasty in relegating incense to an accessory: smoke offerings can make up the central act in a ceremony or enchantment. Incense has also been worked with for millennia in the process of purifying and consecrating a person, place, or thing. As you might imagine, it resonates to the element of Air.
- A **magical oil, ritual oil, condition oil,** or **anointing oil** is an oil worked with to anoint candles, talismans, sacred objects, and, in some cases, yourself. Oils are the building blocks of many of the other materia magica we will be discussing; once you have a formula or recipe for an oil that you like, you can add that oil directly to sacred baths, sachet powders, incenses, and more! Oils are fluid so they resonate with the element of Water; however, depending on what ingredients you include in the making of the oil, other elements may resonate as well.
- **Magical sachet powders** are interestingly one of the least known about and utilized magical ingredients, but they are so handy! Powders can be blown into the air, sprinkled on the ground, and added to all of the objects you might normally work with oils for. I work with powders in all my candle work. Powders also have the benefit of being ideal for dressing papers, cash, and documents that need to be magically gussied up—but in a way that no one will know. (Working with oils on paper will obviously leave a stain.)
- **Sacred bath preparations** are found in all cultures and throughout time. Preparations for a sacred bath can be elegantly simple or remarkably complex depending on who is crafting the instructions. A sacred bath can be inexpensively put together by working with common household ingredients like salt, olive oil, and white vinegar (an excellent recipe for cleansing). The preparations can also become more exotic . . . calling on special kinds of salt, dried herbs, magical oils, and even minerals like quartz crystal. Typically sacred bath preparations consist of all herbal

mixtures (in which case the herbs are dried, mixed, and then packaged), salt bath mixtures that may contain salt along with other minerals and/or salt and dried herbs and roots, or oil-based scrub baths where the sacred bath mixture always includes either salt, sugar, coffee grounds, or a mixture immersed in oil (usually a base oil like almond) to create a body scrub and sacred bath formula all at the same time.

- **Sacred waters and special sprays** are some of the more undervalued available magical ingredients next to magical sachet powders. Especially popular in places with warmer climates (because they are usually water or alcohol–based and therefore cooling to the skin), sacred waters can be gathered easily from natural springs, rivers, lakes, and oceans. Or you may join thousands of other homegrown folk magicians and work with blessed water in the form of holy water—most Catholic churches have it for the taking. Sacred waters and sprays are also aligned with the element of Water.

It is important to note that these are broad categories meant to cover much ground. You may have indispensable magical materials that are not found on this list, and that is completely fine! It is always a good idea to begin by asking yourself what materials and objects feel magical to you.

Using Vs. Working With

When I started my formal magical training, I found that it was common for folks to talk about "using" various things, like magical ingredients, tools, even Holy Helpers. As I was taught in my family traditions, we do not engage with the various components of magical ritual and ceremony in order to "use" them. Rather, as magic-makers we are charged with coming into right relationship with each of the items we work with—whether that is the humble quartz crystal on your desk, the incense you burn in the morning, or the sacred plant growing in your garden. This approach does require more responsibility and attention—but the results are well worth the effort.

Magical Timing

Magical timing refers to aligning your magical work so that it coincides with specific celestial or terrestrial events. There are many approaches to magical timing. Three of my favorites are working by sunrise/sunset, lunar phases, and days of the week.

Sunrise/Sunset

- Sunrise is a wonderful time to do drawing/beginning work.
- Sunset contrarily is a great time to do banishing/ending magic.

Lunar Phases

- The waxing moon (period from the new moon to the full moon) is a time when the moon grows in strength. Doing abundance and drawing work during this time is recommended.
- The waning moon (period from the full moon to the new moon) is the time when the moon appears to be diminishing—so logically enough, this is when doing banishing work makes sense.

Days of the Week

The days of the week provide us another magical framework. Here are some general qualities associated with each day of the week and how you can work with them.

- **Monday:** Ruled by the moon, a great time to do healing work, work involving women/the feminine, and work to change someone's emotions
- **Tuesday:** Ruled by Mars, an excellent day to start an exercise regime, do work to strengthen someone, increase courage and bravery, or create miscommunication and fights
- **Wednesday:** Ruled by Mercury, the perfect time to focus on new ideas, networking, communication, clarity, and wisdom, also a good time to make someone be quiet
- **Thursday:** Ruled by Jupiter, this is the time for wealth-building, career success, money, security, abundance, and parties.
- **Friday:** Ruled by Venus, a perfect day for all work related to love, romance, passion, and sex
- **Saturday:** Ruled by Saturn, this day deals with commitments made and broken, binding and restriction as well as banishing and elimination.
- **Sunday:** Ruled by the sun, an awesome day for any blessing or abundance work

Of course, when it comes to magical timing, the most commonly asked question is: how long will it take for any magical work to actually manifest results? It is perfectly natural to want to know this given the time, energy, and resources that individuals dedicate to meaningful ritual, but it is also a complex question. One rule of thumb, which was presented to me as just that—a rule of thumb—and has recently been taken as biblical law by some is the Rule of Three: three days to see a sign, three weeks for movement toward your goal, and three months for a completed goal. The Rule of Three is handy in that it gives us an outline and a progression of sorts. You do not go about looking for a complete manifested result at the outset: you begin by looking for some encouraging signs, then you perceive slight movements in the direction you wish to head, and finally you will, with some luck, obtain a concrete result. I advise my clients to begin counting days, weeks, and months after their ritual has come to an end.

For example, if you are doing a ritual for a more loving marriage and the work will last for seven days, you do not start that work on a Friday and then look for results on Saturday. You wait until the ritual has fully concluded and then begin paying attention to signs, dreams, and practical information. While the Rule of Three gives us a helpful guideline, I have seen results manifest sooner, later, and in rather unexpected ways for different people. In the meantime, pay attention to possible signs around you indicating that the work either is or is not taking. Typically, you will find movement several weeks after the ritual has been performed, and you will see the desired outcome in several months.

If you do not spot positive signs or experience positive movement, it is unlikely that you will have a positive outcome fully manifest. A different angle or new approach may be in order. Keep in touch with your Sacred Arts advisor. If they provide divination services, you may want to check in about what they think a reliable time frame would be. If they do not provide such readings, ask them to recommend you to a reader who can.

And as always, whether you are performing work on your own behalf or a pro is doing work for you, during this time you want to have full faith that the best outcome for all will be achieved while at the same time remember that magic works when you do.

Colors and Their Meaning

Colors are worked with in a variety of ways in magic. This list can help you decide which ink to use when writing your petition, how an altar may be best ornamented, or what color of candle is best for a given situation:

- **Black:** Most people think of black candles when they want to do cursing work, and this makes me sad. Yeah, you can use black for cursing, but it's also a wonderful candle for banishing and protecting.

- **Blue:** Healing, wisdom, and spirit guidance
- **Brown:** Court case work, legal issues including keeping the law away from your business
- **Green:** Money, abundance, prosperity, and connection to green, earth energy
- **Orange:** Road opening, creativity, creative empowerment
- **Pink:** Love, tenderness, romance, intimate connection
- **Purple:** Power, personal authority, mastery, and success
- **Red:** Sex, personal empowerment, creativity, love
- **White:** Can be worked with for any purpose and is especially good for cleansing/blessing work.
- **Yellow:** Communication, clarity, brilliance, insight

Two final ingredients for successful magical work are using the proper method of deployment and disposal, and personal concerns. We are focusing on these because from a nuts-and-bolts practical perspective, they are not only two of the most important additions, but also two that are commonly overlooked.

Methods of Deployment and Disposal

It is vital to understand that any magical working, ritual, or ceremony has a beginning, middle, and end. Usually practitioners—even advanced practitioners—are aware of the beginning and middle part of their work, but creating the perfect ending to a magical act is a subject of much confusion. This need not be so. The first thing to understand about deployment is that the nature of the magic tells you a great deal about the appropriate manner of disposal. If you have done a working for something or someone you wish to draw or summon to you, it makes sense to leave the magical remains close by, right? That means you might bury them in your front or backyard, or if you live in an apartment, in a potted plant you keep inside. Perhaps you might leave a long-term working like a container spell on your altar for all to see, or you might burn certain items and sprinkle the ashes in your flower bed.

If working with sacred waters and washes, you might sprinkle your doorstep or wash down the sidewalk with one designed to attract positive people and experiences. Special areas of interest around the home for burial include the front yard, where things are buried or magical remains are disposed of with the intention to bring something or someone new into your life. The backyard is appropriate for the burial or disposal of magical remains when you want something or someone already present to stay in your life. The threshold of the home is believed to be especially powerful, so anytime you want to influence someone for good or ill, burying or disposing magical remains at the threshold over which they walk is a powerful thing to do. Accounts of witches in Scotland and England burying items at the threshold of a home go back to at least the 1300s!

However, at some point you will likely do work that is of a cleansing, banishing, or even baneful nature, and when it comes to disposing of those remains, you want to make sure that the items are placed far away from you and your living space. When banishing something or someone, my number one favorite method of disposal is to take all magical remains, burn them to ash, and then carry the ash to a four-way crossroads and scatter it in the four directions. You may also take magical remains and dispose of them in water that is moving away from you: a river or running creek will work well for this but a lake or ocean will not. Another option is to take magical remains, weight them, and sink them to the bottom of a body of water with the intention that whatever or whoever is plaguing you will go down into the depths never to be seen again.

In some cases of defensive or attack magic, we see violent methods of disposal: throwing War Water–filled bottles against an enemy's door or on their steps so that they have to physically walk through the mess or laying down magical sachet powders in a similar fashion. When I lived in San Francisco, I rode the bus and walked through a neighborhood where there was activity between rival gangs. I cannot count how many times I saw broken spell bottles and powders that had been thrown down!

Also remember the general correspondences of east and west. East is a good direction to dispose of things that are positive in nature, and west is a good direction to work with for banishing and cleansing.

Some magical workings will have elaborate instructions on disposal: pay attention to those and follow the guidelines. Generally speaking, here are some of my favored methods:

- **Backyard:** Whereas the front yard is primarily for situations where you seek to draw someone or something, the backyard is worked with to dispose of remains from rituals that seek to keep someone or something with you, close to you, and cooperating with you.

- **Bodies of water:** In cases where you have worked to banish or release someone or something, throw the remains of the work into a body of water like a river that is running away from you. If you wish to succeed over someone else or want to sink a person or situation, go ahead and sink the work to the bottom of a lake, pond, or ocean . . . just make sure that any tidal motion is not likely to bring it back to where you are on shore!
- **Crossroads:** The crossroads has long been the go-to place to dispose of magical work that needs to be dispersed to the four directions. This may be cleansing, uncrossing, or baneful work. Usually, sacred bath instructions specifically recommend disposing of bathwater here. If you are disposing of sacred bathwater at a crossroads, follow the directions of your Sacred Arts advisor. If you wish to get rid of solid ritual work such as candle wax/stubs, incense ash, or petition papers, then you may bundle the work up in an appropriate colored cloth, tie it up, and bury it at the crossroads. Another option is to burn the ritual remains, collect the ashes, and scatter them at a crossroads.
- **Front yard:** The front yard has long been worked with as a place to dispose of the remains of magical work seeking to draw someone or something to you or to protect the home. For instance, water that has been used in magically cleansing your home can be poured out the front door or sprinkled on the sidewalk running in front of your house. Ritual remains may be tied up as I mentioned above and buried in the front yard as well.
- **Large trees:** Burying or breaking certain types of work at the base of large, healthy trees is also a time-honored method of disposal.
- **Where a target walks:** If you have targeted a specific person, either burying the remains of the work or scattering the ashes of the remains of the work in a place where that individual will walk is a time-honored method of making sure the magic influences them.

Personal Concerns

Personal concerns are often not discussed even in texts solely dedicated to magic because the idea of using bodily fluids, hair, nails, and dirty laundry in magical work is sometimes seen as gross, unclean, or a low form of magic. However, when we turn to history, we see that personal concerns were worked with all the time by our magical ancestors, and many old rituals call for certain personal concerns specifically. Here is a quick gloss to orient you:

- **Blood** of course is one of the oldest personal concerns, but working with blood need not take us immediately into the realm of sacrifice and slaughter. Magic around women's menstrual cycles is ancient and profound—why else would there be so many taboos around it?! Blood is considered the life force and vitality of an individual. Working with a little dried blood in healing rituals, for instance, can make the magic that much more effective.
- **Bone** calls up the spirit of whatever animal—be it beast or man—it came from.
- **Dirty laundry/shoes** are requested in plenty of old-timey enchantments: the inclusion of clothes that have been worn—especially undergarments—comes into play usually for love, sex, and romance work. A pair of worn shoes can be worked with in a variety of ways both for blessing and more baneful magic depending on the desires of the magic-maker!
- **Fingernails** affect the hands, which in turn can alter our ability to work, to possess skill, to gain in prosperity, to heal and to harm. Usually, it is fingernail shavings that are worked with, not entire nails!
- **Hair** from the face or head can affect the mind as well as the heart and might be pulled from a brush, picked up by running a piece of tape along a pillow, or pulled from a razor.
- **Saliva** is worked with to effect someone's ability to speak and to make kisses especially sweet or sour. An excellent way to get a sample is by cutting a few bristles off a used toothbrush.
- **Sexual fluids** are used in variety of love, romance, attraction, and sex spells and less frequently in binding or breakup rites.
- **Toenails** effect the feet, and in many cultures the feet are believed to be one of the most vulnerable parts of the body, taking in whatever they walk over, be it good or ill. Again, as with fingernails, just a shaving is fine.
- **Urine** is often seen as one of the most vital bodily fluids and may be used to mark off territory or dominate, while feces is almost always used for baneful magic and cursing work.

Further Development Tasks

- Consecrate a deck of tarot cards (preferably RWS or based on RWS interpretations) to work with as you read this book.
- State in writing and/or verbal form your intention for making tarot magic.

Chapter Two

Kiss Me Again!

Love, Marriage, Romance, and Reconciliation

I love love! Love, romance, reconciliation (reuniting partners), making love, and marriage are all topics that intuitive readers get asked about a lot. More than money, much more than health or personal empowerment, everyone wants to know about love. The first thing the discerning reader needs to be aware of is that there are several different subtopics or categories within the general condition of love, romance, sex, and passion work.

- **Seeking a new love:** This is pretty self-explanatory. Whenever a querent is looking for a new love, they want to draw the right partner to their side. Sometimes this person is known, and sometimes it is better for the querent to focus on an ideal partner they have yet to meet.
- **Relationship and/or marriage blessing:** It's exactly what it sounds like. In these cases, the couple has been together usually for a longer period of time. Maybe they are married, in a civil union or a domestic partnership, or simply involved in a committed relationship. What is typically sought is more tenderness, deeper love, and more affection/communication.
- **Lovemaking:** Whenever we do magic specifically around lovemaking, we are seeking to increase both physical and emotional intimacy between our querent and their partner(s). Whether the querent simply desires to draw someone to them for some fun bedroom activities or wishes to rekindle lovemaking in a long-term relationship, the focus is on the procreative organs, heart center, and in some cases levels of physical energy and vitality.
- **Reconciliation:** Reconciliation is one of the issues I am asked about quite regularly. The permutations are many and varied. In some cases,

the desire to reconcile is completely unrealistic, and in others it actually is quite likely. Many magical folks agree that this is some of the toughest work to do. That said, there are few things as rewarding as playing a small part in bringing people who truly love one another back together in a meaningful way.

- **Queer relationships:** If you are a member of the LGBTQIA2+ community and start looking at old magic formulas, you might notice that they are often very gendered and geared toward straight, cis, heterosexuals. While this might be initially frustrating, don't lose heart! There are many love rites out there (and more every day) written for the LGBTQIA2+ community, and most of the rituals and ceremonies for love and romance that speak to queer querents but are nested within a heterosexual framework can be tweaked by identifying what ingredients are associated with "the man" or the "masculine" and what ingredients are associated with "the woman" or the "feminine" and doubling up or changing out where appropriate.
- **Polyamorous relationships:** Another area to consider is multiple partner relationships. Polyamory (meaning "many lovers" in ancient Greek) is a lifestyle choice, and if you don't know much about it, I recommend that you educate yourself if/when you encounter a querent engaged in this type of relationship because the concerns for polyamorous relationships are different or differently emphasized than those relevant to two-person, monogamous, or exclusive couples. Once those unique challenges and gifts are understood, the general techniques for working on a polyamorous situation are very similar to those of other love and romance situations.

Special Magical Considerations for Love, Romance, Sex, and Passion

The Need for Cleansing in Matters of the Heart

As I wrote earlier, cleansing is important in magic generally, but I have found that sometimes it is overlooked in love work. This is unfortunate because it's so useful. Think about it. If someone has a fight with their lover and wants to engage in ritual to bring them back or simply to bless and strengthen their now stressed relationship, then first they will need to remove the negative vibes. Or perhaps a querent wants to draw a lover to their side—someone they have yet to meet. Cleansing might not seem so important in that situation, but doesn't it make sense to create a small ritual aimed at removing any negative thoughts or feelings the querent might be harboring about love and romance . . . especially if they have experienced some bad relationships? Of course, it does! When cleansing prior to love work, it's important (as always) to be clear in our intention, which is not only that we might be purified and made ready to be in right relationship with our partner(s)—soon to be or otherwise—but also that we might be in right relationship with ourselves.

Gendered Roots and Rocks

Another funny aspect of folk, plant, and herb magic is that some roots and rocks are gendered. Lodestones for instance are often assigned gender so that you have a he or a she stone. Some roots like High John/John the Conqueror are thought of as more masculine, and others like Queen Elizabeth Root are thought of as feminine. That said, it's important to understand that within magic gender is not the same thing as biological sex. Women (including yours truly) can and do work with High John, and men can and do work with Queen Elizabeth. While these are two of the most famous gendered roots, there are others. The right plant magic resources will guide you, and as always, you also need to trust your own intuition when it comes to magical work.

Special Considerations in Tarot for Love and Romance

The Major Arcana

As always, these archetypal cards speak to multiple areas concerning love and romance. They may deliver warnings, encouragement, or sage advice about what needs to be emphasized or cut out completely from a love relationship.

The Suits

Coins

Here the focus is on security and the ways that love and money/security/practical concerns dance with each other. A focus on the body and embodying love is also incredibly important for folks who receive a reading heavy on Coins cards, as is the role that beauty plays in the love we give and the love we receive. Since these cards are associated with the element of Earth, they often encourage taking practical action when it comes to love and romance or may indicate where a practical concern is creating a barrier of some kind.

Swords

Because it deals with cutting, severing, separation, and delineating boundaries, the suit of Swords, attuned to the element of Air, is often not what we really want to see in large numbers when reading about love. Depending on the situation and the questions asked, these cards can offer helpful advice such as indicating that it's time for the querent to cut their losses and move on. In their more benevolent form, Swords are concerned with all issues of communication (so essential to good relationships) and our ability to assess our situation with clarity and wisdom.

Wands

Ruled by Fire, Wands direct our attention to their strong, erect shape as well as the fertile flowering upon them and immediately help us focus on lovemaking and the physical, hot, passionate aspects in love and romance. These cards are often the ones that speak most openly about sex and sexual matters. They can also speak to fears and inner conflicts we may have around romance and love. In some cases, Wands can and will point to physical considerations that are affecting the physical relationship for better or worse.

Cups

Emotional and romantic are two words that describe the energy of this suit beautifully. These cards, attuned as they are to the element of Water, often convey messages about true love, self-love, and the beauty of family love. They can also warn of emotional triggers our querents need to be aware of and will help them not sabotage good relationships. Fundamentally Cups cards are concerned with our abilities to give and to receive. At their deepest level, Cups cards remind us about the powerful healing found in true love.

Major Arcana Cards

Note: Keep in mind that the interpretations offered here are launch points. You will and should have your own interpretations that may or may not align precisely with those suggested. Each description also includes a consideration should the card be reversed or in challenging positions. These reverse card interpretations may also be reliably applied to the card in question when it is in an upright position but surrounded by other cards that are more challenging.

The Fool. Starting a new love adventure! This does not necessarily mean that the querent is embarking on a brand-new relationship, but it can. Generally, when positively placed, the Fool indicates that the querent is allowing more trust and openheartedness into their relationships. Contrarily, this card can express that the querent is not heeding signs right in front of their face about a relationship (like ignoring the fact that she is totally cheating or thinking he is not interested because he gained a few pounds due to the stress he is dealing with at work) when in a reversed position. In reconciliation cases the Fool often reveals that renewed affections are not likely, but if it is drawn in context with other positive cards, it can open up the possibility of a new, beautiful beginning.

Magical Techniques: sacred vessels, lodestones, textile magic, and spirit work

Intentions: clarity/wisdom, success/mastery, attraction, road opening, blessing, protection, beginning, mental/psychic/dream influence, and cleansing

The Magician. It is time to draw inspiration from what is above and below—meaning what is in your body as well as what is in your mind but also applying to all opposite forces: heaven and earth, masculine and feminine, etc. The interplay between these apparent opposites contains important messages for the querent regarding love and romance. The Magician can also serve as a reminder to protect what is most tender about your relationship. Whenever the Magician appears in any kind of reading, his presence can be taken to mean that working with magic to address/transform the situation is a smart move. When it comes to love, romance, passion, and sex, this is true across the board and especially for reconciliation cases. When reversed or in a challenging position, this card can indicate that there are illusions and trickery around the relationship that need to be seen for what they really are. There may also be an indication that pursuing one's goal through magic is not the correct approach.

Magical Techniques: all

Intentions: success/mastery, victory, attraction, blessing, and mental/psychic/dream influence

The High Priestess. One of the biggest messages in the High Priestess card is that it's time for the querent to take back their sense of sovereignty in or from a relationship. This is especially the case for women, but it can apply to men as well. The card can also indicate that the couple needs to have a magical pursuit they hold in common. If pulled by someone, male or female, who is in a relative position of authority and having a hard time getting a date, the card can suggest that one reason for this lack of activity is because the querent is seen as intimidating. Sometimes the High Priestess reveals that the querent will be happier by themselves or in a noncommittal relationship. In cases of reconciliation the card often indicates a favorable, but often slow resolution. Reversed, the High Priestess indicates a cool, aloof, or impersonal demeanor that would lead others to believe the querant is not interested in romance or matters of the heart.

Magical Techniques: magical words/prayers/petitions, physical manipulation, spraying/washing/spitting/asperging, and spirit work

Intentions: clarity/wisdom, success/mastery, road opening, blessing, protection, healing, loss/removal, mental/psychic/dream influence, and cleansing

The Empress. The Empress often indicates a wife or wifely role and sometimes mom as well. She is a woman solid in her power, maternal but also super sexy. Sometimes she reminds us that in the middle of all the "mom chores" some sexiness is getting lost. She may suggest that the querent is in a prime position to attract whomever they would like to. In cases where someone is having an extramarital affair, this card signals the spouse, and if it is in a positive context with other cards, then it indicates that the spouse will win any legal/financial battles. For reconciliation cases that do not involve extramarital affairs, the card signifies a positive outcome. If in a negative or reversed position, the Empress can point to an indulgent, demanding, and shortsighted individual.

Magical Techniques: sacred vessels, lodestones, physical manipulation, and textile magic

Intentions: success/mastery, victory (especially in competitive situations), attraction, blessing, and gain/increase

The Emperor. Are the categories around love, sex, and romance too rigid? Sometimes the Emperor indicates a partner who is very controlling of the purse strings, possibly the breadwinner. This control, whether it manifests financially or in some other manner, is killing the romance and love and must be addressed. Sometimes this also points to apathy around lovemaking. But conversely, it can denote stepping into your power and authority around love. In reconciliation cases the Emperor often tells us that a rigid mindset needs to be overcome in order for there to be success. His presence can also point to the possibility that reconciliation won't happen unless one or both partners fully step into their power. When reversed, the Emperor reveals that the imbalance in power has become too great and is no longer sustainable.

Magical Techniques: sacred vessels, lodestones, and physical manipulation

Intentions: clarity/wisdom, success/mastery, victory (especially in competitive situations), attraction, protection, gain/increase, and stability

The Hierophant. This card often shows us that it's time for the relationship to move into the next phase, whether that means declaring exclusivity, getting engaged, or getting married. The relationship is ready to be blessed and consecrated by whatever magical authority the couple recognizes (whether or not it is legally binding). Sometimes this card indicates that the role of religion/spirituality in the lives of our lovers needs to be either more or less emphasized depending on where it shows up in a reading and in what context. The presence of the Hierophant can also illustrate a need for general blessing on one or both people in the relationship. In cases of reconciliation, this card signifies that there should be deep cleansing and blessing and renewed spiritual alignment for one or both people. When reversed, the Hierophant tells us that there is a lack of institutional support for the couple. Sometimes this occurs when folks from different classes, countries, or cultures get involved with each other, and in those cases some road opening and blessing work can be very helpful!

Magical Techniques: candles/oil lamps, magical words/prayers/petitions, and spirit work

Intentions: clarity/wisdom, road opening, blessing, protection, and cleansing

The Lovers. Obviously this is an important card for our topic! The Lovers can point to the beginning or continuation of a happy love affair, but the card also warns of potential obstacles and temptations that one or both partners need to be aware of as their love grows. The Lovers is a card of decision-making, so when it shows up in a reading, it can tell us that the situation is now calling for a choice to be made. This card may also point out that a new lover or potential lover is shortly arriving on the scene. When it comes to reconciliation, we very much want to see this card because it indicates a strong possibility for a favorable outcome to such work.

Magical Techniques: lodestones, candles/oil lamps, and physical manipulation

Intentions: clarity/wisdom, victory, attraction, and blessing

The Chariot. When it comes to love, there are always obstacles. The Chariot reminds our querent of this. Positively positioned within a reading, it also tells them to disregard the obstacles, for they will be overcome. The Chariot asks the querent to be quite discerning about their desires, encouraging them to pay attention to what they are pursuing from a place of pure appetite versus what they are pursuing from a place of deep wisdom. Finally, the Chariot reminds us that tension is not always a bad thing requiring removal. Sometimes tension is the stuff that makes a relationship sing! In cases of reconciliation, the Chariot may indicate that travel or movement is required for the reconciliation to really take effect. When surrounded by positive cards, the Chariot ultimately gives us a message of victory and success, but it is victory and success won through work and balancing opposing forces. When in a reversed or challenging position, the Chariot indicates there is too much conflict and disagreement to get any kind of momentum in the situation. It can also tell us the situation is simply stuck and not able to move.

Magical Techniques: magical words/prayers/petitions, physical manipulation, healing, and spirit work

Intentions: success/mastery, victory, and road opening

Strength. When we get the Strength card in love, romance, sex, and passion readings, it tells us several important things:

1. All people, but especially women, need to be aware of their strength and power within the relationship and in some cases take that power back.
2. It's OK for the querent to be by themselves, and it might even be necessary for them to take some solo time before finding a relationship that really rocks.
3. People who fill one's head with negative ideas need to be silenced.

This card indicates endurance for difficult times, but it also illustrates self-love and the ability to overcome said difficulties. In reconciliation cases Strength can often indicate that the reconciliation will not happen but this will actually be a good thing. In other cases, it expresses that a romance might be saved by one partner reclaiming their power and becoming very clear on their boundaries. When reversed, the Strength card is usually a warning that the querant does not currently have the internal reserves to deal with the situation on their own and may need the support of family, friends, and their wider community.

Magical Techniques: sacred vessels, candles/oil lamps, and mental/psychic influence

Intentions: clarity/wisdom, success/mastery, victory, attraction, protection, loss/removal, and mental/psychic/dream influence

The Hermit. In cases of love and romance, the Hermit card usually indicates issues around communication and/or fear. The card can turn up when one or all parties in a romantic affair are hiding something from the other member(s). Another possibility is that one person refuses to be transparent and communicate with the other. Sometimes the Hermit also tells us that the querent is in a pattern of isolating themselves and not engaging with others. If this is the case, then that pattern may need to be disrupted before a relationship is possible. The Hermit card can also announce that the querent needs to take some time on their own before getting involved with anybody else. In cases of reconciliation the Hermit card shows us that the road will be long and tough and ultimately a reconciliation may not happen at all. However, if the card is positively positioned, it can indicate that there is simply a need to open the road of communication. The deeper message of the Hermit is that every relationship has its own cycles and this time in the relationship is more of an in-breath, quieting period. When the Hermit is reversed, it shows that the querant is ready to get out there, be seen, and be social.

Magical Techniques: candles/oil lamps, magical words/prayers/petitions, and spirit work

Intentions: clarity/wisdom, blessing, protection, healing, beginning, ending, and cleansing

The Wheel of Fortune. The Wheel of Fortune informs us that what goes up must come down and vice versa. If things have been rough for the lovers in question, then a better situation will soon reveal itself. However, if things have been smooth sailing, then it may be time to prepare for a coming storm. Because of its link to the power of Fate, the Wheel of Fortune can imply that the partner(s) you are reading for (whether they are together or not) are in some way destined to be in each other's lives. If the situation that is being read on is too turbulent and dramatic, then the Wheel of Fortune advises that all parties involved determine what their highest priority is and focus on that. In cases of reconciliation, the Wheel of Fortune almost always needs to be read with another card because it can indicate that the situation may go either way. It can also suggest that parted lovers are in some way either fated to be together and/or fated to learn something important from each other. When reversed, the Wheel of Fortune usually indicates that a pattern in the relationship needs to be disrupted or broken. It might also tell us that one or more parties are trying to "force" something into being . . . and meeting significant resistance along the way.

Magical Technique: spirit work
Intentions: clarity/wisdom, success/mastery, blessing, protection, and stability

Justice. In the world of love, the Justice card really asks us to focus on fairness and reciprocity. This card indicates that what the querent puts into the relationship is what they will get out of it, but it also reminds them that at issue are concerns around equality and reciprocity. This card may express that it is time to make a relationship legal in some manner. Justice also shows up to remind us of the role that politics and justice do or don't play in a relationship. If one partner in the relationship is very politically active but the other is not, then there may need to be some rebalancing or a discussion.

In reconciliation cases the Justice card often indicates the querent is only partially ready to reconcile, that a part of them is also seeking revenge or feels a need to make the other person pay. Contrarily, the card can also point to the possibility of a successful reunion being difficult unless previous inequalities in the relationship are addressed honestly and with a desire to change for the better. When reversed, the Justice card indicates a fundamental imbalance in the relationship and that it will be difficult to make any headway until that foundational challenge is addressed.

Magical Techniques: candles/oil lamps, magical words/prayers/petitions, and physical manipulation
Intentions: clarity/wisdom, victory, protection, and stability

The Hanged Man. He of course tells us that there needs to be a radical shift of perspective when it comes to relationships and love affairs. Often the Hanged Man also shows us that pride, and an unwillingness to seek compromise or to sacrifice for the greater good of the union, is a root obstacle when it comes to finding happiness and harmony. Sometimes this card can also indicate that money and specifically debt are causing disharmony in the relationship and these are the areas that really need to be addressed. In cases of reconciliation, the Hanged Man can be a messenger of good or bad news. His presence can signal that one or more of the parties involved are finally ready to make the sacrifices required to be in a relationship with each other and/or that a limiting perspective on romance has been banished in favor of one more fitting to the relationship. But be warned: his presence can also tell us that someone is not ready to get rid of a rigid perspective in order to make a relationship work. When the Hanged Man is reversed in a reading, he often affirms that the situation is seen correctly by all parties or that the time for sacrifice is now over.

Magical Techniques: sacred vessels, magical words/prayers/petitions, physical manipulation, textile magic, and spirit work

Intentions: clarity/wisdom, road opening, healing, cursing/reversing, ending, loss/removal, and mental/psychic/dream influence

Death. Often this card indicates that the relationship is dying or already dead. This message typically goes hand in hand with something new coming into being, which may be one or more partner(s) recognizing that they want to be out of a relationship for a while or a new lover coming in. Sometimes Death can tell us that a relationship will be affected by an actual, physical death.

Depending on the context in which the Death card is pulled, it can also illustrate that seeds of intention around love and romance that were sown long ago by the querent are now ready to be harvested. If pulled for cases concerning reconciliation, the message is almost always that an attempt to reconcile will not meet with success. In these cases, cleansing, banishing, and blessing are required. When reversed, the Death card can tell us that the relationship is alive and well, though, depending on surrounding cards Death reversed, it may also be a warning that one or more people involved in the relationship are refusing to let something die that really needs to. Death reversed can also sometimes indicate pregnancy.

Magical Techniques: spraying/washing/spitting/asperging, textile magic, and spirit work

Intentions: clarity/wisdom, protection, cursing/reversing, ending, loss/removal, and cleansing

Temperance. Temperance advises that what the querent needs right now is patience and moderation. That's the message whether the querent is looking for love, currently in a relationship, or hoping for reconciliation. If surrounded by negative cards or in a reversed position, Temperance may indicate that drinking, drugs, and partying are having a problematic effect on the individuals in the relationship or the relationship itself. This card can also speak to fertility, pregnancy, and family planning. If it shows up for a querent who is currently sexually active and could either get pregnant or get someone else pregnant, then that possibility needs to be highlighted so that everyone can make the best decision. When it comes to those seeking reconciliation,

Temperance issues an invitation to pause and consider where you have been and where you want to go. Often, when this card is pulled for love, it indicates that healing is required before the relationship can proceed to the next level.

Magical Techniques: sacred vessels, physical manipulation, spraying/washing/spitting/asperging, and spirit work

Intentions: clarity/wisdom, road opening, blessing, protection, healing, stability, banishing, mental/psychic/dream influence, and cleansing

The Devil. Temptations, infidelity, drugs, alcohol, illicit sex, and sabotage are all tricks that the Devil tries to play when it comes to romance and love. As in other scenarios, this card first and foremost indicates addictions—be they chemical, physiological, or psychological—and the need to eliminate them from one's life. When surrounded by a number of positive cards, the Devil can suggest the querent is in a situation where there is struggle but this is temporary and soon will be resolved if the querent just sticks with their current course of action. When read in a more negative context or in a reversed position, the Devil indicates a lack of freedom and independence in the situation that is harming all parties. The ancient understanding of the Devil is that it is a challenger, an adversary, and so generally, when it comes to love, the message is that until the Devil is taken care of, a happy relationship will not be possible. The same is true for cases of reconciliation.

Magical Techniques: candles/oil lamps, physical manipulation, textile magic, and spirit work

Intentions: clarity/wisdom, victory, blessing, protection, cursing/reversing, loss/removal, banishing, mental/psychic/dream influence, and cleansing

The Tower. In cases of love and romance, the Tower is often interpreted as signifying a devastating breakup or divorce. If those events have already occurred or are occurring at the time of the reading, then the Tower simply tells us that they are the focus for the querent and nothing else will happen until they are resolved. If there is a question about breaking up or divorcing and the Tower shows up, then the indication is that a breakup/divorce is quite likely. Sometimes the Tower can demonstrate that some other extremely destabilizing force is at work in the relationship, like a significant health or financial issue, and that the relationship can survive but will not emerge from the event unscathed. Remember that the Tower always advises us to look beyond appearances and deeply into the rubble. There is a reason that things fell apart: the universe wants the querent to pay attention, and if they will do so now, then they will save themselves difficulties down the road. In cases of reconciliation, obviously the Tower indicates a solid no or, at the very least, not at this time. When reversed, the Tower usually tells us that the situation has moved from a crisis point into stabler territory, or, in some cases, that a crisis was averted altogether.

Magical Techniques: sacred vessels, physical manipulation, textile magic, and spirit work

Intentions: clarity/wisdom, blessing, protection, healing, cursing/reversing, ending, loss/removal, stability, banishing, and cleansing

The Star. A breather in the midst of chaos, the Star often illustrates a deep need to return to a place of self-love and tells us that this must be in play before a relationship can begin or resume. The Star can indicate that the querent and/or the relationship(s) the querent is asking about have emerged from an intense and challenging period. Healing is both advised and required when this card shows up. When the Star appears, it is time for all parties involved to take stock of where they have been, where they are, and what direction they want to pursue now. Looking at the natal charts of all parties is especially useful according to this card. This is another card that can also indicate fertility and pregnancy. In cases where reconciliation is sought, the Star tells us consulting with an astrologer and clarifying direction and priorities must occur before there can be a successful reunion. When reversed, the Star reveals that something about the situation is not in alignment. It may also indicate some astrological turbulence ahead that all parties need to be aware of.

Magical Techniques: sacred vessels, spraying/washing/spitting/asperging, and spirit work

Intentions: clarity/wisdom, blessing, protection, healing, beginning, stability, mental/psychic/dream influence, and cleansing

The Moon. The Moon reveals difficulties in a love relationship specifically linked to uncontrolled emotions, financial stress, and/or desires that are creating problems in the current relationship. Often this card indicates that the individuals involved are trying to "work on it," but the work is only addressing surface tensions as opposed to the underlying issues. In some cases, the work is failing because one or more individual(s) involved are too comfortable with the current state of the relationship and are unwilling to get into more challenging territory. Depending on the situation, the Moon can also indicate a mother, mother-in-law, or maternal figure who is significant in some manner either positively or negatively. The Moon may also speak to the fact that a woman in the situation is going through hormonal changes and this needs to be considered in the overarching analysis. Like the Star and Temperance, the Moon can indicate fertility, and pregnancy. When reversed, the loss of fertility and/or a pregnancy is a possibility as are illusions and delusions that serve no one. In cases of reconciliation the Moon usually points to a doubtful reunion.

Magical Techniques: sacred vessels and mental/psychic influence

Intentions: clarity/wisdom, blessing, healing, gain/increase, beginning, ending, and mental/psychic/dream influence

The Sun. An especially positive card for reconciliation, the Sun indicates rebirth and magical transformation. This card can be worked with in cases where the relationship has been going on for years and requires a jolt of heat and electricity! In some instances, the Sun can tell us that a baby will soon be in the picture! If you are reading for a querent who has just ended a long-term relationship and the Sun emerges in a positive context, then often your querent will get into a new and quite satisfying union in a short time. The Sun is known to "shed light" on situations, so sometimes this card comes up when those involved in the relationship need to have an honest conversation with each other. This is a great card for finding a new lover or beginning a new relationship. When reversed, the Sun tells us that the relationship is missing a vital force or factor that will allow it to move to the next level. It may also warn of using pregnancy/children to try to "save" or otherwise manipulate a relationship.

Magical Techniques: candles/oil lamps and spirit work

Intentions: success/mastery, road opening, blessing, protection, cursing/reversing, gain/increase, and beginning

Judgement. A deep concern about bad decisions in the past and skeletons in the closet are two of the things this card points to. It often indicates a past transgression the querent or their lover(s) have not totally forgotten or forgiven. Judgement's appearance in a reading may also signal a need for the querent and/or all parties involved to exercise more discernment in the choices they are making. Sometimes this card can advise the querent to make a relationship more official and legal. In issues where there is a legal concern (such as a divorce or custody battle), if the Judgement card shows up, I recommend you pull another card to get a sense of whether the outcome will be favorable or not. In cases of reconciliation, Judgement indicates that the person seeking to reconcile will have a lot of hoops to jump through before they are deemed "worthy." When the Judgement card appears reversed in a relationship reading, it suggests resistance to important transitions or awakening in one's love life. This reversal often points to avoiding necessary relationship revelations or refusing to heed calls for transformation.

Magical Techniques: sacred vessels, magical words/prayers/petitions, and spirit work

Intentions: clarity/wisdom, success/mastery, victory, protection, healing, cursing/reversing, loss/removal, stability, banishing, and cleansing

The World. This is an all-around awesome card but especially when it comes to amore! The World often tells us that those involved in a relationship are deeply in love with one another. If the querent is looking for love, then the World card indicates they will have an easy time drawing the right partner(s) to their side. In some cases, it shares that each person is totally head over heels with the other and the object of affection is seen as the highest, the best, the most delightful—a fantasy come to life! The card usually bodes well for reconciliation cases too and often indicates that someone has not fully gotten over another person. In some cases, the World can be a double-edged sword, suggesting that one of the partners feels that the other is too good, too smart, too successful and therefore "out of their league." When reversed, the World suggests completion that feels somehow unfinished or delayed. This reversal often points to relationships that are struggling to reach their full potential or natural conclusion.

Magical Techniques: sacred vessels, candles/oil lamps, textile magic, and spirit work

Intentions: success/mastery, victory, attraction, blessing, gain/increase, beginning, and ending

Court Cards

King and Queen of Coins. In love matters the King and Queen of Coins can often indicate in-laws, parents, neighbors, and of course, work supervisors or colleagues. If the astrology is right, they can also represent either member of the couple, too. Because they deal with the element of Earth, this pair suggests issues of security, the way that finances effect a relationship, and aspects of the relationship (or of people in the relationship) that are hidden and unknown. In reconciliation cases the King and Queen of Coins almost always signify that the couple needs to focus on financial success—whatever that means and looks like for them—and practical matters. In some cases, it can also indicate in-laws that have to be dealt with. Like all Coins cards, the King and Queen of Coins emphasize drawing and attracting abundance. When reversed, both the King and Queen of Coins suggest a lack of awareness or responsiveness to the practical and/or financial issues directly impacting the relationship. Money trouble is often a major culprit.

Magical Techniques: sacred vessels, lodestones, and physical manipulation

Intentions: success/mastery, victory, attraction, gain/increase, and stability

Knight of Coins. As a helper figure, the Knight of Coins expresses that now is a good time to stop and smell the roses. If the individuals involved have been "working" very actively on their relationship, then this is the moment to pause and enjoy the fruits of their labor thus far. When reversed, he tells us that a romance may be stalled out, stale, and in need of reinvigoration. As a measure of time and speed, this Knight signals that things are progressing very slowly and patience is required.

Magical Techniques: sacred vessels and lodestones

Intentions: success/mastery, gain/increase, and stability

Page of Coins. This card calls attention to looking for a new start, a fresh beginning, or a new way of relating to both romance and money. Sometimes in romantic situations and certainly in reconciliation work, the Page of Coins can indicate that the querent has a pie-in-the-sky kind of attitude. They are looking at the best version of events and refuse to consider what will happen if anything less than perfection manifests. In cases of reconciliation especially, this card can indicate a dreamy stance that ignores real problems. When reversed, the Page of Coins may suggest that those involved in the relationship are immature and acting without any concern for consequences.

Magical Techniques: sacred vessels, lodestones, and physical manipulation

Intentions: clarity/wisdom, success/mastery, attraction, and stability

King and Queen of Swords. As I wrote earlier, Swords are not really the cards we want to see in great numbers when looking at love issues. However, the King and Queen of Swords can be very informative, reminding the querent to pay attention to reason as well as passion, emphasizing the need for clear and loving communication and keeping them aware of the dance between giving themselves over to their partners completely and maintaining boundaries. In cases of reconciliation the King and Queen of Swords can be positive or negative. They can indicate that the door of communication is open and the way is clear, so write that letter, make that call, etc. But they can also—especially when reversed or negatively positioned among other cards—suggest that the relationship is over and cannot be brought back. When reversed, the King and Queen of Swords suggest that there has been a total communication breakdown and the relationship/connection is on its way out.

Magical Techniques: magical words/prayers/petitions, physical manipulation, and spirit work

Intentions: cleansing, blessing, clarity/wisdom, road opening, banishing, and mental/psychic/dream influence

Knight of Swords. The Knight of Swords as a helper shows up quickly and may depart just as quickly. Sometimes his presence indicates that the situation needs a quick burst of acute magical work but then can be left alone. In other cases, the Knight of Swords tells us that the querent will get movement fast. Things will fall into place with apparent ease, but sometimes they will not stay put for very long. In reconciliations the Knight of Swords indicates that fast action is vital to success and communication between the estranged partners is essential. When reversed or in a challenging position, the Knight of Swords indicates that one or more parties may be leaping to incorrect conclusions and acting rashly as a result.

Magical Techniques: magical words/prayers/petitions, physical manipulation, and textile magic

Intentions: clarity/wisdom, road opening, and mental/psychic/dream influence

Page of Swords. In many cases the Page of Swords is a young person who is just starting out in their "adult" life. They may be in school or thinking about going to school or newly graduated and figuring out their next career move. What the Page of Swords is not ready for is a relationship. Typically, this card indicates that if a romance has started, it will be short-lived, or if the two people are really deeply devoted, it has a good chance of becoming a long-distance relationship. In reconciliation cases the Page of Swords points to at least one of the partners being more concerned and preoccupied with questions about their general future than they are in reuniting romantically. It does not expressly take reconciliation off the table, but it does lessen the likelihood of it happening. When reversed, the Page of Swords suggests that one or more individuals involved is too immature to be in a relationship and/or is not ready to communicate clearly.

Magical Technique: magical words/prayers/petitions

Intentions: clarity/wisdom, road opening, banishing, and mental/psychic/dream influence

King and Queen of Wands. The focus now is on sex and physical intimacy. Sometimes these cards simply indicate that the sexual aspect of the relationship is strong and vital. In other cases, they may point to lovemaking that is lacking and needs to be addressed. In reconciliation cases, the King and Queen of Wands can and often do signal that the relationship the querent seeks to return to is solely based on physical connection. If that is acceptable to the querent, then it is fine, but if not, the reconciliation will not hold. This card also indicates a favorable field for love magic, and in cases where someone is seeking to attract a new lover, the King and Queen of Wands express that their vitality is on fire. When reversed, the two tell us that the situation is lacking passion, energy, vitality, and verve. They may also indicate that physical attraction is not present.

Magical Techniques: candles/oil lamps, magical words/prayers/petitions, physical manipulation, and spirit work

Intentions: success/mastery, victory, attraction, and gain/increase

Knight of Wands. When we get the Knight of Wands, we are told that doing magical work, especially utilizing the element of Fire, is a really good way to go. However, we are being informed that we are dealing with a situation where one or more of the people involved are not sure about what they want. Usually with this card there has been sex or some level of physical intimacy, but the relationship may or may not be exclusive and there may or may not be labels involved. The Knight of Wands indicates that a fear of commitment—of going "all the way"—is at the root of this one step forward, one step back attitude. In cases of reconciliation this card signifies that the road will be long and it may or may not lead to a happy resolution. When reversed, the Knight of Wands indicates that the challenge is creating any kind of momentum at all.

Magical Techniques: candles/oil lamps and spirit work

Intentions: road opening, success/mastery, victory, and mental/psychic/dream influence

Page of Wands. This card often comes up when people are seeking a new lover and want to know if they will find one. The Page of Wands is looking, looking, but he is in a desert. Sometimes this means that a person is expecting the impossible—the perfect lover to arrive tied up in a bow on their doorstep—without them ever having to go out, meet people, and play the dating game. When reversed, this card indicates that the querent or the person the querent is seeing is emotionally immature. They may talk a good game, but if the querent is looking for a forever relationship, this is not the right time or candidate. In terms of reconciliation this card signifies extreme youth and can often signal love's first real heartbreak.

Magical Techniques: candles/oil lamps, magical words/prayers/petitions, and spirit work

Intentions: attraction, road opening, and blessing

King and Queen of Cups. Fire rules sex and passion, but the Water of Cups rules deep and romantic love. Like the King and Queen of Coins, the King and Queen of Cups can indicate secondary players: parents, friends, even a married couple that has an ideal relationship. However, they may also represent the lovers themselves, in which case we can know that the love is true, deep, and overflowing. In cases of reconciliation either of these cards can bode well for a happy ending. When reversed, the indication is that the situation is lacking love, romance, and/or the deep feelings required to take it to the next level. The cards reversed may also suggest there is a chemical dependency or substance abuse issue that is getting in the way of the relationship.

Magical Techniques: sacred vessels, spraying/washing/spitting/asperging, textile magic, and spirit work

Intentions: clarity/wisdom, blessing, healing, gain/increase, and mental/psychic/dream influence

Knight of Cups. First and foremost the Knight of Cups is a magical helper who can assist in getting a love situation off the ground or especially help to heal a relationship that has ended and might be reconciled. As far as being a speedometer goes, he reminds us that good things come to those who wait. The Knight of Cups can feel plodding at times, but he also always gets where he is going. When reversed, the Knight of Cups suggests that there is a need for healing, especially heart healing, in the situation that is not being acknowledged or addressed.

Magical Techniques: sacred vessels, spraying/washing/spitting/asperging, and spirit work

Intentions: clarity/wisdom, blessing, healing, gain/increase, mental/psychic/dream influence, and cleansing

Page of Cups. This card often indicates a young man or woman who is somewhat fly-by-night. They often come across as sensitive, magical, deep, and/or artistic, and usually their heart is in the right place. They will listen, however, to their emotions and intuitions, and if something bright catches their eye, it will be difficult to hold their attention. These are fun lovers but tough folks to get a commitment from. If the querent can secure such a commitment, it will be deep and lasting in most cases. In a reconciliation, the card's message really depends on what the querent wants. If they want the relationship back but are not looking for a long-term commitment, then it may work out beautifully. In a reversed position, the Page of Cups tells us that communication is a key challenge in the current situation and things will not move forward until that is addressed.

Magical Techniques: sacred vessels, spraying/washing/spitting/asperging, and spirit work

Intentions: clarity/wisdom, blessing, healing, mental/psychic/dream influence, and cleansing

Pips

Aces

Coins: A solid foundation for something long term to grow and flourish

Swords: The road is open for communication, a meeting of minds, and sometimes topped off by sexual union.

Wands: Sex, lust, and often a new man/masculine energy on the scene

Cups: True love, commitment or the querent's ideal type of relationship, deep feelings

Intentions: clarity/wisdom, victory (especially in competitive situations), road opening, blessing, gain/increase, and beginning

Twos

Coins: Emotional desires and practical concerns are at war with each other—the couple is stressed over money and/or lack of planning.

Swords: Uncertainty about the future causes concern and often the erecting of boundaries. Lovemaking and physical affection may wane.

Wands: A desire to move forward with a new lover but also an indicator that healing/getting over an old lover has not yet happened and is a current obstacle

Cups: The meeting of minds and hearts and developing a beautiful partnership—sometimes romance at the office!

Intentions: clarity/wisdom, road opening, and mental/psychic/dream influence

Threes

Coins: Can indicate marriage or a long-term partnership; often love and a desire to hold a significant place in the community go hand in hand.

Swords: Breakups, divorce, broken hearts—often because one or both partners were seeing others; infidelity

Wands: The wait is over, and good intentions put to drawing lovers or having right relationships are showing fruit.

Cups: Finding joy and support in friends, going out and being social in order to find a new lover, making sure you make time for others

Intentions: clarity/wisdom, attraction, cursing/reversing, gain/increase, and loss/removal

Fours

Coins: Holding back the heart center, available in many ways that do not count but refusing or having a hard time making that intimate step forward into real connection

Swords: Letting something go—often an event that has happened in the couple's past that now truly needs to be released and forgiven

Wands: Marriage, joy, parties, and festivities where love for each other is proclaimed; also sometimes pregnancy!

Cups: A lack of commitment or follow-through; trying to decide if one wants to be in a monogamous relationship or have freedom

Intentions: clarity/wisdom, success/mastery, blessing, protection, and stability

Fives

Coins: Feeling lack—of love, of support, of security, or of resources. Focusing on the negative and refusing to see what is positive or possible.

Swords: Sabotage, often in the form of a lover being dishonest and sometimes indicating that a supposed friend is actually competing for the same person. Querent needs to watch their back.

Wands: Internally and externally conflicted over a relationship—often passion and desire want to go in one direction while duty and love wish to pursue a different direction. Anger may result. Also, lots of nasty bickering.

Cups: Sadness, not fully getting over a lover from the past, not fully letting go, inability to forgive oneself for something that happened once upon a time

Intentions: protection, cursing/reversing, mental/psychic/dream influence, cleansing

Sixes

Coins: Being played: one person's favors are being shared with at least one partner that you may not know about. Can also indicate affairs with married men or women. A return to an already imperfect balance.

Swords: The road is closed; communication is shut off; the desire to move to a more peaceful state in the family or relationship is being blocked.

Wands: Victory through competition—often beating someone else out for a person's love and affection

Cups: A past lover, sometimes childhood sweetheart, coming back on the scene and possible rekindling of an old romance

Intentions: clarity/wisdom, success/mastery, victory, blessing, protection, and healing

Sevens

Coins: Something that the couple has been waiting a long time for finally manifests!

Swords: Lies are being told; at least one person in the relationship is not being honest. In some cases, the querent may be lying to their reader or themselves.

Wands: Feeling trapped in a relationship, wanting to get out but also feeling like one cannot just leave.

Cups: A tumultuous relationship with lots of highs and lows and more than a few outbursts. Can indicate mental imbalance for one or more partners but can also signal an immature relationship ethic addicted to drama.

Intentions: clarity/wisdom, road opening, protection, cursing/reversing, banishing, and mental/psychic/dream influence

Eights

Coins: Steady work in a relationship, taking one day at a time

Swords: A relationship, possible relationship, or desire to reconcile is being sabotaged from the outside by mean and spiteful people. Jealousy and family tensions are usually to blame.

Wands: Connection, communication, and energy, but be careful not to come on too strong or to put too much stock into early movement.

Cups: Leaving a relationship, getting out now, accepting that it's over and working to move on. In rare cases a long-distance attachment.

Intentions: attraction, blessing, protection, healing, gain/increase, and stability

Nines

Coins: Typically indicates a woman who is successfully drawing her desire to her!

Swords: Psychic work being done on the querent or their lover; anxiety, fear, and insomnia. All is not well.

Wands: Past relationship trauma has made a potential or actual partner have shaky judgment and lots of fear around love.

Cups: Open to the possibility of a relationship but unwilling or unable to make the first move

Intentions: clarity/wisdom, victory, attraction, protection, cursing/reversing, banishing, and mental/psychic/dream influence

Tens

Coins: A solid foundation, close-knit family bonds, familial wealth radiating out into the greater community

Swords: Being stabbed in the back and deeply betrayed. Get out of the relationship if you are still in it, and seek out healing and support.

Wands: Long road ahead—especially if looking for reconciliation—but depending on other cards pulled it could be worth it!

Cups: Happy family, a relationship culminating in marriage/children or whatever the querent's ideal happens to be

Intentions: success/mastery, victory, blessing, protection, healing, gain/increase, ending, stability, and cleansing

---

Further Development Tasks

- Name three ways you might integrate images from the tarot into love rituals that you would perform.
- Give three of your own interpretations for a pair of Kings and Queens (you choose the suit) with an eye toward love and romance.

Magic-Making

Attracting a Lover with a Lodestone

You Will Need

A lodestone

Whiskey or another sacred libation (can also be holy water)

Ritual anointing oil for attraction or olive oil (optional)

A petition listing the qualities that you want to attract

Personal concerns from the individual you wish to attract (optional)

A china plate

Magnetic sand or magnetic filings

Process

1. Hold the lodestone in your hand and ask it if it is willing to work with you to attract the right partner. (You may want the lodestone to be the opposite gender from you, or that may not matter to you.)

2. If you receive a yes, then ask the lodestone what its name is.

3. Once you receive the name, wash the lodestone down with whiskey, calling it by name and thanking it for its assistance.

4. Anoint the lodestone in a five-spot pattern with the ritual anointing oil if you are working with that. You may also work with regular olive oil to do this.

5. Take your petition, and if you are working with personal concerns, place those in the center of the petition. Fold the paper once toward you, turn it clockwise 90 degrees and fold it toward you again. Repeat this until the paper is about the size of a Post-it note.

6. Then set the paper in the center of the china plate and set the lodestone on top of the paper. Feed the lodestone a little magnetic sand, and then pray over it for the right person to come into your life.

7. Once the right person has shown up, bury the plate, petition, and lodestone in your backyard.

Reconciliation Devotional Candle

You Will Need

A glass-encased devotional candle that is pink, white, or blue

A knife, ice pick, or other sharp and narrow implement

Three Balm of Gilead buds

A pinch of dried white rose petals

A pinch of dried pink rose petals

A pinch of dried violet petals

Ritual oil for reconciliation (optional)

Pink and blue glitter (optional)

Small chunk of rose quartz

Process

1. Poke three holes into the candle using the knife, ice pick, or other sharp and narrow implement.

2. Place the three Balm of Gilead buds at 12, 6, and 9 o'clock, praying as you do so for healing upon all parties in the relationship.

3. Sprinkle the white rose petals on top of the candle (a tiny bit will do!), praying for peace between all parties.

4. Sprinkle the pink rose petals, praying for a return of love and tenderness with all parties.

5. Sprinkle the dried violet petals, praying for a return of sweetness and passion to the relationship.

6. If you are working with ritual oil for reconciliation and/or glitter, drizzle the oil on the candle and top that with glitter if you like.

7. Place the rose quartz near the edge of the candle, praying as you do for a return to true and deep love.

8. Pray over the candle as a whole your wish for reconciliation.

9. Bless the candle by gently tapping its base on a hard surface three times sealing your work.

10. Light the candle in a place where it may be left alone undisturbed.

11. Once the candle has finished burning, you may divine in its remains to gain further insight into your situation.

Chapter Three

Money, Honey! Part One: Personal Prosperity, Wealth, and Abundance

Whenever I work with a querent in the areas of money, abundance, and wealth, I always like to point out that there is one theme underlying all these concepts: the idea of security. The trick is to understand that security has many different meanings depending on who you are and what you value. I have clients who don't care about the number in their bank account, but they must have a home that they own free and clear in order to feel OK. On the flip side, I have globe-trotting nomadic patrons who don't feel secure unless they are headed to some wonderful destination where they don't know the language or culture—in their case, a home that ties them down to one spot is the opposite of security. My point is that your understanding of security is going to influence your attitudes about money, abundance, and everything else.

Working with Magic for Personal Gain

Some believe it's not OK to work magic for personal gain, and there is good reason for this. The forces we call upon when we create or participate in magical enchantments are potent, universal, and often do not "get" terrestrial human concerns (in part because they do not have the same relationship we do to time and space). Corollary to this, is the fact that many people throughout the ages have taken the attitude of using magic for personal prosperity as opposed to the one I encourage my community members to cultivate which is that of aligning themselves with benevolent forces already at play in the world and in our lives. The distinction is sharp and useful. One form of magic is coercive, while the other is cooperative. When we cultivate an attitude of walking in alliance and kinship with unseen forces, then we can cocreate much together—including a stronger sense of security and personal abundance.

Special Magical Considerations for Personal Abundance Work

The first thing I recommend to anyone interested in personal wealth and abundance is to create an altar that serves as a physical location for any magical work aimed for prosperity (personal and/or business). This altar can also act as a focal point for our ongoing relationship with the fundamental question: Where do I locate security? Such an altar space is versatile, and it would be appropriate to work on other conditions there as well such as healing, fertility, and blessing. In this case, the altar space takes on a general sense of drawing/increasing what is beneficial into your life. We begin with an altar because personal wealth is something that we return to again and again, and it is also an area where we have deep work to do in most cases. Our definition of what wealth looks like may change, but it's a common theme running through our lives. It also makes sense to have a permanent working altar for this condition because much of what we will talk about magically are things to place on the altar.

But before getting into all the magical goodies that can help us build up our wealth, I want to make a quick note about gambling, lotto playing, and lucky numbers.

First off, despite a modern prejudice, there is much precedence for magic relating to gambling, lucky numbers, and lotto playing. After all, these areas more than any other are luck-driven, and one of the many aspects of magic is increasing one's luck. However, years of professional work with querents coming from all economic corners lead me to say this as well—if gambling of any type is one of your ways of raising money, well and good so long as it's not an addictive behavior. If it is, please seek help. If you want to create an altar specifically dedicated to gambling luck, do so, but realize that this space should be a secondary altar that is "backed up" by a primary abundance altar. Now let's peek at a few specific magical techniques you will want to take note of:

- **Prosperity boxes:** These are a specific kind of sacred vessel. These boxes may be mirrored or not, and you want something inside to represent the person you are working on. In this case, if you are creating a prosperity box to increase your own personal prosperity, then the person is you! Ingredients could be as elementary as some of your nail trimmings or as elaborate as a little doll baby. The box is then filled with a variety of money and prosperity drawing curios and left on the altar. Some folks like to add petitions to their boxes, and others like to burn candles on their boxes once a week to activate them.

- **Cash shrines:** Another specific kind of sacred vessel, a cash shrine is something we will see more in the realm of business prosperity, but some people do like to have a place on their altars where they put extra cash. This can be "donated" to a saint like San Martin de Caballero, or it can be set underneath a lodestone and used as "hunting money."
- **Dressing cash:** Falling under the category of magical words/prayers/petitions is the dressing of cash. This is another wonderful trick that involves working with magical sachet powder sprinkled onto cash money, checks, and even in your wallet for a specific intention—usually to grow/increase and keep your money.

Special Considerations in Tarot for Personal Abundance Work

The Major Arcana

When we remember that the Major Arcana cards point out large forces at play not only in our personal lives but in the universe itself, we can begin to get a feel for the expansive quality they imbue on the questions of personal security and financial health. Often the Major Arcana will direct the querent to work or focus on specific areas of their life with regard to money and financial health; in other cases they will warn them of what could happen and how to work with natural forces instead of against them.

The Suits

Coins

As an entire suit Coins speak directly to money and moneymaking, but because they point to the underlying theme of security, Coins also signal concrete actions that can either help support you or become problematic for your relationship to money. Coins are all about practicalities. These cards can tell you to write up and stick to a budget. They can also speak to you about deep tangibles . . . like calling on your ancestors for financial insight.

Swords

The saying "people who fail to plan, plan to fail" was made for the suit of Swords. Swords relate to our mind and intellectual processes, so these are the cards that help us plan for the future, strategize, and create smart tactics around personal finances. Swords can support us in cutting off people who would use our resources carelessly, and they can also be called upon to cut out things like debt. Swords speak to career and profession and, in some cases, may indicate a need to go back to school or receive technical training in order to come into right alignment with money and security.

Wands
Wands invite the querent to look at the connection between money, physicality, vital energy, creativity, and passion. One question that may emerge from this network of relationships is: Is my/one's personal current sense of security sustainable? If the things that make us feel secure are also making us unhealthy (like a desk job where we never move around) or drain our energy, then we may need to assess the trade-off and decide whether or not it is worthwhile. Hot feelings like irritation and anger may come up with these cards . . . especially as they have to do with personal finances. The good news is that the deepest work of Wands is transformation: if something needs to change in your life when it comes to money, then these are the cards to point that out and help you achieve your goals.

Cups
Money and emotions are very tied up with one another. Cups highlight this and encourage us to look closely at the intersection between our emotions, work habits, earning potential, and spending habits. Cups speak to cooler and deeper emotions like sadness, melancholy, and love . . . all of which do play a role in your relationship to money. These cards will help you discover what that relationship is.

Major Arcana Cards

Note: As with the previous chapter, card interpretations include a meaning should the card be reversed and/or surrounded by more challenging cards. When it comes to a financial reading either in this chapter or the next, reversals may universally be read in one more way: an indication that the querent's current financial state is "under water." The exceptions to this general rule would be the Hanged Man and the Wheel of Fortune.

The Fool. His appearance can indicate that someone is being foolish when it comes to their personal prosperity or that they need to be especially aware of changing tides in their financial situation right now. A new chapter could be unfolding, and the querent will need to use all their resources to take advantage of it. Prudence, symbolized by the white rose that the Fool carries, is an important virtue to cultivate when it comes to money, and in some cases this card indicates that there are hidden ways of generating more wealth the querent is not aware of or has not acknowledged. In reversed form, the Fool may indicate that the querent needs to stop their pie-in-the-sky financial thinking and get serious about the details.

Magical Techniques: candles/oil lamps, magical words/prayers/petitions, and physical manipulation

Intentions: clarity/wisdom, success/mastery, road opening, blessing, beginning, and mental/psychic/dream influence

The Magician. The Magician shows up to remind us that when it comes to wealth and security-building, all the resources we need are at hand. The Magician also gives a nod to ritual and ceremony, indicating we would be wise to focus our efforts in those areas on personal wealth and abundance. Now is the time to build your personal prosperity altar! You may also want to invest in some basic ingredients for money and wealth-building magic. When reversed, the Magician indicates that magic is not the appropriate avenue through which to pursue wealth at this time and the focus should be on practical actions. A reversal here could also tell us that the querent does not have everything they need to address their financial situation and they may require outside help or advice.

Magical Techniques: all

Intentions: success/mastery, victory, attraction, road opening, blessing, protection, and mental/psychic/dream influence

The High Priestess. Sometimes money situations are broken, requiring help and repair. Other times, intuition guides us in one direction, and practical concerns encourage us to go in a different direction. The High Priestess shows up in times like these to let the querent know they should heed their intuition when it comes to financial health. She might also demonstrate that higher education or spiritual endeavors/work are directly tied to the querent's earning potential. For instance, if the querent is considering going back to school and the High Priestess comes up in a reading, the indication is that a return to school would be a sound choice. When reversed, the High Priestess suggests that the querent is closed off to their own inner knowing, or perhaps unwilling to do healing work around their relationship to money . . . and either of these will create problems for them down the road.

Magical Techniques: magical words/prayers/petitions, spraying/washing/spitting/asperging, textile magic, and spirit work
Intentions: clarity/wisdom, blessing, protection, healing, and mental/psychic/dream influence

The Empress. While her mate focuses on personal sovereignty as it relates to wealth and money, the Empress encourages the querent to utilize personal wealth to make the world a better, more beautiful place. This card comes up to remind us that we need to support our creative habits with time, tools, and, in some cases, actual money. If you paint, now is the time to buy supplies. If you write, now is the time to carve out space every week to do so. If you dance, put on the music already! Work with your creativity to craft a prosperity box or work with a goddess like Lakshmi who is known to aid in matters of personal prosperity and wealth. In her reversed form, the Empress indicates indolence, laziness, and refusal to work toward your goals.
Magical Techniques: sacred vessels, lodestones, physical manipulation, and textile magic
Intentions: success/mastery, victory, attraction, blessing, gain/increase, beginning, and stability

The Emperor. As mentioned above, the focus here is on personal sovereignty, skill, and mastery when it comes to prosperity. The Emperor indicates that the best way to improve your financial situation is to improve your skills and abilities as they relate to money and moneymaking. This card can also point to a boss, supervisor, or even benevolent family member whose approval and favor may do a lot for the querent. If the card seems to speak to the querent themselves, then there is a reminder to be generous and help others get set up for success. When reversed, the Emperor expresses selfishness, greed, or an inability to get approval from banking institutions.
Magical Techniques: sacred vessels, lodestones, and physical manipulation
Intentions: success/mastery, victory, blessing, gain/increase, beginning, and stability

The Hierophant. The Hierophant indicates that the querent's personal prosperity is tied to their magical and charitable sensibilities. If money is always tight, this card suggests that they try giving some to a responsible not for profit charity—religious or otherwise. The Hierophant can signal that the querent's relationship to personal prosperity is a spiritual concern and should be treated as such. Tithing may be of interest in this case, and lineage and legacy work is recommended. When the Hierophant is reversed, it can indicate the querent's relationship with a nonprofit and/or religious organization is imbalanced and needs to be reassessed.

Magical Techniques: candles/oil lamps, magical words/prayers/petitions, spraying/washing/spitting/asperging, and spirit work

Intentions: clarity/wisdom, road opening, blessing, protection, healing, and cleansing

The Lovers. When this card comes up, it often points to the querent's romantic relationships—and in some cases past trauma around romance—as a place to explore when trying to answer questions about money and personal prosperity. This card can indicate that the querent's partner has a strong influence over their financial situation—for better or for worse depending on context. The Lovers often signal a significant decision needs to be made by the querent with respect to their situation. Look to the cards around the Lovers to get a sense of what the decision should be. When reversed, the Lovers reveal a lack of harmony and unison when it comes to the querent's relationship to finances. It may also let the querent know it is time to stop putting off the hard decisions.

Magical Techniques: lodestones, candles/oil lamps, and physical manipulation

Intentions: clarity/wisdom, success/mastery, victory, attraction, and blessing

The Chariot. The Chariot contains a message of victory and success. When we look at it from the vantage point of personal wealth, it also serves to point out that two things that may seem diametrically opposed are actually the keys to the kingdom. Example: a specific amount of debt provides the querent with a distinct financial goal to achieve. When we pull the Chariot card, the querent may be looking at luxury travel in the name of moneymaking but may also need to get creative with a current tension and be open to doing something rather dramatic, like moving. When reversed, the Chariot indicates that the querent's relationship to personal abundance is out of balance and requires a strong course correction. Depending on how serious the situation is, the querent may need to let someone else (like a financial advisor) take the reins for a while.

Magical Techniques: candles/oil lamps, magical words/prayers/petitions, physical manipulation, and spirit work

Intentions: clarity/wisdom, success/mastery, victory, road opening, and blessing

Strength. The Strength card can indicate the querent needs to control spending habits, debt, or other big forces threatening their financial well-being. They may do this by first assessing their situation and then moving to make practical changes. This card may sometimes say that the querent is surrounded by people whose opinions are louder than they need to be and who are not encouraging the querent when it comes to good financial practices—in which case setting strong boundaries and protecting themselves from naysayers is the way to go. When reversed, the Strength card shows the querent is fighting a losing battle against external pressure. They need to be willing to ask for and receive help to stabilize the situation.

Magical Techniques: candles/oil lamps, magical words/prayers/petitions, physical manipulation, and spirit work

Intentions: success/mastery, victory, blessing, protection, healing, and mental/psychic/dream influence

The Hermit. The Hermit shows up to remind the querent that our relationship to personal prosperity begins with our relationship to ourselves. It may be time to go inward and get clear on what they want, need, and no longer desire. The Hermit may also indicate that the querent either is living too simply, barely scratching out an existence, and extra support from family members and community is needed or needs to simplify their relationship to abundance and desire for the finer things in life. When reversed, the Hermit suggests there are some deep lessons around money and finances that the querent has not yet learned. Things will not change until the querent takes the time and space to master those lessons . . . and in turn share them with others.

Magical Techniques: sacred vessels, candles/oil lamps, magical words/prayers/petitions, and spirit work

Intentions: clarity/wisdom, blessing, and protection

Wheel of Fortune. The Wheel of Fortune speaks to our personal fortunes directly and reminds us that while many things are not destined, every now and then something is. If the querent has been experiencing a hard time in their personal finances, then this card announces the tide is turning in their favor. If, however, things have been going well, this card reminds the querent to prepare for lean times ahead. When reversed, the Wheel of Fortune indicates that a reversal of fortune is likely but with prayer and diligence you may be able to escape it, especially if it is negative!

Magical Techniques: Magic is contraindicated with the Wheel of Fortune card, but spirit work is acceptable.

Intentions: clarity/wisdom, gain/increase, loss/removal, stability, and cleansing

Justice. The Justice card speaks to fairness and reciprocity and reminds the querent that when it comes to personal finances, what you give is what you get. There is a great freedom with this card because the querent has the ability to chart their own course. This card also obviously points out that balance is required. If the querent is involved in legal issues or a court case, depending on the cards around the Justice card either a positive or negative outcome directly affecting the querent's financial well-being is indicated. When reversed, the Justice card signals there is a taker in the situation and they are not giving in equal measure. This could be the querent, but more likely it is someone adjacent to them. In this case, identifying the individual and removing them is the best course of action.

Magical Techniques: candles/oil lamps, magical words/prayers/petitions, and physical manipulation

Intentions: clarity/wisdom, gain/increase, loss/removal, stability, and mental/psychic/dream influence

The Hanged Man. When we receive this card, it reminds us that we should shift our perspective if we want to make headway with our personal finances and our relationship to prosperity. Often that perspectival shift also requires letting go of something we no longer need. In the short term this can feel like a painful sacrifice, but in the long term it is an excellent choice for the querent to make. When reversed, the Hanged Man carries the opposite message: maybe our querent has sacrificed too much in order to be financially secure. We might ask if the sacrifices are worth the trade. This card when upright, and most of the reversals in this chapter, can also signify that our querent is under water financially.

Magical Techniques: candles/oil lamps, magical words/prayers/petitions, physical manipulation, textile magic, and spirit work

Intentions: clarity/wisdom, protection, healing, cursing/reversing, ending, loss/removal, and banishing

Death. When we receive the Death card after asking about personal prosperity, it usually means one of two things. The first is the possibility that something in the querent's life needs to "die back" so that more abundance can smoothly come to life in their world. The second is that they may be impacted financially—positively or negatively, depending on the position of the card and other cards around it—by the actual death of someone or something, like an older family member who left them an inheritance or the metaphorical death of their spouse's job. When the Death card is reversed, it can indicate that the querent needs to shift their attention from releasing/banishing to calling in and attracting. It can also indicate that an inheritance the querent thinks will be theirs does not live up to the hype.

Magical Techniques: candles/oil lamps, spraying/washing/spitting/asperging, and spirit work

Intentions: clarity/wisdom, victory, attraction, protection, cursing/reversing, ending, loss/removal, banishing, and cleansing

Temperance. With the Temperance card the querent is reminded that slow and steady wins the race and trying to accomplish too much too quickly is really just going to leave them confused and lost. Advise them to be patient and act with prudence. If the querent has a big idea about what to do with their money, how to manage their money, or how to make more money, and this card appears, it is a sign that the querent needs to wait for a while before making any significant change. The Temperance card can also suggest the querent would be well-served by developing a hobby or outside of work interest and money could be made in such a manner. When reversed, this card indicates that now is a time for action, not hesitation, and the querent needs to move in a decisive manner.

Magical Techniques: sacred vessels, physical manipulation, spraying/washing/spitting/asperging, and spirit work

Intentions: clarity/wisdom, road opening, blessing, healing, stability, and cleansing

The Devil. When this card shows up, the message is loud and clear: the querent has a person, bad habit, or pattern of belief holding them back and definitely negatively impacting their earning capability. This card can also indicate that the querent understands themselves to be enslaved by their current situation and unable to make choices or move forward, but in reality they have more freedom—and choices—than they think they do. Another message of the Devil? If things look too good to be true, then they probably are. When this card is reversed, it indicates that there is blessedness around the situation right now and you don't need to deal with devilish drama!

Magical Techniques: candles/oil lamps and spraying/washing/spitting/asperging

Intentions: victory, protection, cursing/reversing, loss/removal, banishing, and mental/psychic/dream influence

The Tower. The Tower is one of the better-known cards in the tarot deck partially because it often portends doom and disaster. However, the Tower card also creates an opening for deep awareness. The querent needs to prepare for things to get rough financially, but also get ready for new information that can impact their life positively in the long term. If the querent is already having a very difficult time financially, then the Tower card indicates they need to look for the treasure among the ruins and rubble. When reversed, the Tower is a reminder that the querent should build their finances up in such a way that they will be sustainable and capable of withstanding even the most tumultuous storm.

Magical Techniques: sacred vessels, magical words/prayers/petitions, physical manipulation, and spirit work

Intentions: clarity/wisdom, protection, cursing/reversing, ending, loss/removal, stability, banishing, mental/psychic/dream influence, cleansing

The Moon. The Moon indicates obstacles standing between the querent and their financial health. Often these obstacles come from two major sources: the querent's personal appetites and the querent's practical responsibilities. Sometimes they both play a role in the situation. If this card comes up in a reading, it is a good idea for the querent to assess their role in any financial stress and also to seek guidance from magical allies. The Moon also speaks to illusions, and so determining if the querent has any false impressions or delusions about money and their financial situation is a good idea. Yet another interpretation of this card has to do with healing: the Moon's presence can indicate healing around finances is needed and/or is happening. If the Moon shows up reversed, then this suggests the querent is deep into fantasy and escapist thinking about finances. Some cleansing and a focus on clarity and wisdom are advised.

Magical Techniques: sacred vessels, spraying/washing/spitting/asperging, and spirit work

Intentions: clarity/wisdom, blessing, healing, mental/psychic/dream influence, and cleansing

The Sun. The Sun in many ways can be read as the opposite of the Moon. Here the roads are open, and the way is clear. Everything is sparkly and full of possibility and potential. The Sun also is about resourcefulness, so when reading for a querent who is not feeling so full of possibility, assist them in thinking about what they already have or can do that can be a source of money. If the Sun shows up in a challenging position in the reading, it can indicate that the querent is being tested by abundance—which is quite possible! Another interpretation for the Sun in a challenging position is that the querent's desire for children may not be realistic given their current financial situation. When the Sun shows up reversed, there is a sense that things are not clear, not optimistic, and not hopeful. The querent may feel weighed down to the point of not knowing what to do or what actions to take. In these cases, blessing work is helpful.

Magical Techniques: candles/oil lamps, magical words/prayers/petitions, and spirit work

Intentions: clarity/wisdom, success/mastery, victory, attraction, road opening, blessing, protection, and healing

Judgement. The Judgement card often points to a querent having certain ideas or preconceptions about where they need to be financially. Those coulds and shoulds often kill real creative thinking and solid action, so when this card crops up, it may indicate that it's time to get back to basics and remember one's true worth. Another possible interpretation of the Judgement card is that it shows up to let the querent know a situation that previously seemed "dead and buried" may crop up again and create positive or negative effects for the querent when it comes to their finances. Always, this card indicates the querent needs to use their head and their discernment when assessing financial questions and concerns. When Judgement is reversed, it signifies a lack of discernment has created a problematic situation which may require some effort before it is finally resolved.

Magical Techniques: sacred vessels, physical manipulation, spraying/washing/spitting/asperging, and spirit work

Intentions: clarity/wisdom, blessing, protection, healing, ending, loss/removal, banishing, and cleansing

The World. When this card shows up, it indicates that victory and success belong to the querent! Personal prosperity and a strong sense of security are all part of the package! The World refers to the entire story and reminds us that everything is connected—the querent would do well to remember this is as true in finances as it is for everything else. The World also signifies the ending of one cycle and the beginning of a new cycle, so the querent may see that play out in their personal finances. If the World is reversed, it can suggest that the querent is too fixed on a specific aspect of their financial situation and not taking the whole into the account. It can also say that the querent is not operating from their truest sense of self.

Magical Techniques: all

Intentions: clarity/wisdom, success/mastery, victory, attraction, road opening, blessing, protection, healing, beginning, ending, and stability

Court Cards

King and Queen of Coins. The King of Coins shows up to speak about authority but in a less grand, more practical way than the Emperor does. He also checks in and asks: Is the querent utilizing all of their talents to the best of their abilities? Is there a hidden thing the querent does, person the querent knows, or idea the querent has that could greatly contribute to their personal abundance? Whereas her husband is really focused on the querent and what they have going on, the Queen of Coins looks to others. She tells us that right now to solidly address our desire for personal wealth and abundance we need to be a blessing to other people—practically and magically as well. When reversed, the King or Queen of Coins suggests the querent is ignoring practical concerns and/or obvious financial challenges and nothing will improve until they deal with those issues head-on.

Magical Techniques: sacred vessels, lodestones, physical manipulation, and spirit work

Intentions: clarity/wisdom, success/mastery, attraction, road opening, blessing, gain/increase, and stability

Knight of Coins. When it comes to personal abundance, the Knight of Coins turns up to remind us that we need to take it easy. He has been engaged in combat and riding through the wildwood. Now he is showing up and standing still on his horse. This period might feel like a waiting game, but it actually should be viewed as a much-needed break. Now is the time to catch our breath and make a plan, not take action. When reversed, this Knight can indicate that cash flow is especially going to be challenging for the querent in the coming days.

Magical Techniques: sacred vessels, lodestones, physical manipulation, spraying/washing/spitting/asperging, textile magic, and spirit work

Intentions: success/mastery, blessing, protection, and stability

Page of Coins. The Page of Coins is the ambitious, yearning part of the querent's personality. When this card comes up, it is first and foremost a clue we may need to reinvestigate what it is that really says wealth to the querent—what abundance can really look and feel like. This is because the querent is reaching and stretching out for security but not quite finding it, perhaps because they are looking in the wrong directions. The Page of Coins also tells us that because the querent is in a place where they are grasping, they may not have the lucidity to make the best possible decisions. Consequently, they should proceed with caution and prudence. When reversed, the Page of Coins suggests that the querent needs to educate themselves about financial matters . . . little in their situation will improve until they do.

Magical Techniques: sacred vessels, lodestones, physical manipulation, and spirit work

Intentions: clarity/wisdom, attraction, road opening, gain/increase, and stability

King and Queen of Swords. These cards indicate it's time to get serious about the connection between the querent's personal wealth and career, job, or vocation. Perhaps they need to ask for a raise, go back to school, or fully commit to the professional path they are on. Whatever the point, the King and Queen of Swords encourage them to get to it quickly and with a solid plan in place. When reversed, the King and Queen of Swords speak to a lack of planning, strategy, and/or training in connection with financial difficulties. In this context, they advise the querent to make a plan, develop a strategy, and receive the training they need in order to have the right relationship with their money.

Magical Techniques: magical words/prayers/petitions, physical manipulation, and spirit work

Intentions: clarity/wisdom, success/mastery, victory, road opening, protection, and mental/psychic/dream influence

Knight of Swords. This helper figure is showing up to instruct the querent that they need to establish better boundaries around financial matters and communicate their needs to others with more clarity and precision. Also, the

Knight of Swords warns the querent not to rush in to a new job, an opportunity that looks too good to be true, or a serious relationship change that could have long-term effects on their personal finances. When reversed, this card often indicates the querent needs to act.

Magical Techniques: magical words/prayers/petitions and physical manipulation

Intentions: clarity/wisdom, victory, road opening, and protection

Page of Swords. The Page of Swords signals issues around thinking about and planning for the future are very present for the querent right now. When this card appears, it is a good idea for the querent to think about their future in terms of finances and what financial concerns are priorities for them. This card may also indicate the querent needs to go back to school or get some specific training around either their particular skill or finances in general. When reversed, this card suggests a lack of clarity and understanding that is resulting in scattered thoughts and confusion. In these cases, a resetting and cleansing are a good idea.

Magical Techniques: magical words/prayers/petitions, physical manipulation, and spirit work

Intentions: clarity/wisdom, success/mastery, road opening, gain/increase, beginning, mental/psychic/dream influence, and cleansing

King and Queen of Wands. The King and Queen of Wands deal with our deep passions and our ability to manage our energy and create magical change in our lives. Refinement, artistry, and creative self-expression are all areas tied to these two figures. When they show up in a reading, it is a clue to the querent that their personal prosperity is tied to following their passions, marketing their creativity, and managing their energy. Like all face cards, the King and Queen of Wands can indicate actual people involved in the querent's situation, but they can also represent attitudes, beliefs, or influences the querent has internalized for better or worse. When either of these cards is reversed, the indication is that the querent is creatively blocked or refuses to link their creativity to their finances . . . and this is causing problems.

Magical Techniques: candles/oil lamps, physical manipulation, and spirit work

Intentions: clarity/wisdom, success/mastery, victory, attraction, road opening, blessing, and protection

Knight of Wands. The Knight of Wands specifically shows up to talk about energy and energy management. The feeling is that there is something going on in the querent's life that requires discernment but also making a decision. They need to act instead of doing a one step forward, one step back kind of dance. Often, if there is a difficult decision the querent is facing, doing some spirit work with a Holy Helper is a good choice. This card can also warn the querent that they are entering a time of financial flux where things break their way for a while and then setbacks occur. When reversed, the Knight of Wands indicates that putting off a decision is creating instability and interrupting flow.

Magical Techniques: candles/oil lamps, physical manipulation, and spirit work

Intentions: clarity/wisdom, success/mastery, victory, attraction, protection, and stability

Page of Wands. The Page of Wands deals with looking for answers in all the wrong places when it comes to personal prosperity. This is a card of "drying up," so the querent may feel that they have literally run dry—they have no good options or good solutions. The answer, the Page of Wands advises, is to look within and call upon what talents, resources, and connections or possible connections are already in place. When reversed, the Page of Wands can indicate overwhelm—things are not dry! In fact, there are so many ideas and possibilities that the querent is not sure which one to choose!

Magical Techniques: candles/oil lamps, physical manipulation, and spirit work

Intentions: clarity/wisdom, success/mastery, victory, attraction, protection, and stability

King and Queen of Cups. When we recollect that the King and Queen of Cups speak to our emotions, it won't be a surprise that, when we get either of these characters, they are encouraging the querent to look at the feelings around personal prosperity and money. The Queen of Cups specifically refers to intuition, particularly the querent's ability to use theirs for insights into their personal prosperity. The King of Cups points to making one's feelings around personal abundance work in their favor and not counter to it. In either case when these cards show up in challenging positions, they often indicate the querent is likely to spend money when they are emotionally stressed out and/or the querent is responding emotionally—and often with depression—to their current financial situation. In either case gentle healing is in order.

Magical Techniques: sacred vessels, spraying/washing/spitting/asperging, and spirit work

Intentions: clarity/wisdom, blessing, protection, healing, stability, mental/psychic/dream influence, and cleansing

Knight of Cups. The Knight of Cups often refers to a magical helper, and that is the primary meaning of the card in this case. The querent should seek out a magical helper when it comes to increasing their personal prosperity. The Knight of Cups can also indicate that slow and steady wins the race. The querent may feel like their peers are racing past them with more success—but the truth is they may well come out best in the end! The Knight of Cups can also express that the querent is doing deep healing work around money at this time and patience is needed.

Magical Techniques: sacred vessels, spraying/washing/spitting/asperging, and spirit work

Intentions: clarity/wisdom, blessing, protection, healing, stability, mental/psychic/dream influence, and cleansing

Page of Cups. The Page of Cups signals something that may feel contradictory to some of the other aspects in the Cups cards. In cases of personal prosperity it indicates the querent may want to stop listening to their intuition or dampen it down a bit and focus on some of the practical considerations in dealing with their personal finances. This is because the messages they are receiving from their inner contacts are not loud and clear—or if they are, something is getting lost in translation and the advice as the querent perceives it is usually not very good. When reversed, this card suggests that the querent is ignoring their intuition at their own peril.

Magical Techniques: sacred vessels, spraying/washing/spitting/asperging, and spirit work

Intentions: clarity/wisdom, blessing, protection, healing, stability, mental/psychic/dream influence, and cleansing

Pips

Aces

Coins: New beginnings or a new and clearer relationship to personal prosperity and finances; starting out on a solid footing

Swords: Victory and success in the querent's personal finances come through clear communication, strong social connections, and a smart career moves. Say yes to the opportunity.

Wands: Energy, vitality, and creative ideas are positioned to open up a new road of revenue.

Cups: Love, emotions, marriage, and partnership are all poised to be special blessings on the personal financial situation and signify a new start.

Intentions: clarity/wisdom, road opening, blessing, beginning, and cleansing

Twos

Coins: The querent needs to work on balancing their emotional needs and desires with practical realities.

Swords: Setting up boundaries is essential to improving the querent's personal relationship with money, and in some cases road opening work is a must!

Wands: A desire to move forward and open new roads for personal prosperity is hindered by an attachment to the past.

Cups: Partnership—either in love or business—will increase the health of the querent's personal finances.

Intentions: clarity/wisdom, success/mastery, road opening, and blessing

Threes

Coins: Collaborating with two partners and/or making long-term plans will lead to a better financial forecast.

Swords: Heartbreak and emotional turmoil are taking their toll on the querent. In some cases, this card can refer to a loss or gain in personal finances coming out of divorce or separation.

Wands: The querent is waiting for a return on an investment that has been a long time coming; seeking out patience and support is a good move.

Cups: Celebrating with friends and getting social (stepping away from mundane concerns) will improve the querent's relationship with their personal prosperity.

Intentions: success/mastery, victory, attraction, road opening, blessing, protection, and gain/increase

Fours

Coins: The querent refuses to give up the best part of themselves and so does not have as much security or abundance as they otherwise might.

Swords: It's time to tie up loose ends and leave a few things in the past where they belong. Once the querent does, the road to personal prosperity will be more open and freer.

Wands: Marriage, partnership, and/or community support are all important to the querent's overall sense of prosperity right now.

Cups: It's time for the querent to decide and commit to something or someone. Until they do, the energetic drain of their indecision will affect their finances for the worse and other areas as well.

Intentions: success/mastery, victory, blessing, protection, and stability

Fives

Coins: Impoverishment and a scarcity mentality that is easily triggered. Financially speaking, times may be tough, but there are resources available to the querent that they are not taking advantage of. Contrarily, this card may indicate a young person who is on their way financially, living lean but preparing for a solid and well-funded future.

Swords: Sabotage and betrayal are present in the querent's current situation: they need to watch their prosperity and their backs.

Wands: Conflict, anger, and irritation are all playing a big role in the querent's life right now and, as a result, keeping them from fully investing in their relationship to security and prosperity.

Cups: Regret over past decisions, depression, and melancholy are eating away at the querent and need to be addressed for the money river to flow fast and clean.

Intentions: clarity/wisdom, protection, healing, cursing/reversing, loss/removal, banishing, and cleansing

Sixes

Coins: The querent will get a fair share or has a good reciprocal relationship to their personal prosperity, but they are probably not going to get more than their fair share.

Swords: The road feels blocked, and the querent may not have a very clear idea about what they want or need to do as far as their personal finances go, but they are making more headway than they think!

Wands: Victory and success go to the querent—usually after there has been a bit of competition!

Cups: A lover or friend from the past may show up and assist the querent in financial matters. Another possibility is that the querent returns to a previous situation that enriched them.

Intentions: success/mastery, victory, blessing, healing, gain/increase, and stability

Sevens

Coins: I consider this the return on investment card. It indicates the querent will get a good return on their work and efforts.

Swords: The querent needs to be aware of lies and deceit around their relationship to personal prosperity. These can be lies told to the querent themselves or lies someone else is telling.

Wands: Feelings of being trapped and having no way out have a negative influence on the querent's personal finances.

Cups: Big emotional mood swings exert an effect on personal finances through spending habits and a lack of clarity around money stuff.

Intentions: clarity/wisdom, success/mastery, protection, stability, and banishing

Eights

Coins: Steady work is the way to win. If the querent just keeps putting one foot in front of the other, they will overcome.

Swords: Slander, lies, and gossip are creating issues for the querent when it comes to their finances. This may be negative self-talk, talk from others, or possibly both.

Wands: More information and clarity around finances and financial priorities need to be gathered. The querent may receive news in the near future that directly informs their financial situation.

Cups: The querent may need to make a move before they are able to have the kind of personal financial situation they want for themselves. The move could be relocating or changing jobs.

Intentions: clarity/wisdom, blessing, protection, cursing/reversing, gain/increase, loss/removal, banishing, and cleansing

Nines

Coins: The querent has a wonderful relationship to their personal prosperity. There is enough money for all their needs and many of their wants and a good amount of flexibility in their schedule. This is a good card to meditate on for those trying to manifest that reality.

Swords: Nightmares, insomnia, and stress. The querent needs to realign themselves with their ideas surrounding personal prosperity and, practically speaking, make sure that they are getting enough rest.

Wands: In this case excess energy and conflict-filled situations have left the querent feeling like they don't have good judgment and the other shoe is going to drop. It's not a good time to make decisions.

Cups: The querent has a good attitude: open and positive about their relationship to prosperity. However, they may sometimes take too passive of a role when it comes to earning.

Intentions: clarity/wisdom, success/mastery, blessing, protection, cursing/reversing, banishing, mental/psychic/dream influence, and cleansing

Tens

Coins: Mega prosperity and wealth; concern turns to legacy-building and legacy-leaving.

Swords: Betrayal, chronic fatigue, and death. The querent needs to seriously assess a situation or person around them and reverse course—for their money and their health!

Wands: Effort needs to be made now to improve the situation with the querent's personal finances and sense of abundance. Typically, I pull a second card to make sure that the effort is worth it!

Cups: A card that indicates the querent locates true wealth and abundance in their family and in their love relationships

Intentions: success/mastery, victory, blessing, protection, healing, cursing/reversing, gain/increase, ending, stability, banishing, and cleansing

---

Suggestions for Further Development

Answer the following questions for yourself:

- What is my relationship to personal prosperity?
- What does security mean to me?

Magic-Making

My Favorite Money Mantra

Let me share my personal favorite money mantra:

money come, money stay, and money grow!

Dress Me Up, Take Me Out!

This is a way to dress cash money for smart spending.

You Will Need

Cash spending money in whatever denominations
and combinations you want

A pen

A sachet powder for wealth and prosperity or
ground sassafras, cinnamon, and cinquefoil

Process

1. Take each bill and at the very bottom inscribe RTM, which stands for Return to Me, with the pen.

2. Fan the bills out.

3. Keeping your focus on your desire to attract more money, sprinkle the sachet powder or herbal blend over the cash.

4. Using your hands, move the powder toward yourself so that it covers all the cash money, and as you do this, pray that when you spend this money, it returns to you increased.

5. Place the money in your wallet, and then go out and make smart choices about what you purchase.

◆ *Chapter Four* ◆

Money, Honey! Part Two: Business Prosperity and Career Success

In the area of personal prosperity, we always begin by considering what makes us feel secure, but in the arena of business prosperity and career success, we have a more objective agenda. For those who are self-employed there is an obvious need to make money; for those working for others there is also a need to make, and keep making, money and also to have room for promotion and advancement. In both instances these things can be easy to say and difficult to manifest. With a little divination know-how and potent engagement with magic, however, you can be way ahead of the game! First, let's look at the different variables we encounter in this area and the magic that goes along with them. I am going to start by assuming that your querent is working for somebody else, since for 90 percent of the population that is the case. When working for someone else, whether at a large company or a small family-owned business, there are a few constants to be familiar with: the boss or supervisor, colleagues, the querent's work, and wages and salaries.

- **The boss or supervisor:** This is the person or people who have a higher rank than the querent. The title may refer to a manager or a CEO depending on where the querent works, but if they want to keep their job and have the best experience possible, they need the boss on their side. Magically speaking there are two ways to encourage people to work with you. The first is through sweetness, employing techniques like sweetening spells, lodestone attraction work, and the use of certain herbs like five-finger grass and vanilla to facilitate a cooperative relationship. The second is through more coercive means so that the boss really has no other choice. This is done with dominating herbs and roots like licorice root, Master Root, and Master of the Woods as well as hot pepper and High John the Conqueror root.

- **Colleagues:** Colleagues are tricky. On the one hand, querents need to get along with them and not have waves or ripples in the community pool. On the other, we want to make sure that they do not try to take credit for the querents' work, refuse to accept responsibility for mistakes, or make things harder than they must be. As with working with the boss, when we look at colleagues, we may befriend them and "work toward the good" with sweetening work or take a more coercive approach. However, with colleagues a couple of other possible directions come up. We may need to shut the mouths of gossipy colleagues by doing Shut Your Mouth–style workings. We may also want to make sure that when it comes to any kind of competition, we have the advantage and victory.
- **The work:** Then there is the actual work the querent is doing. They should be skillful and happy in the work so that they receive the money, promotions, and praise they deserve! The type of magical work we focus on here is to build up, increase, and maintain skill levels. Obviously having the boss on the querent's side and cooperative colleagues helps, but the work speaks for itself. In some cases, this might also involve magical work to change jobs or find a position the querent is more qualified for.
- **Wages and salaries:** Making sure that wages are delivered on time and fairly and are all they could be is the top priority with career success magic.

Now, if you are working for yourself or with a querent who is self-employed, then some of these issues are nonexistent while others take on a different level of emphasis. In these special cases, we focus on:

- **Colleagues:** The boss or supervisor is not mentioned here because the querent is usually their own boss. Colleagues are quite important in the world of freelance work and self-employment, however—even more important in some respects than if you work a typical office job. When it comes to working with colleagues in our freelance lives, we want to focus on communication, collaboration, and good vibes. It is also great if you can get to a mutually beneficial referral system.
- **Work:** Just as in cases of working for someone else, in a freelance situation and self-employment the actual work a person is doing deserves equal emphasis and attention. Growing, refining, and promoting the unique skills the querent brings to the table are essential—and often overlooked. This is because while large companies slate money for the

further development and refinement of skills, small or microbusinesses often do not.

- **Wages and salaries:** Keeping a business flush and prosperous depends on growing, keeping, and increasing money as well as maximizing all the various sources of revenue available. Depending on what kind of special case business you have, you may want to consult with a lawyer/accountant about what business structure would be most financially advantageous to you. In such situations, I always recommend doing a little attraction magic to make sure the right people show up to your side!

Special Considerations in Tarot for Business Prosperity and Career Success

The Major Arcana

The Major Arcana cards always invite us to look at and consider the significant overarching themes at play in our work and lives. When we are reading for business success and prosperity, they are going to focus on our attitudes about business, our relationships with those we have business with, our financial stability or lack thereof, and our personal attitudes about our careers. Depending on the cards drawn, we may find we are in a place of relative security and ease or we have some upcoming difficulties we need to be aware of, but the key in thinking about the Major Arcana is that we need to focus on the big picture.

The Suits

Coins

As was the case with our last chapter, Coins are quite useful when we are asking about financial success. Coins bring up the issue of security, which we have explored in detail. When many of these cards show up, we need to ask—is there job security here, a possibility for promotion and advancement? Because they are ruled by the element of Earth, Coins warn us first impressions may be misleading. Something can look very legit, but if it sounds too good to be true, it probably is. Likewise, something may not look that attractive at first, but underneath the surface there may be a great deal of good fortune and possibility. Coins, along with some of the Major Arcana and court cards, also talk about our relationship with the "rulers" in the workplace—bosses, managers, and supervisors are all indicated here because they are the ones who control the purse strings. And of course, Coins deal with money, wages, salary, promotions and demotions, and practicalities. If a good number of Coins come up during a reading, it indicates the job is too tied to money for good or ill, the money is not worth the work or vice versa, or there will be a great return in this situation.

Swords

Along with its resonance to cursing work, the suit of Swords has a lot to say about business. These cards often refer to white-collar professions: doctors (especially surgeons), lawyers, and academics. Swords emphasize long-range vision, clarity of thought, mental agility, and articulate communication. Of course, depending on the Swords card you pull as well as the position it is in, you may find that any of these areas are currently being challenged or blocked as well. When we get a lot of Swords around questions dealing with business success and prosperity, it means we need to pay special attention to the types of plans we are making (especially for the long term), the way we are communicating with others, and how we are keeping our skills sharp and up to date. Many Swords may also indicate it's time to go back to school or to get serious about finding a "real" job.

Wands

As we have already learned, Wands are ruled by the element of Fire. In turn, Fire is the ruling principle for our passion, sex lives, physical health, energy, and creativity. When reading for business success and prosperity, a preponderance of Wands underscores the element of creativity in business and may also emphasize the need for a physical element in one's work. It's important to understand that when we talk about creative work, we do not necessarily mean someone has to be an artist, musician, dancer, or poet. All kinds of jobs require creativity and innovation. Wands also tend to rule technology and electronics, two areas where innovation absolutely rules. The physical aspect of this suit may indicate someone needs to pursue a more physical path such as coaching a team sport or working as a yoga instructor. It may also suggest the querent's current work needs a more pronounced physical aspect to it. More than any other suit, when it comes to business success and prosperity, Wands signify potential conflicts, miscommunication, and disagreements as well as competition and victory through conflict.

Cups

Cups deal with emotions and intuition, and at first it may seem unclear how those things apply to business prosperity but they do! A plethora of Cups asks: How is the querent feeling about their business? Are they doing work they really want to do? Is there any anger, resentment, or depression around work attitudes? Are they feeling ignored or undervalued? (One of the issues the element of Water points out is the tendency to give, give, and give and never receive anything back in turn.) On the flip side, is the querent asking for what they want and deserve? Are they setting boundaries, communicating effectively, or wallowing in self-pity and passive-aggressive behaviors? These are the questions that Cups cards want us to consider. The truth about business, whether one works with someone else or has their own, is that there should be a basic level of happiness and joy. If that is not there, then it is nigh impossible to "fake it till you make it." There is, however, another element to Cups and that has to do with good fortune, magic, and windfalls. Cups are magical. A casual perusal of fairy tales reveals vessels that are never empty, the holy grail with the ability to restore life and confer immortality, and cornucopias that overflow with the good things of life. Pulling many of the more positive Cup cards can indicate your work and actions have been noticed and rewards are around the corner.

Major Arcana Cards

The Fool. This card signals starting a new job or venture, relocating, or changing from an existing job, having trust that "everything will work out in the end"—but also having prudence and discernment. The Fool may also show up to indicate that something in the querent's professional life is calling for their attention. In a reversed position the Fool indicates the querent may be lacking some vital skills when it comes to their work or they have a track record of making poor choices around career.

Magical Techniques: candles/oil lamps, magical words/prayers/petitions, physical manipulation, and spirit work

Intentions: clarity/wisdom, attraction, road opening, blessing, gain/increase, beginning, and mental/psychic/dream influence

The Magician. The Magician points to having (or drawing to you) the tools needed to get the job done, using magic to improve your situation, or protecting an idea until it's ready for the world. It's about embracing change and transformation in your work. In a challenging or reversed position, the card indicates a work colleague or supervisor is being tricky or duplicitous and the querent needs to watch their back.

Magical Techniques: all

Intentions: clarity/wisdom, success/mastery, attraction, road opening, blessing, and mental/psychic/dream influence

The High Priestess. This card often indicates the need to go into (or the querent's current presence in) the fields of health and healing and/or religion and the Sacred Arts. Intelligence, articulation, and intensive study will be part of the professional experience. The querent should be careful not to isolate themselves. The High Priestess can also represent academic posts, especially for women, and in some cases points to the need to return to school or get certified in a specific skill set. In a reversed position, this card can indicate health issues getting in the way of work or that a lack of skill or certification is holding the querent back.

Magical Techniques: sacred vessels, magical words/prayers/petitions, spraying/washing/spitting/asperging, textile magic, and spirit work

Intentions: clarity/wisdom, success/mastery, blessing, protection, healing, and mental/psychic/dream influence

The Empress. Manifesting one's work into the world, physical labor, reaping the harvest from work you have already done, getting a "queen" at your job on your side, coming down from the ivory tower or sanctuary and working with the hoi polloi . . . are all indicated with this card. The Empress can also represent women who find their life's work in being wives and mothers and all that goes into those roles. In a challenging or reversed position this card can signal a female boss or colleague who is being difficult to the querent for whatever reason, as well as indulgence, and/or laziness.

Magical Techniques: lodestones, physical manipulation, and textile magic

Intentions: success/mastery, victory, attraction, blessing, gain/increase, beginning, and stability

The Emperor. He is the boss man and speaks to career development, promotion, growth, and not becoming stuck or too rigid. The Emperor may show up to encourage the querent to get their boss on their side, to warn that the boss is a potential problem, or indicate that the road to success lies in becoming your own boss. The Emperor can also represent lending institutions like banks and loan companies. In a challenging or reversed position this card can indicate the relationship between either the person or institution that this card represents and the querent is not great. It may also signify the querent needs to root themselves in their own deep sense of authority.

Magical Techniques: sacred vessels, physical manipulation, and spirit work
Intentions: success/mastery, victory, blessing, protection, gain/increase, and stability

The Hierophant. This card often indicates a supervisor or manager who is responsible for a larger group of people. Sometimes in a typical work setting this card can represent HR. The Hierophant can also suggest the charitable arm of a business or that the querent should consider going to work for a charity. Fundamentally this card speaks to order and making sure everything in the querent's work is organized. The Hierophant in a reversed position can indicate that religion is invading the workplace to an inappropriate degree, the querent is refusing to listen to their own inner guidance, or the head of the organization is in some manner corrupt.
Magical Techniques: candles/oil lamps, magical words/prayers/ petitions, spraying/washing/spitting/asperging, and spirit work
Intentions: clarity/wisdom, success/mastery, blessing, healing, and mental/ psychic/dream influence

The Lovers. Work relationships, being headhunted by another company, and/or workplace romances that will affect the querent's job are all expressed with this card. The Lovers can also indicate the querent has an important decision coming up in their work/career sector and they need to listen to their heart when coming to a decision. In a challenging position the Lovers card especially advises that the querent be aware of problematic workplace romances and/or temptations that are tricky in some way. When reversed, this card can also indicate the querent's situation is being made harder by someone at work who refuses to commit to a choice.
Magical Techniques: candles/oil lamps, magical words/prayers/petitions, physical manipulation, and spirit work
Intentions: clarity/wisdom, success/mastery, victory, and attraction

The Chariot. Luxury travel for business or a willingness to relocate if paid for it, working with a difficult team successfully, overcoming obstacles in a way that leads to recognition and promotion—these are all situations this card speaks to. The Chariot can also point to special projects and launches and give advice on how to make them successful. This card may also indicate the need to host or attend a retreat or conference. At its deepest level, the Chariot is an ancient allegory for the soul, so when the card shows up in a positive position, it is a powerful message your work is aligned with your soul. When reversed, the Chariot indicates travel plans may fall through or be delayed, a move would not be the best idea for your current career path, or you are dissatisfied with your current career choice on a soul level.

Magical Techniques: candles/oil lamps, magical words/prayers/petitions, physical manipulation, and spirit work

Intentions: clarity/wisdom, success/mastery, victory, road opening, blessing, and gain/increase

Strength. Now is the time to call upon your inner resources and the power of quiet. There are wild forces around you that need to be tamed and redirected. Women in the workplace have the potential to be great allies, teachers, and mentors. Transformation is afoot, but it is subtle and easy to miss. Sometimes the Strength card indicates the querent would be happiest in a career that involves the outdoors and/or animals. In a challenging or reversed position this card can suggest there is a woman at work who is too aggressive or demanding. It can also sometimes indicate a female employee is experiencing sexual harassment or unequal treatment at work. Taking a step back, taking a breath, observing closely, and then acting decisively are the way to play the game right now.

Magical Techniques: candles/oil lamps, magical words/prayers/petitions, physical manipulation, textile magic, and spirit work

Intentions: clarity/wisdom, success/mastery, victory, protection, and stability

The Hermit. This card signifies working in solitude or keeping one's silence in the workplace. Committing to an intense period of education and/or development will serve the querent's overarching career goals even though it means they may get overlooked in the immediate moment. The Hermit can also indicate a teacher, mentor, or guide showing up to help the querent out in their career journey or perhaps that the querent themselves should consider taking on such a role. In a reversed or challenging position, the Hermit may signal a mentor or potential guide is sabotaging the querent. Another possible meaning is that the querent actually needs to use their voice and not remain silent.

Magical Techniques: sacred vessels, candles/oil lamps, magical words/prayers/petitions, and spirit work

Intentions: clarity/wisdom, success/mastery, blessing, protection, healing, and mental/psychic/dream influence

Wheel of Fortune. As always, this card indicates the situation is about to change. Aspects of work and career that have been challenging are about to get easier, while elements that have been easy may become more of a challenge. When this card appears, the querent may expect some personnel changes as well; perhaps a new supervisor, boss, or work colleague is going to come into the picture and stir things up. If things have been especially challenging, this card can indicate a change is needed. When in a reversed position, the Wheel of Fortune can denote resistance to change is making things harder than they need to be or the situation has grown too stagnant and needs to be shaken up.

Magical Technique: spirit work

Intentions: blessing, protection, gain/increase, beginning, ending, and loss/removal

Justice. This card brings an emphasis on fairness in the workplace, equal pay issues, glass ceilings, and workers' comp-type cases. As far as work and career go, Justice indicates whatever you put into a situation is what you will get out of it. Depending on context, this card may advise the querent to pursue a career in a legal profession or to consider going to law school. The Justice card may also speak to the querent about weaving political concerns/activism into their work and career. When reversed, the Justice card indicates there is a serious imbalance in this area of life and/or something unfair is occurring in the querent's place of work.

Magical Techniques: candles/oil lamps, magical words/prayers/petitions, physical manipulation, and spirit work

Intentions: clarity/wisdom, success/mastery, victory, gain/increase, beginning, ending, loss/removal, stability, banishing, and cleansing

The Hanged Man. When the Hanged Man shows up, he reminds the querent that not all is as it seems and a change in perspective may be beneficial. In the context of work and career, this card often indicates that the querent is about to undergo a trial by fire or apprentice with a tough boss. There may be fierce competition where not everyone is left standing. The querent will be expected to make sacrifices for this work. Sometimes this card can indicate job cuts and layoffs. When the Hanged Man card is reversed, it suggests that the querent has given and sacrificed enough, and now is a time of rest and healing. The reversal of this card can also remind the querent that while their perspective is good, some perspectives are more accurate than others.

better choice. Sometimes this card indicates the querent lacks options due to financial constraints, in which case finding aid to alleviate those constraints is recommended. In other cases, the Devil can signify a colleague or boss who is making the querent's life a living hell. When reversed, the Devil card signals the querent may be in a situation that is really toxic or dangerous to their health (mental, spiritual, psychic) but some element is so tempting (usually, but not always, money) that they find it incredibly hard to walk away.

Magical Techniques: candles/oil lamps, magical words/prayers/petitions, physical manipulation, spraying/washing/spitting/asperging, textile magic, and spirit work

Intentions: clarity/wisdom, success/mastery, victory, protection, cursing/reversing, loss/removal, stability, banishing, mental/psychic/dream influence, and cleansing

The Tower. The Tower card can be unsettling when it shows up, and this is especially true in the area of work and career. Loss of a job or job security, dramatic internal restructuring, crises in other parts of the querent's life affecting their job negatively are all valid interpretations. The Tower can also indicate something difficult and unexpected, like a work-related injury. The querent must remember that wherever it shows up, the Tower promises deep and meaningful transformation. It may not be pleasant going through, but the querent will come out changed for the better on the other side. In a reversed position this card can indicate a "eucatastrophe"—meaning a dramatic event that works out in strong favor for the querent. Sometimes when reversed, this card can also assure the querent the hardest or worst part is over.

Magical Techniques: sacred vessels, candles/oil lamps, magical words/prayers/petitions, physical manipulation, spraying/washing/spitting/asperging, textile magic, and spirit work

Intentions: clarity/wisdom, blessing, protection, healing, cursing/reversing, ending, loss/removal, banishing, and cleansing

The Star. Realignment of self with respect to work and livelihood, possibly a period of relative tranquility regarding big changes, the team or department getting "on the same page," beginning of a new development or project—these are all possibilities the Star points to. This card also always indicates looking to the querent's natal chart and/or considering the astrology for significant work events (like launches) is a smart move. The Star can also remind the querent of the need to go on retreats to refuel their creativity. When reversed, the Star card often indicates the querent has, in some respect, lost their way. They are floundering and in need of direction and restoration.

Magical Techniques: sacred vessels, spraying/washing/spitting/asperging, and spirit work

Intentions: clarity/wisdom, road opening, blessing, healing, stability, and cleansing

The Moon. Blockages, inability to move up the ladder or break though the glass ceiling, not enough pay or good enough pay, appetites (from food to sex to harmful substances) that negatively impact work, and out of control emotions can all be indicated by this card. Sometimes the Moon shows up as a warning to the querent some aspect of work/career that looks too good to be true actually is. The Moon can also indicate the querent has a natural gift for the arts, healing, metaphysical, or food industries and their current work is unsatisfying and difficult because they are in the wrong area. The Moon is also a reminder about cycles: there is a flow to everything and remembering that may give the querent much needed support. When the Moon shows up reversed, the message is that the situation has left reality and is getting lost in fantasy-making. The querent needs to stop trying to escape, listen to their inner knowing, and commit to moving forward.

Magical Techniques: sacred vessels, spraying/washing/spitting/asperging, and spirit work

Intentions: clarity/wisdom, blessing, healing, gain/increase, beginning, ending, loss/removal, stability, banishing, and mental/psychic/dream influence

The Sun. The querent has the freedom to shine through possibilities, promotions, and new projects. This card often indicates the querent is finally going to be recognized for what they do and bring to the table. Sometimes the Sun can announce that a pregnancy/baby is going to change the querent's relationship to work and career in a dramatic (but usually positive) manner. In a challenging or reversed position the Sun can indicate the querent is under the threat of being replaced with a younger/less experienced individual and should take steps to protect their position.

Magical Techniques: candles/oil lamps, magical words/prayers/petitions, physical manipulation, and spirit work

Intentions: clarity/wisdom, success/mastery, victory, road opening, blessing, gain/increase, and stability

Judgement. A need for evaluations, tests, certifications, and sometimes a sense of being judged by colleagues or supervisors in a nonofficial capacity are all possibilities when this card shows up. Judgement can indicate a situation where the querent needs to bring a heightened level of discernment or awareness to bear. Judgement can also suggest the querent would do well in professions related to law, law enforcement, or working with the dead. Sometimes this card can point to a very influential boss or supervisor who either works with or against the querent's interests. A test may need to be retaken, a certification renewed. The querent would do well to have a Plan B and C in their back pockets. When reversed, the Judgement card suggests an inability to make clear decisions due to clouded judgment or fear of evaluation, potentially leading to missed opportunities for professional advancement or financial growth. The reversal may also indicate excessive self-criticism or avoiding necessary reviews of business practices, creating stagnation where honest assessment would lead to improvement.

Magical Techniques: candles/oil lamps, physical manipulation, spraying/washing/spitting/asperging, and spirit work

Intentions: clarity/wisdom, victory, blessing, protection, healing, cursing/reversing, ending, loss/removal, banishing, and cleansing

The World. This card tells us the querent is poised for victory, success, and the completion of a significant project, goal, or cycle. There is a sense of having finally arrived. Recognition and honors, revelation of true self, work, and purpose, and awards are all indicated by this card. There is also a sense that the querent can show up to professional situations as their most authentic self. When the World card is in a challenging position, it can often indicate the spotlight is on the querent in a way that makes them uncomfortable and/or they have been given too much responsibility for their current skill level. It may also indicate the achieving of a significant goal or the completion of a big project is delayed.

Magical Techniques: sacred vessels, lodestones, candles/oil lamps, magical words/prayers/petitions, textile magic, and spirit work

Intentions: success/mastery, victory, blessing, gain/increase, beginning, ending, and stability

Court Cards

King and Queen of Coins. These cards can embody a manager, boss, supervisor, and in some cases people who can assist you in getting/keeping/staying in a job. If you work for yourself, this card can indicate your work persona. The King of Coins often suggests there are hidden aspects to the work, the company, or the person in charge that the querent is not aware of—things that can directly affect the querent's relationship with them for good or ill. The Queen of Coins signals now is the time to be generous with your work, your skill, and your money. When either of these cards are reversed, the querent's relationship with whomever the card may represent is strained. The King specifically may suggest that secrets concerning work and career are going to become problematic and in the case of the Queen, that the querent is giving too generously or has too many outgoing expenses.

Magical Techniques: sacred vessels, lodestones, and physical manipulation

Intentions: success/mastery, blessing, protection, gain/increase, and stability

Knight of Coins. This is a helper figure who comes to assist, especially when there is a transition or a need to increase cash flow. He may point out practical steps and that it's a good idea to make a to-do list. The Knight of Coins also speaks to the need to take a pause or break before making a significant career move. Reversed, the indication is the querent is stuck, unsure of what to do next, or waiting too long to make their move.

Magical Techniques: sacred vessels and lodestones

Intentions: success/mastery, blessing, protection, healing, gain/increase, and stability

Page of Coins. This card indicates the yearning and quest for more stability and income health. The Page of Coins suggests that the querent desires promotion or a wage increase. Sometimes the Page of Coins recommends that in order to get ahead the querent should develop a practical skill set that will make their work more valuable. When reversed, this card warns against get rich quick schemes.

Magical Techniques: sacred vessels and lodestones

Intentions: clarity/wisdom, success/mastery, attraction, road opening, blessing, gain/increase, and stability

King and Queen of Swords. The King and Queen of Swords often point to those at a supervisory level, especially in white-collar professions. This could be the boss and management eyeing the querent for promotion and/or increased responsibilities. These cards could also indicate the querent has the skills needed to move up the ladder . . . and if they don't, they should make every effort to get them. Often these figures support and encourage writing, public speaking, and other forms of work-related communication. At their deepest level, these cards are about clarity, wisdom, goal-setting, and goal-achieving. When reversed, the King and Queen of Swords indicate something is getting lost in communication, the querent is not getting on the right side of the figures in power, or they need to refine their skills.

Magical Techniques: magical words/prayers/petitions and spirit work

Intentions: clarity/wisdom, success/mastery, victory, protection, gain/increase, loss/removal, and mental/psychic/dream influence

Knight of Swords. Rash action and/or loose lips that could end up coming back to bite the querent if proper care is not taken, getting involved in complicated work situations too quickly or adding too much to one's plate, leaping before looking—this card speaks to all of these themes. The Knight of Swords also warns about being too hasty in either offering or accepting help from someone else, especially if the querent is not sure they can be trusted. When it comes to workflow, the Knight of Swords indicates projects and goals are being achieved quickly, perhaps faster than expected—just make sure no details are lost in the speed. When reversed, this card signifies things are either moving too quickly or too slowly and so adjustments should be made. It can also indicate the querent is operating under a big assumption that is not entirely accurate.

Magical Technique: magical words/prayers/petitions

Intentions: clarity/wisdom, road opening, protection, stability, and mental/psychic/dream influence

Page of Swords. This card can point to a lack of clarity, serious revisiting of going back to school or seeking out professional training, or the need to obtain certification in a specific skill or ability. The Page of Swords can also point to a promising entry-level or internship position for the querent that could lead to an excellent job in the future. Generally, what we see here is a level of immaturity that is about to become more mature through experience and opportunity. The time for learning is now! When reversed, the Page of Swords can indicate the querent is suffering from paralysis by analysis and/or they are engaging in a lot of unhelpful negative self-talk.

Magical Technique: magical words/prayers/petitions

Intentions: clarity/wisdom, attraction, road opening, blessing, gain/increase, beginning, and mental/psychic/dream influence

King and Queen of Wands. Typically these cards represent colleagues or the creatives in a job or department. Often they speak directly to those involved in PR, marketing, and social media management. They thrive on excitement, creativity, artistry, and change. If the King and Queen of Wands show up, they are telling you that in the realm of work your supervisors are looking for those qualities in you and what you are doing. If either card represents the querent, then the message is to bring more creative thinking to their current career. These cards can also sometimes speak to a workplace romance or affair. For self-employed folks, they speak to marketing and visibility. When reversed, the King and Queen of Wands indicate a lack of practical thinking in work and career is becoming problematic. Creativity is wonderful, but it needs to be grounded in order to manifest. These cards can also indicate an issue with anger or impatience at work when they are in a challenging position.

Magical Techniques: candles/oil lamps and spirit work

Intentions: success/mastery, victory, attraction, road opening, blessing, and protection

Knight of Wands. He often shows up when a venture, promotion, or project is going to be more difficult than it initially appeared. The querent can proceed as planned but should also move ahead with caution. Now is a good time to call in reinforcements to help control and manage the situation. He might also ask if the querent is holding back at work; if the answer is yes, then colleagues and supervisors are aware of this. This card can also indicate events like launches and rollouts will not go as planned and experience blocks and delays. When reversed, the Knight of Wands tells us getting a creative project off the ground is going to be difficult, marketing/visibility is a real challenge, or there is a general lack of clarity about direction and mission.

Magical Techniques: candles/oil lamps and spirit work

Intentions: clarity/wisdom, success/mastery, and stability

Page of Wands. This card indicates the querent wants more control and power than they have when it comes to work. This card may also suggest the process of looking for leads and coming up empty or speak to a situation where making sales is especially hard. The Page of Wands can also indicate the querent needs to have a creative vision and plan before proceeding. Going back to school and focusing on something like graphic design, PR, or marketing or even just taking a class in one of these areas could be a great move for the querent. When reversed, the Page of Wands indicates the querent is feeling out of options, out of answers, and out of steam.

Magical Techniques: candles/oil lamps and spraying/washing/spitting/asperging
Intentions: clarity/wisdom, success/mastery, blessing, and stability

King and Queen of Cups. The boss or influential colleagues are wondering about the querent's emotional state and how it is affecting their work: Are they happy? Content? Enthusiastic? Depressed or stressed out? Is there generosity and sharing or holding back? This could also indicate there is a deep, intuitive connection between the querent and the supervisors/colleagues these cards may represent. These cards may also show up to encourage the querent to take on a more emotional/psychological approach to their work or to seek out a career in the arts. When reversed, both the King and Queen of Cups indicate the querent is not heeding their own intuition and/or is trying to stifle an artistic impulse in the name of practicality.
Magical Techniques: sacred vessels and spraying/washing/spitting/asperging
Intentions: clarity/wisdom, blessing, protection, healing, mental/psychic/dream influence, and cleansing

Knight of Cups. As a helper figure, the Knight of Cups indicates the querent may need to call on help . . . or they may be called on to offer help. This card can signal a project or desired goal will move along at a slower pace but it will be thoroughly completed. Remember: slow and steady wins the race. The card may also speak to things like being looked over for a promotion, with the promise that ultimately the querent will benefit. When reversed, the Knight of Cups warns against trying to hurry along a situation or individual as well as the perils of refusing to ask for or offer help.
Magical Techniques: sacred vessels and spraying/washing/spitting/asperging
Intentions: clarity/wisdom, success/mastery, blessing, healing, mental/psychic/dream influence, and cleansing

Page of Cups. The Page of Cups can signal an emotional imbalance at work and/or because of work, uncertainty of next steps, changes needing to be made but it being unclear which ones or how. It can indicate that the querent is being falsely led by poor or incorrect intuition. This card can also tell us that the querent needs to do some soul-searching, possibly go back to school, or consider changing fields because where they currently are does not feel like the best fit.
Magical Techniques: sacred vessels and spraying/washing/spitting/asperging
Intentions: clarity/wisdom, road opening, blessing, healing, mental/psychic/dream influence, and cleansing

Pips

Aces

Coins: Start a new venture, take the new job, or finally ask for the raise—this is a windfall of money and good fortune.

Swords: Communication is now vital; bring opposing forces together, and victory is assured.

Wands: Now is the time for creative passion to infuse one's work. Be courageous, try new things, and don't let anger or short tempers sabotage the good work that has been accomplished.

Cups: One's cup is running over with goodness—rewards, praise, promotion, and amazing clients are yours. Enjoy!

Intentions: clarity/wisdom, success/mastery, victory, attraction, road opening, blessing, gain/increase, and beginning

Twos

Coins: Balancing work and life and stretching the dollar are indicated. Is it time to ask for a raise or look for a new job?

Swords: Set boundaries and heed one's own counsel first. Focus on the present and stop trying to forecast into the future.

Wands: Let go of a work grudge to open the field for advancement.

Cups: There are excellent partnership possibilities; can also indicate going into or succeeding in a health-related field.

Intentions: clarity/wisdom, success/mastery, victory, attraction, road opening, blessing, gain/increase, loss/removal, and stability

Threes

Coins: Collaboration with others, often in slightly different fields or departments, will build something lasting. Often money does not immediately come, but the work is worth it.

Swords: Heartbreak effecting work or workplace romances gone awry, betrayal at work of a romantic or nonromantic nature, or a firing/decision to leave

Wands: Investments in work and/or school are finally paying off. Success can be seen on the horizon, but watch out for overly ambitious plans and impatience.

Cups: Powerful relationships with colleagues and promising collaborations will bear fruit.

Intentions: clarity/wisdom, success/mastery, attraction, and blessing

Fours

Coins: Seeking outside funding or the need to seek outside funding. Also, a refusal to be generous with time, money, or other resources is holding you back from promotion and excellence.

Swords: Something needs to be addressed and let go of or "put to bed." It could be criticism at work, not getting the promotion, or really any career-related activity that might stick in the querent's craw.

Wands: Call in community support and rely on colleagues. Can indicate a prosperous partnership or merger and abundance.

Cups: Indecision, unsure about which direction to follow in a professional sense, wanting to "have one's cake but eat it too"

Intentions: success/mastery, blessing, protection, and stability

Fives

Coins: Poverty, illness, feeling crunched from all sides, often finding a partner and wallowing in self-pity and misery, passive-aggressive behavior

Swords: Sabotage, theft, dishonorable actions, often from a competitor or rival

Wands: Disagreements, miscommunication, and outright fights with colleagues and direct supervisors, internal conflict and in some cases malicious gossip

Cups: Regret, refusal to let go of a past action or decision, feeling stuck and frustrated. In some cases, feeling like the job that the querent left was superior to the one they currently have.

Intentions: clarity/wisdom, protection, cursing/reversing, loss/removal, banishing, and cleansing

Sixes

Coins: Restoration of fairness, sometimes an increase in salary (though usually with an equal increase in responsibility) and in some cases being forced to "share the wealth"

Swords: Making an effort to move from a tumultuous state (one's department, job, or choice of career) into a more peaceful and tranquil place. Sometimes feeling blocked in that effort.

Wands: Victory and success, usually through competition and conflict—often gained with a partner or invisible helper

Cups: A higher-up remembering the querent and helping them or a reference putting in a good word—collegial help too

Intentions: clarity/wisdom, victory, attraction, blessing, protection, cursing/reversing, gain/increase, loss/removal, and stability

Sevens

Coins: Return on investment—the time the querent has taken and energy they have spent on this project was worth it.

Swords: Lies, deceit, and colleagues or supervisors taking advantage and passing the querent's work off as their own

Wands: Feeling trapped in work, creatively stagnant, possibly henpecked by superiors and colleagues

Cups: Emotionally unsure about work. One day it seems great and the next it seems terrible. Walking on eggshells, often as a result of internal restructure or mergers. High stress.

Intentions: clarity/wisdom, success/mastery, victory, blessing, protection, cursing/reversing, gain/increase, loss/removal, and cleansing

Eights

Coins: Steady and honest work, sometimes being a workaholic and not recognizing how much capital has been created

Swords: Being surrounded by enemies, talked about negatively, in a hostile takeover, or engaging in negative self-talk

Wands: Lots of energy, possibly a new member to the team or a new colleague with good questions, creativity, and potential. Information is coming in.

Cups: A need to relocate but not with expenses paid or fully paid, feeling compelled to seek work elsewhere or leave

Intentions: success/mastery, blessing, protection, cursing/reversing, gain/increase, and stability

Nines

Coins: Freelance work, independence in work, virtual commuting and calling one's own shots, having some control over the schedule and great money

Swords: Work anxiety is keeping the querent up at night. There are dreams and nightmares about work, very high stress, and the lack of rest affects the job.

Wands: Lack of clarity and a feeling of impending doom, waiting for the other shoe to drop, deep mistrust of colleagues and immediate supervisors sometimes resulting in poor decisions

Cups: Possibility, potential, security, and strength. Taking on a position of authority and knowing your worth and value.

Intentions: clarity/wisdom, success/mastery, attraction, blessing, healing, cursing/reversing, banishing, and mental/psychic/dream influence

Tens

Coins: Great financial stability and security, big returns and wealth-building that allow the querent/their work to truly leave a legacy and give back

Swords: Ultimate betrayal related to work, project given to someone else, getting fired or laid off, chronic fatigue or other health issues, severe work-related injury, extremely unfair treatment

Wands: A great deal of work and effort required at this time. Pull other cards to determine if there is a worthwhile payoff or not.

Cups: "Happily ever after," rising to great prominence, having control, authority, and making great money, working well in a team or with colleagues.

Intentions: clarity/wisdom, success/mastery, victory, blessing, protection, healing, cursing/reversing, gain/increase, ending, loss/removal, stability, banishing, mental/psychic/dream influence, and cleansing

---

Further Development Tasks

- Define your own relationship to work.
- Name three magical materials you might advise someone to work with in augmenting their prosperity.

Magic-Making

Shoe Trick

When it comes to work and career, we often have to deal with supervisors or those in positions of power, and of course, we want to make sure everything goes our way. Shoe tricks are very popular for these purposes. To encourage someone to do what you want them to, one easy trick is to write their name in pencil three times; turn the paper 90 degrees and write your name over their name in permanent ink; anoint the paper in a five-spot pattern with an appropriate ritual anointing oil; and then stick it in the bottom of your left shoe. Wear the shoes (with the petition paper inside) into your meeting with the individual.

Peace at Work Sacred Vessel

This magic is to make everyone get along.

You Will Need

Petition paper

Pen and pencil

Ritual oil for job or career success

A miniature jar full of honey

Pinch of dried lavender

Ground and dried cinquefoil

A pinch of cardamom seed

A potted plant that you can have on your desk/area at work

Process

1. Write your petition paper by putting down all of your colleagues' names in pencil, then, turn the paper 90 degrees, and write your name in pen over their names. Repeat your name as many times as you need to so it completely covers their names. Then write in pen a petition for getting along. Something like: kind, respectful, cooperative. Repeat these words again and again in a circle around all of the names.

2. Anoint the paper in a five-spot pattern with a ritual oil for job and career success.

3. Fold the paper toward you, turn it 90 degrees and fold it again. Continue this process until you can place it inside the honey jar.

4. Add the herbs to the honey jar, and as you do all of this, hold in your heart and prayers that everyone in your workplace gets along with one another.

5. Place the honey jar in the base of the pot and then put the plant over it.

6. Put the plant someplace visible in your office so it can send out its good vibes!

◆ *Chapter Five* ◆

Reader, Heal Thyself:

Healing

When we consider healing through magic and divination, we should be aware of three different levels of healing. These might stand on their own or be found in any combination. For instance, a querent might only have a body problem or they might be facing interrelated issues. The levels are:

- **Physical healing:** Many magical people and intuitive sorts are drawn to physical healing because they themselves have experienced health problems. In today's world the Sacred Artist who feels called to this path of physical healing would do well to seek out training in either conventional or alternative medicine and healing modalities.
- **Emotional healing:** There are many rites and ceremonies for emotional healing, and this is an area where the intuitive shines brightest. Really, anytime we are doing intuitive work we are engaging with feelings, desires, and sensitivities. If you wonder what emotional healing is exactly, we need not get fancy or potentially overwhelmed. Emotional healing is required whenever our hearts are hurt and/or we feel angry, betrayed, ashamed, and/or guilty. In those times and spaces, we need support for our emotions regardless of what is happening to us physically. Botanicals like rosemary, lavender, and angelica root are known for bringing about peace and tranquility. Some folks love to work with flower essences around these issues as well.
- **Spiritual healing:** Spiritual healing deals with soul work. Some traditions believe the soul can be killed or destroyed, but many others do not. Whatever you believe, when we talk about healing on a spiritual level, we are discussing healing at the soul level. Often this level holds traumas made evident in a querent's natal chart and which may have been carried through multiple generations.

Remember, You Are Not a Doctor . . . (Unless You Are)

Divination and ceremony are not substitutes for medical knowledge, but assuming that someone who does require the services of a doctor or mental health care provider would not also benefit from magical or magical intervention is simply wrong. If you are working with a querent who has contacted you because they are suffering physically, you must ensure they see a medical doctor, medical herbalist, etc. If you are working with someone who has a psychiatric disorder, then they need to be working with a mental health professional too. When such providers are in place, creating ceremony for an individual can augment the healing process in a variety of ways. Moreover, in many cultures even today, the healing process is not considered complete unless and until it has been ritualized in a sacro-magical manner.

Identifying Causes for illness

In cases of disease and affliction one thing the magician is especially interested in is the cause. Not so long ago, most people believed illness, heartbreak, and affliction were brought on by means of magic. This, for instance, is why in Celtic countries there are so many taboos and folk beliefs warning about faeries, especially during what many consider to be the "dark" part of the year—the days ranging from the summer solstice to the winter solstice—because the fey were believed to bring about illness when angered or insulted. It also speaks to why we have so many cultures with a wariness of the evil eye. In magic, healing and hexing are often paired arts; the worker who is proficient in one is believed to be capable of both.

This turns our attention to another common culprit in illness: hexing or cursing. Magical convention indicates that if you have been bewitched and fallen ill because of enchantment, then the only way to remove that bewitchment and completely heal is through breaking the spell. In fact, in the form of Mexican folk magic practiced by curanderos/as there is an entire subset of specialization for "spell breakers." This type of work may be accomplished through sympathetic magical acts; for instance, if you cannot find the actual materials worked with to cause the evil eye, you could make an evil eye and pierce or burn it to dispel any negativity. Many people believe that magic aimed at healing on any level must be performed on your behalf by someone else. Typically, in healing magic the best time to begin your work is on the full moon so that as the moon wanes the affliction also wanes.

Special Magical Considerations for Healing Work

There are a few magical forms for cleansing that are different from other types of magical work we have already covered. These are specific to the art of healing and being healed.

- **Egg cleansing:** An egg cleansing is an act especially popular where I live in the Southwest. This practice is also sometimes referred to as a *limpia*, although this term precisely means a sacred bathing ritual that may or may not be accompanied by the rolling of an egg over the body. The belief is that you start at the head and roll an egg down a person's body to the feet. The egg will absorb any illness and negativity. The egg is then either smashed at a crossroads or at the base of an old tree or it is broken into a bowl and peered at for divination purposes.

- **Footbaths:** Feet are funny! From ancient Chinese medicine to African magic to Celtic shamanism, the feet, hands, and head are all regarded as especially powerful areas of the body. When it comes to feet specifically, there is a prevalent belief that you may easily take in negativity through them. For this reason, healing is sometimes administered through the use of a magical footbath. The bathing of feet also has deep roots; think of Mary Magdalene washing Christ's feet with her tears and then cleansing them with her hair and anointing them with precious spikenard oil. Foot-bathing is potent. And as the Magdalene demonstrates, this is a two-part process. There is the washing of the feet with a special soap or herbal blend (made according to the complaint/situation of the querent) and then the anointing the feet with oil or ointment. Typically, the oil or ointment used to anoint the feet may have blessing and protective qualities to it. In many cases, the querent is advised to burn or donate the pair of shoes they showed up in and bring a brand-new pair of shoes they have never worn before to depart in.

- **Medical massage:** This form of healing is sometimes referred to as "hands-on work" and usually involves the physical manipulation of the body—thus the massage part—with the addition of cooling or spicy oils and ointments, all of which have special significance. Obviously, this form of healing is especially good for chronic aches and pains, arthritis, and rheumatism. When employed by a practitioner you trust, it can be an incredibly rewarding magically and physically healing experience. A great current example of medical massage can be found in the oil and herb massages provided by Ayurvedic practitioners to rebalance one's dosa.

- **Cleansing at a distance:** Typically when someone needs cleansing to accompany their healing work, they seek out the cleansing in person or take a sacred bath. However, in some cases a person is not able to travel physically, and/or they do not believe they have enough power or vitality to perform a sacred bath effectively for themselves. In other cases, the person has a magical worker they have worked with over a long period of time, and they believe this person is best suited to help them even though they may be physically far away. It is in cases like these that cleansing at a distance in employed. Usually, a candle or poppet stands in for the person and then the querent's dis-eases are rolled away and health and blessings are attracted back in through magical bathing, censing, or the egg cleansing method described above. Cleansing and healing at a distance may also be performed with anatomically correct models of the body and its various parts—the kinds you would buy for a science or health class. These models are usually made of hard plastic or resin and so can be anointed with oils, special washes, and waters, filled with herbs, roots, curios, and/or personal concerns, set up on an altar, and blessed with hands-on work.

Special Considerations in Tarot for Healing Work

The Major Arcana

As always these are the cards that alert us to big, archetypal patterns. When you pull a significant number of Major Arcana cards for questions around healing, the first thing to do is note what themes or patterns are emerging and then try to determine what they have to tell the querent. Can you create a story with the cards showing up, or do the cards have certain themes in common (colors, botanicals, elements, or figures)? Perhaps just as important is a gut check of how these Major Arcana cards, as well as the other cards drawn, make the querent feel. Do they feel good, bad, or indifferent when seeing certain Major Arcana cards?

The Suits

Coins

Coins, ruled by the element of Earth, connect to our physical bodies, and specifically to teeth and bones. Coin cards can provide information about strength and level of physical endurance. These cards can also suggest problems around weight gain. **Emotionally** Coins can often indicate a priority around a sense of safety and security. A number of Coin cards may also point to practicalities that are not in place. Does the querent have a primary care provider they like? Do they have health insurance? Are they avoiding medical care due to financial stress? **Spiritually,** the Coin cards can indicate the querent is either not on earth enough—not grounded enough, not present enough in their body—or conversely they are too much of the earth and not as free as they might otherwise be.

Swords

Since this suit is ruled by the element of Air, Swords correlate to a couple of specific areas and also recommend a certain approach to issues. When looking at **physical illness,** if many Sword cards come up it indicates that the pulmonary system may be at risk and/or the querent may have lung/respiratory issues. They may also suggest trauma to the head on either a physical and/or mental level and that care by a mental health practitioner is a good recommendation. The need for a good doctor, surgeon, and/or specialist is often implied by Swords.

In cases of **physical or emotional** healing, if several Swords show up, it may indicate a lack of clarity and lucidity in mental processes. When the issue is around **spiritual or soul healing,** Swords are often associated with one's will. Lack of will, weak will, unclear will, or damaged will are all possibilities that need to be considered. A damaged will is akin to a damaged sense of self: often we see difficulty in erecting and maintaining boundaries, in consistent follow-through, and in feeling like there is purpose and direction in our lives.

Wands

Since this suit is ruled by the element of Fire, Wands deal with the blood, circulatory system, and heart in the realm of **physical healing.** They can also indicate the querent requires more exercise and physical activity. The Wands can point out physical causes for a great demand or marked lack of demand for sex. Finally, the Wand cards may deal with digestion and gut health. In the work of **emotional healing** Wands often point out the querent is suffering from stress, anxiety, inflammation, and in some cases an overabundance of anger. These cards can also suggest challenges around fear and physical intimacy. When it comes to **spiritual healing**, Wands indicate the querent may be experiencing trouble with the hips, sex organs, lower abdomen, and lower back, which rules our ability to connect through sex and physical intimacy, as well as our feelings (and fears) around basic survival. Finally, Wands indicate trauma and anger that need to be addressed on a spiritual level.

Cups

When it comes to healing, the realm of Water, symbolized by the Cups cards, rules. Water indicates healing or the need for healing unlike any other element. On the **physical level**, we are composed of over 70 percent water, so Cups speak to comprehensive healing. Specifically, the element of Water points to our urinary systems including bladder and kidneys, as the organs that filter and eliminate waste through water. Like Wands, Cups can also indicate issues with blood, sinuses, and the reproductive system. **Emotionally** Cups are probably the most resonant and can signal issues of depression, anxiety, light indecision, or chronic bipolar behavior. Cups cards also denote trauma, especially of a sexual nature, and they can sometimes refer to addictive dependence on drugs or alcohol. On the **spiritual level** Cups cards indicate our heart center and our ability to give, to be generous, loving, and intimately connected. They also rule our third eye center and psychic health, including dreams both good and bad as well as our intuitive abilities. Magically when we see a large number of Cups, we are looking at doing work through sacred vessels, spraying/washing/spitting/asperging, textile magic, or spirit work.

Major Arcana Cards

The Fool. The querent would be wise to add prayer and spiritual practices to their healing regimen, but not rely solely on such practices. Easy physical movement like going for a walk is recommended here. If the querent is disabled, then they may consider getting a companion animal. When reversed, the Fool indicates the querent needs to get some experts involved in their situation . . . taking a wait and see approach or relying on a faith healing-type approaches is dangerous at this time.

Magical Techniques: lodestones, magical words/prayers/petitions, physical manipulation, and spirit work

Intentions: clarity/wisdom, success/mastery, attraction, road opening, blessing, protection, and beginning

The Magician. A magical approach is advised for healing. Do honor all elements of wellness, but now is the time to seek specialized help and expertise. Don't keep hiding from or tricking oneself about the truth of a situation if healing is needed. If the querent is in any kind of recovery and the Magician is pulled, the indication is they have all the resources they need to fully recover and heal. When reversed, the Magician may suggest the Sacred Arts are taking either too big or too small of a role in the healing of the querent and adjustments need to be made. There is also a possibility of a charlatan or con artist advising the querent, so now is the time to really vet all health care providers.

Magical Techniques: candles/oil lamps, magical words/prayers/petitions, physical manipulation, textile magic, and spirit work

Intentions: clarity/wisdom, success/mastery, victory, attraction, road opening, blessing, protection, healing, gain/increase, stability, and mental/psychic/dream influence

The High Priestess. She may indicate a health care professional or a resonance with this field. There is a need for healing on a spiritual and emotional level, repairing what is broken. Specifically address spiritual and emotional wounds and dealing with phobias. The High Priestess can often indicate the presence of deep trauma that needs to be worked on with a professional. When reversed, the High Priestess can signal a refusal on the part of the querent to heal and/or that people around the querent are not as intelligent and wise as they may seem to be.

Magical Techniques: sacred vessels, magical words/prayers/petitions, spraying/washing/spitting/asperging, textile magic, and spirit work

Intentions: clarity/wisdom, success/mastery, blessing, protection, healing, cursing/reversing, gain/increase, loss/removal, mental/psychic/dream influence, and cleansing

The Empress. This card often concerns issues around pregnancy, including miscarriage and motherhood, as well as issues around feminine reproductive organs and women's health. The Empress may also advise the querent to pay more attention to their food and diet. In a challenging or reversed position the Empress can indicate obstacles with any of the areas listed above, but she can also point to excessive weight gain, sometimes leading to or complicated by other health issues like diabetes or high blood pressure.

Magical Techniques: sacred vessels, lodestones, and textile magic

Intentions: success/mastery, victory, attraction, blessing, protection, gain/increase, and stability

The Emperor. He deals with issues around fatherhood and paternity as well as men's health, including prostate issues. Bones, strength, teeth, and joints are all emphasized by this card. The Emperor can also indicate the querent either needs more or less sedentary time, depending on what cards show up around it. In a challenging or reversed position the Emperor can indicate loss of strength and vitality—sexual and otherwise.

Magical Techniques: lodestones and physical manipulation

Intentions: success/mastery, victory, blessing, protection, gain/increase, and stability

The Hierophant. The Hierophant may be a doctor or a spiritual advisor the querent is consulting on health matters, or the card may show up to point out the querent could excel in one of these areas themselves. It could also indicate either taking on or returning to a spiritual tradition is a good idea at this point. This card can also suggest the querent will do their best healing if they have a team around them all pitching in to help out. When in a challenging position, the Hierophant may indicate the querent is getting bad advice from a spiritual advisor and/or health professional.

Magical Techniques: candles/oil lamps, magical words/prayers/petitions, and spirit work

Intentions: clarity/wisdom, road opening, blessing, protection, healing, mental/psychic/dream influence, and cleansing

The Lovers. This card usually indicates physical problems are coming from emotional or spiritual issues tied to a current relationship or past romance. Sometimes it can express that a romantic partner needs to be medically evaluated and/or there is a physical, emotional, or spiritual cause for lack of sex or overabundance of sex. It also indicates the querent needs to make an important health-related decision. When reversed, the Lovers shows the querent's choice to delay on making a decision is compounding health issues.

Magical Techniques: lodestones, candles/oil lamps, and physical manipulation

Intentions: clarity/wisdom, success/mastery, victory, attraction, road opening, blessing, stability, and mental/psychic/dream influence

The Chariot. The Chariot tells of victory and success, especially in the face of difficult health circumstances. This card often indicates a multipronged approach would be best . . . for instance, an approach in which working with more conventional medicine is complemented by holistic healing modalities.

In a challenging position it can signal victory will not be complete or there might be unexpected lasting issues. Sometimes this card can indicate that in order to see real improvement, the querent needs to physically relocate or be willing to travel to find the right care providers.

Magical Techniques: candles/oil lamps, magical words/prayers/petitions, physical manipulation, textile magic, and spirit work

Intentions: clarity/wisdom, success/mastery, victory, road opening, blessing, and stability

Strength. This card points to endurance, and sometimes a need to seek a second medical opinion. Strength can sometimes indicate thyroid issues, especially in women. On an emotional level, there may be some anger issues that need to be addressed. This card can also be an indicator that womb health is not all it should be for the querent. It can also tell us that now is not the time for action, but instead for rest. Of course, Strength indicates a need to continue to build up physical strength. In a challenging position this card can suggest more physical strength is needed and/or the querent does not feel able to fully articulate their health challenges.

Magical Techniques: candles/oil lamps, magical words/prayers/petitions, and physical manipulation

Intentions: clarity/wisdom, success/mastery, victory, blessing, protection, and stability

The Hermit. The Hermit tells of going inward, sometimes in a depressive manner, but usually as an appropriate response. The card can indicate challenges with vision and/or mobility in some cases. It may also indicate traveling to find the best expert for a given condition is a wise move. Sometimes the Hermit expresses the querent would do well to take on healing studies themselves. When in a challenging position, it can signal a refusal to talk about or seek counsel concerning health issues and a general lack of communication when it comes to wellness.

Magical Techniques: candles/oil lamps and spirit work

Intentions: clarity/wisdom, blessing, protection, healing, loss/removal, and banishing

Wheel of Fortune. This card indicates a need to maintain ongoing vigilance in all areas of health. If the querent doesn't have a good team of health care professionals around them, they should begin to gather one. Most essentially, there is a recommendation that the querent become aware of what their standard of health looks and feels like so that they can adopt that as a working baseline. The Wheel of Fortune can also point to dramatic fluctuations in everything from hormones to blood pressure. When in a reversed position, the indication is that the querent is stuck in a stagnant pattern with regard to their health and healing.

Magical Technique: spirit work

Intentions: clarity/wisdom, gain/increase, beginning, ending, loss/removal, and stability

Justice. The querent will get out what they put into their health. Eating right, exercising, and in general being accountable for every level of health are the best approach now. Yoga, balancing exercises, and hugging the midline are all important. Practice getting up and sitting down on the floor without using your hands and cultivate a good relationship with your physical strength. When Justice is reversed or in a challenging position, it indicates a health situation is coming up that is not fair or asked for but must still be navigated. It may also indicate partnership is lacking between the querent and their health care team.

Magical Techniques: magical words/prayers/petitions, physical manipulation, and spirit work

Intentions: clarity/wisdom, gain/increase, beginning, ending, loss/removal, and stability

The Hanged Man. This card denotes a condition in decline, often indicating the need for healing work at a spiritual level or soul healing. This card may also suggest the current treatment regimen someone is on needs to be reevaluated and perhaps even the diagnosis itself be checked. Occasionally the Hanged Man points to the need for the querent to sacrifice something in order to have overall better health—anything from choosing where to live based on medical providers to undergoing a specific therapy or procedure. When reversed, the Hanged Man indicates the querent is improving, getting stronger, and needs support to "keep the good work going."

Magical Techniques: magical words/prayers/petitions, physical manipulation, textile magic, and spirit work

Intentions: clarity/wisdom, protection, healing, cursing/reversing, ending, loss/removal, banishing, mental/psychic/dream influence, and cleansing

Death. When this card is looked at in a physical health situation, it may indicate a terminal case. On an emotional or spiritual level, however, Death often says that a death or loss has not been properly dealt with, remembered, or grieved and this is creating issues. This card can also indicate someone close to the querent may be about to die and the querent needs to safeguard their health as they are likely to be exceedingly vulnerable during this time. The Death card can also suggest the querent look at lineage patterns and case histories around health for insights into their own situation. When reversed, Death signifies life will win out and, in cases where the prognosis is grim, a second opinion should be sought.

Magical Techniques: sacred vessels, candles/oil lamps, spraying/washing/spitting/asperging, textile magic, and spirit work

Intentions: clarity/wisdom, success/mastery, protection, healing, cursing/reversing, ending, loss/removal, and banishing

Temperance. This card often indicates the ability to get pregnant (even if all hope was lost), remission of disease, self-care, and patience. Moderation in food and drink and cutting out all alcoholic beverages and mind-altering substances are advised when Temperance appears. Swimming/water sports and balancing exercises are also indicated by this card. When Temperance shows up in a challenging position, it often signals there is an issue with addiction of some kind and this is creating other health issues.

Magical Techniques: sacred vessels, spraying/washing/spitting/asperging, and spirit work

Intentions: clarity/wisdom, road opening, blessing, protection, healing, stability, and cleansing

The Devil. The Devil tells of chemical addictions causing health problems at all levels. Repetitive and problematic behaviors may be creating emotional distress or someone in the querent's life is exhibiting these qualities. This could also indicate there is someone in the querent's life who is tempting them to engage in behaviors that are not good for their health. When reversed, the Devil often shows us that the querant may require external help to free themselves from harmful situations. The Devil reversed can also point to a possibility of relapse.

Magical Techniques: spirit work

Intentions: banishing, clarity/wisdom, cleansing, cursing/reversing, ending, loss/removal, mental/psychic/dream influence, and protection

The Tower. Sudden and acute illness or injury on any level, magical healing needed after trauma, sometimes severe issues with the musculoskeletal system, and ultimate destruction of harmful agents are some indications for this card. The Tower always refers to crisis, and originally crisis was a medical term. This card can signify a chronic condition is turning acute and/or swift decisions may have to be made. When reversed, the Tower suggests a situation is stable, at least for now. In some cases, this card reversed may indicate the querent is doing a good job building their health back up after a setback.

Magical Techniques: sacred vessels, textile magic, and spirit work

Intentions: clarity/wisdom, protection, healing, cursing/reversing, ending, loss/removal, stability, banishing, and cleansing

The Star. This card speaks to healing and soul alignment, remission of disease, seeing disease clearly and making different life choices as a result. Looking to one's natal chart for information about physical, emotional, and spiritual health concerns may be called for. The Star also signals bringing all levels of health back into balance with one another. When reversed, there is a lack of clarity around health and the underlying causes of dis-ease. This card may also indicate a challenging health situation is returning once again.

Magical Techniques: sacred vessels, lodestones, spraying/washing/spitting/asperging, and spirit work

Intentions: clarity/wisdom, road opening, blessing, healing, gain/increase, stability, mental/psychic/dream influence, and cleansing

The Moon. Sometimes this card specifically refers to "female problems," including inability to get pregnant, but it may indicate emotional distress as well or that the querent is blocked on a spiritual or emotional level. Mental health can be especially highlighted by the Moon based on the long-standing connection between the Moon and our emotional/mental state. Self-care is very much recommended by this card, as is looking to the female lines of ancestry for insight into current conditions. When reversed, the Moon can indicate a deep mental/emotional challenge that needs to be addressed and healed.

Magical Techniques: sacred vessels, spraying/washing/spitting/asperging, and spirit work

Intentions: clarity/wisdom, blessing, protection, healing, gain/increase, beginning, loss/removal, and mental/psychic/dream influence

The Sun. The harbinger of vitality, good health and a positive state of being, the Sun can also point to pregnancy, fertility, and/or the arrival of a young child. Often it announces a need to get outside, get vitamin D, and/or work with animals. This card can specifically speak to equine therapy as a positive medicine for the querent. If the Sun is in a challenging position, it can point to a compulsive focus on youth and youthfulness as we age. It can also indicate a general lack of vitality or point to declining health.

Magical Techniques: candles/oil lamps and spirit work

Intentions: clarity/wisdom, success/mastery, victory, attraction, road opening, blessing, protection, healing, gain/increase, beginning, and ending

Judgement. This card recommends seeking out good doctors or health care providers, trusting judgments, and calling upon one's own judgment in health matters. The Judgement card can sometimes indicate there will be a rapid (usually positive) turn in an individual's health. If this card shows up in a challenging position, it can express that certain judgments need to be questioned or reconsidered or a second opinion is advised. It may also indicate there is going to be a rapid downturn in health and vitality.

Magical Techniques: sacred vessels, physical manipulation, spraying/washing/spitting/asperging, and spirit work

Intentions: clarity/wisdom, success/mastery, victory, blessing, protection, healing, cursing/reversing, and cleansing

The World. Health and healing are complete—there is success, victory, the shedding of old skin and old dis-ease to celebrate new life. The querent is stronger, fitter, and feistier than they have been in the recent past. The World can also indicate the querent's entire life situation needs to be taken into account when assessing their health . . . not just the obvious symptoms but rather the whole. In a challenging position the World card tells us the querent is stuck, doesn't have as much vitality as they need, and perhaps is taking too narrow of a view of their situation.

Magical Techniques: sacred vessels, lodestones, and spirit work

Intentions: success/mastery, victory, attraction, blessing, protection, healing, gain/increase, beginning, ending, and stability

Court Cards

King and Queen of Coins. These cards indicate a family history of illness in all forms, bones and teeth and the issues surrounding those areas, in some cases doctors or healers, especially those who are researching the history of disease and its external effects, genetic predispositions, and dealing with illness with parents or older siblings/friends. They can signify geriatric care for all levels of healing. Building a strong foundation upon which healing can happen, needing to be more active, and watching out for a sedentary lifestyle and weight gain are all indicated. They can signal strength training and weightlifting. They also speak to ensuring practical issues around health are taken care of: insurance, prescriptions, etc. When the King or Queen of Coins is reversed, the indication is the querent is not working from a solid foundation, may have a hard time keeping up with practicalities, and/or may be suffering from lack of movement.

Magical Techniques: sacred vessels, lodestones, and physical manipulation
Intentions: clarity/wisdom, success/mastery, victory, attraction, blessing, protection, healing, gain/increase, and stability

Knight of Coins. This can indicate a dentist or bone doctor, a spiritual worker who is willing to give you a fair price, helpful reminders about practical issues surrounding health and healing, and also a reminder to get physical. This card may also suggest the querent needs to pause and thoroughly consider all of their options before taking action. When reversed, the Knight of Coins signals the querent needs to take action and move forward.

Magical Techniques: sacred vessels, lodestones, and physical manipulation
Intentions: clarity/wisdom, success/mastery, victory, road opening, blessing, protection, healing, gain/increase, and stability

Page of Coins. This card calls out searching for strength, vitality, good health, and healing modalities, perhaps research into alternative methods and paying special attention to family history. Consider where being cheap on health now will cost you down the road. This card can indicate doing some magical work to attract the right health care team can be a really effective move. When reversed, the Page of Coins tells us the querent needs to put some practical actions in place if they want to achieve the results they are hoping for.

Magical Techniques: sacred vessels, lodestones, and physical manipulation
Intentions: clarity/wisdom, success/mastery, attraction, blessing, protection, healing, gain/increase, and stability

King and Queen of Swords. Often these come up to represent good doctors, surgeons, specialists, and mental health workers. Sometimes these cards can indicate the querent should consider going into a healing field as their primary profession. In a challenging or reversed position, the King and Queen of Swords can indicate issues with airways, breathing, asthma, and pulmonary systems. They may also signal a lack of mental clarity, feelings of anxiety, head trauma, and/or issues around speech and processing information.

Magical Technique: magical words/prayers/petitions

Intentions: clarity/wisdom, success/mastery, victory, protection, healing, cursing/reversing, banishing, and mental/psychic/dream influence

Knight of Swords. Swift movement is advised, but it is also a good idea to look before one leaps. There may be a situation requiring decisive action. It is essential to get clear on what is going on and what the best treatment protocol might be. This card can illustrate a need for emergency surgery and an aggressive attitude with respect to treating illness. When in a challenging position, the indication is the querent needs to slow down, take stock of where they are, and chart a path ahead in a thorough and deliberate manner.

Magical Techniques: candles/oil lamps and magical words/prayers/petitions

Intentions: clarity/wisdom, success/mastery, victory, road opening, blessing, and protection

Page of Swords. More information is needed before a decision can be made. The querent may have to do some reading up and research themselves to have a good understanding of what they are experiencing. Prioritize finding the right health care team. When in a challenging or reversed position, this card can speak to audio/verbal processing challenges, mental confusion, lack of connection, and the feeling that there are no resources that can help the querent in their time of need.

Magical Techniques: lodestones, candles/oil lamps, and magical words/prayers/petitions

Intentions: clarity/wisdom, road opening, blessing, and stability

King and Queen of Wands. These two signify general physical health with a specific emphasis on gut health and blood and heart systems. They can also indicate issues around anxiety, anger, and sex. Paying attention to the way the querent relates to others is important here, especially noting if they get frustrated. Take special care to protect against fire in the home and inflammation in your environment. Make sure all systems mentioned above are in good order, especially electrical issues with heart (as opposed to vascular problems). Wand cards can also point to concerns with eyes and eye health.

When reversed, either of these cards points to inflammation, excess anger, or unresolved issues with any of the systems mentioned above.

Magical Techniques: candles/oil lamps and spirit work

Intentions: clarity/wisdom, success/mastery, victory, attraction, road opening, blessing, protection, and healing

Knight of Wands. Our fiery helper, the Knight of Wands reminds the querent to get out and get physical much like his brother the Knight of Coins. There is a specific emphasis on cardio activity. It can also indicate some issues around the heart on any level which need to be addressed. For emotional and spiritual healing, this card often tells the querent they need to look at their relationship to creativity and creative work. When reversed, the Knight of Wands can indicate there is going to be an interruption of sorts to business as usual; sometimes that can be a smallish health scare.

Magical Techniques: candles/oil lamps and spirit work

Intentions: success/mastery, victory, attraction, road opening, blessing, protection, and healing

Page of Wands. This card can indicate a health plateau—not necessarily good or bad, just blah. It usually signals an emotional block or psychic numbness, working on survival, and a need of support. Sometimes the Page of Wands can indicate the querent would do well to set aside preconceived notions and get a new perspective on their situation. When reversed, the Page of Wands tells us the querent is feeling like they do not have the resources in terms of time, energy, and/or finances to take proper care of themselves.

Magical Techniques: candles/oil lamps and spirit work

Intentions: clarity/wisdom, attraction, road opening, blessing, protection, healing, gain/increase, and stability

King and Queen of Cups. The King and Queen of Cups can indicate gifted, talented, and ethical healers either working with the traditional medical industry or in one of the alternative branches of healing. These two figures can also speak to health issues around emotions, spirit, reproduction, and women's issues. They can also indicate issues with the urinary tract, bladder, and kidneys. On an emotional level, these cards signal challenges around depression, psychic overload, and a feeling of spiritual ennui. When in a challenging position, the cards can suggest any of the above issues are creating obstacles and challenges that need to be addressed sooner rather than later.

Magical Techniques: sacred vessels, spraying/washing/spitting/asperging, and spirit work

Intentions: clarity/wisdom, success/mastery, attraction, blessing, protection, healing, mental/psychic/dream influence, and cleansing

Knight of Cups. This is an effective healer and helper figure who may move slowly compared to others but has a gentle, thorough approach that is often most effective. This card can also show up to indicate the querent needs to be able to ask for, and accept, help and healing. When in a challenging position, this card expresses that the heart is hurting on an emotional or spiritual level. It can also tell the querent they are waiting too long to take action on an issue.

Magical Techniques: sacred vessels, spraying/washing/spitting/asperging, and spirit work

Intentions: clarity/wisdom, success/mastery, attraction, road opening, blessing, protection, healing, stability, mental/psychic/dream influence, and cleansing

Page of Cups. Sometimes we need to listen to our intuition when it comes to healing; other times we don't. The Page of Cups often indicates now is not the time to listen to your intuition and/or go with your gut! It would be better to seek out expert advice. The Page of Cups can also signify that the querent is beginning their healing process . . . and it will be a journey. In some cases it may tell us the querent has a gift for healing and may want to consider study in that field. When reversed, the Page of Cups can speak to psychic or spiritual overload, too many opinions, listening to a doctor or health advisor who is not giving the best advice, or a need to look at other options and possibilities.

Magical Techniques: sacred vessels, spraying/washing/spitting/asperging, and spirit work

Intentions: clarity/wisdom, blessing, protection, healing, mental/psychic/dream influence, and cleansing

Pips

Aces

Coins: Ensure all structures relating to health are sound: insurance, updated doctor visits, bones, teeth, muscles. Make sure you are getting enough strength-increasing activity in the body.

Swords: Surgery or a new approach for treatment might be needed, and the results will be good and successful. Support from partner(s) is essential.

Wands: Get active, get physical. Check the blood and heart, and manage weight.

Cups: This is a good time for fertility and pregnancy. Depression is not an issue. Good relationships and overall health.

Intentions: clarity/wisdom, success/mastery, victory, attraction, road opening, blessing, protection, healing, gain/increase, beginning, mental/psychic/dream influence, and cleansing

Twos

Coins: Health issues are related to finance issues; seek out external support.

Swords: No on surgery, or at least not yet: get a second and maybe third opinion. The querent could be suffering from baneful conditions. Stop trying to future cast; get clear on the here and now.

Wands: Let go of the past in order to have emotional healing and move on. Be careful in world travels. Consider the relationship between health and comfort.

Cups: Health and healing. The perfect health partner has arrived; be willing to look at alternative methods now.

Intentions: clarity/wisdom, success/mastery, attraction, blessing, protection, healing, gain/increase, and stability

Threes

Coins: Collaborating with others for best health, seeking out magical or intuitive advice around health issues, considering the effect home has on health

Swords: Chronic or acute issues around heart and cardio system; heart attack, broken heart leading to physical symptoms, in need of immediate assistance

Wands: Effort put into health in childhood and adolescence is paying off now, arid climates for better breathing.

Cups: Consider the effect diet is having on all areas of health in one's life.

Intentions: clarity/wisdom, success/mastery, attraction, blessing, protection, healing, and gain/increase

Fours

Coins: A closed-off attitude is creating problems in other areas of health.

Swords: Natural death, acceptance of terminal condition, tying up loose ends, making sure that death arrangements have been made, finishing up

Wands: Community support in health, more activity, and better diet choices

Cups: Focusing on one issue while ignoring others

Intentions: clarity/wisdom, success/mastery, blessing, protection, healing, and stability

Fives

Coins: Poor health due to lack of resources and financial wherewithal; a need to seek out community and in some cases federal support; indigent population health issues

Swords: Sneaky health issues that show up without warning

Wands: Anger issues, acute concerns around blood and heart, sometimes issues with vision as well

Cups: Depression and the need for emotional and magical healing; being locked in the past

Intentions: clarity/wisdom, protection, healing, cursing/reversing, loss/removal, stability, and banishing

Sixes

Coins: Receiving aid and help with covering medical expenses

Swords: Emotional difficulties, especially concerning the way we communicate; possible anxiety issues

Wands: Successful outcome to any medical procedure; strong heart, good circulatory system!

Cups: A medical or spiritual professional personally working with you to assist with whatever issue is going on

Intentions: clarity/wisdom, success/mastery, victory, attraction, blessing, protection, healing, and gain/increase

Sevens

Coins: Seeing good effects from changes in diet, exercise, and lifestyle but happening slowly and gradually

Swords: Misdiagnosis, false information, false hope

Wands: Trapped, unsure of which direction to proceed in; issues around anger holding you back from healing

Cups: Mental anxieties and disorders, depression and mania, magical uncertainty and emotional fragility

Intentions: clarity/wisdom, success/mastery, victory, attraction, blessing, protection, healing, gain/increase, and loss/removal

Eights

Coins: A focus on endurance and stamina, good overall health

Swords: A series of health issues, bad luck, emotional and magical concerns; can indicate that someone is suffering from crossed conditions.

Wands: Health in the process of being restored, upward ascent to positivity

Cups: Seeking out a different mode to address health concerns, listening to intuition around difficult circumstances, separating oneself from well-wishers

Intentions: clarity/wisdom, victory, blessing, protection, healing, and stability

Nines

Coins: Eliminating stress will improve overall health.

Swords: Anxiety; insomnia and sometimes sleep apnea!

Wands: Head trauma, lack of clarity, lack of wisdom when it comes to making healthy decisions, hypochondria

Cups: Good overall state of health, watching weight and appetite, moms that are close to due date!

Intentions: clarity/wisdom, blessing, protection, healing, cursing/reversing, loss/removal, banishing, and mental/psychic/dream influence

Tens

Coins: The structures in place are solid for continued good health.

Swords: Chronic fatigue, other chronic issues that are sapping energy and time

Wands: Serious effort must be made if a return to health is really desired. Usually this will involve physical effort.

Cups: Awesome health on all levels, great support, joy!

Intentions: success/mastery, victory, blessing, protection, healing, cursing/reversing, gain/increase, beginning, ending, loss/removal, stability, banishing, and cleansing

---

Further Development Tasks

- Briefly state in your own words what the three levels of healing are and how you understand them.
- Name three ways you could incorporate sacred waters into healing magical work.

Magic-Making

A Prayer Bundle for Health and Vitality

You Will Need

Petition paper

Ritual anointing oil for healing and vitality (optional)

Personal concerns from the individual you wish to bless with health and vitality

A red charm bag, ideally one that is flannel and can be tied

Whole angelica root

Pinch of dried life everlasting

3 dried bay leaves

Incense (optional)

Process

1. Write out your petition for health and vitality.

2. If you are working with a ritual oil, then anoint the petition paper in a five-spot pattern in the corners and center.

3. Place your personal concerns in the center of the paper. Fold it toward yourself; turn it 90 degrees clockwise and fold it toward yourself again. Repeat this until the paper is small enough to go into the charm bag.

4. Anoint the entire angelica root, praying over it as you do so and then place it in the bag.

5. Add the life everlasting and bay leaves.

6. Anoint the bag in a five-spot pattern with the ritual anointing oil if you are working with that. You may also work with regular olive oil to do this.

7. Breathe into the bag and then tie it closed.

8. Hold the bag over the incense and bless it in your own words, allowing it to hang and start swinging much as you would with a pendulum. Once that bag has stopped moving, it is ready to be worn.

9. Ladies, the traditional place to wear a prayer bundle is in your bra. Gentleman, the traditional place for you is in a pocket.

To Heal from an Accident

You Will Need

A tea made of feverfew and ginger

Everything you would normally work with for sacred bathing

Process

1. Add the tea of feverfew and ginger into your bathwater.

2. Take a sacred bath as you normally would with the intention of healing quickly from an accident.

◆ *Chapter Six* ◆

Oh, Officer!

Court Case Success and Legal Issues

Very few people like dealing with law enforcement and courts of law. Certainly none of us like being involved in drawn-out and messy courtroom battles. As it turns out, our ancestors did not like legal troubles any more than we do, and the many magical approaches specifically designed for the remediation of legal conflicts bear testament to this. Some of the oldest magic in the world deals with both civil and criminal legal issues. For a good example of this check out the Icelandic tale Egil's Saga, considered one of the world's first Who Done It? stories, where we find heavy application of runic magic! When we talk about legal cases, it's important to remember that just as we discussed how we are not doctors in the previous chapter, we are also not lawyers and cannot give legal advice. However, we can work with both divination and magic to support querents in many ways. But before getting into all of that, let's look at the types of situations we most usually encounter when we deal with legal issues:

- **Court cases:** A common question from querents is some variant of "will I win my case?" As we will see in the tarot section, there are many possible answers to that question. From a magical perspective court cases deal with several dimensions and possibilities: getting a judge, a jury, lawyers, and witnesses either on the side of the querent or keeping witnesses quiet is often a big part of this work. Other aspects include hurrying a trial along, delaying a trial, or having a trial completely thrown out.

- **Seeking out legal aid:** Sometimes a person is in a situation that calls for legal aid—whether that is having the local police force listen to their story, a lawyer willing to advise them on the best steps to take, or a judge enforcing a previous court ruling. In these cases, magical work can draw the right professionals to the querent's side and to make sure that they receive the full benefits of good advice.

- **Avoiding legal entities:** This is a topic some readers and workers will be uncomfortable with, but it is a time-honored aspect of magic-making so you know I'm going to bring it up! Sometimes, we work with querents who derive their own living from being on the wrong side of the law. You and only you can determine when and for whom—if anyone—you are willing to do work in situations like these, but we will spend some time talking about how to avoid the law and/or legal detection.

Special Magical Considerations for Court Case Work

As we have seen with other magical forms, there are magical workings specific to court cases and legal work. Here are some of my favorites:

- **Beef tongue ritual:** Here the intention is to "sew" up the mouth and tongue of someone who is slandering or bearing false witness against the querent in a court of law. Depending on the ingredients used, the ritual can simply shut the person up or cause them to be confused, garbled, and incendiary in their testimony. Typically, a piece of the target's hair or some of their saliva is required to accomplish this. The Beef Tongue Ritual is actually a combination of sacred vessel and textile magic.

- **Honey jar sacred vessels:** Honey jars are worked with to promote goodwill and cooperation. In court case situations it is customary to work a sweetening jar so that everyone involved (even if they are on the "opposite" side) are "sweet on you" in the sense that they favor your case and want you to win.

- **Sacred bathing prior to court appearances:** When a querent is ready to appear in court, it is traditional to take a sacred bath in the morning before putting on clothes and getting ready. Ideally this bath should be composed of ingredients that foster victory in the case as well as protection.

- **Dressing legal documents and the body:** A querent may take initiative and dress hard copies of legal documents with magical sachet powders designed to increase chances of victory and coming out on top in court trials. They can also dress their body with a magical oil for victory after magical bathing and can use a body-safe sachet powder as well. Top it all off by fashioning a prayer bundle that can be worn in court! Dressing the body/physical documents is a form of physical manipulation magic.

- **Sumac berries:** In legal situations where you know the querent will be found guilty, especially in capital punishment vs. life sentence cases, it is believed that carrying sumac berries in your pocket while praying for three days will result in the most merciful sentencing possible if the querent is truly sorry for whatever crimes he committed. This is another form of physical manipulation magic.
- **Petitioning Archangel Michael:** The Archangel Michael is venerated by Christians, Jews, and Muslims the world over. I have written extensively about Michael, but what you need to know for legal work is that in his role as a saint, this angel is the patron of law enforcement officers. He is also historically a powerful ally for those who are being treated unfairly or unjustly. An altar may be built, talisman worn, and he may be petitioned to aid in legal affairs.
- **Petitioning El Niño de Atocha:** El Niño de Atocha, also known as the "infant of Atocha," is the patron saint for those in prison and those living in unjust societies, under political pressure/corruption, and dealing with immigration issues. He is usually depicted as a young boy. The reason he is associated with those unjustly imprisoned is because according to legend, when Islamic soldiers imprisoned and tortured Christians in Atocha, Spain, in the 1400s all the Christians would have starved to death if a little boy dressed as a pilgrim had not brought them food every day. When the Moors released the Christians, it was believed that the child was actually Jesus Christ himself. Later sightings of the young child were seen during time of political unrest and in one case staving off a rape.
- **Petitioning Santísima Muerte:** Santa or Santísima Muerta is a relative newcomer on the legal scene. She is based on a very ancient Aztec/Nahuatl goddess Mictecacihuatl—the Lady of Death. Santísima Muerte has developed a reputation, especially in states bordering Mexico, as a "narco saint." In truth, she was first petitioned and honored in rites involving ancestor veneration. Then in the 1970s and '80s she began to be invoked as a saint who would help keep husbands faithful to their

wives—kind of a more compelling or scary Lady of Guadalupe. In the last couple of decades, she has gained popularity with those on the wrong side of the law, especially when involved in drug trafficking. It is believed that she protects bandits from the eyes of the law. However, in my work with her I have seen the opposite: she will bring justice to those doing harm when asked to do so.

- **Petitioning Moses:** In Judaism and Christianity (especially some Protestant forms) Moses is the Giver of the Law. Because he was chosen to politically lead the Israelites out of their bondage in Egypt and because he was given the Ten Commandments on Mount Sinai, Moses is invoked when an individual seeks freedom or a just ruling.
- **Petitioning King Solomon:** King Solomon was believed to be the wisest man on earth during his reign. He is remembered for the famous judgment over two mothers both claiming a child to be their own. Knowing that one of the women was lying and that a true mother would never let harm come to her child, he recommended that the child be cut in two and a half given to each woman. The true mother refused, saying that the other woman could have the child, and in so doing got her baby back. He is commonly petitioned when seeking a just and wise judgment or judge.
- **Petitioning Lady Liberty:** Lady Liberty portrayed by the Statue of Liberty is based on the ancient Roman goddess Libertas and primarily concerned with freedom and justice. Many feminists and Neo-Pagans who perform magical work for political purposes invoke her protection and aid.

Some General Remarks on Petitioning

The idea of petitioning a saint or Holy Helper can be confusing to some people, but it does not have to be. Like much of magic, petitioning can be as complicated or as easy as you want it to be. There is no right or wrong way to petition many figures. Here are general steps to take.

- Build an altar in their honor or consecrate a space as sacred to them. Have a representation of them present.
- Engage in prayer, affirmations, or simply converse with them.

- State your need.
- State your form of payment.
- Leave a thanks offering.

Talismans Worked With in Court Case Work

- **Court case root/Little John to Chew root/galangal (Thai ginger):** These are all names for the same root. A member of the Ginger family, court case root derives its name from the old belief that by boiling it (some say for seven minutes and others for nine) in a pot of sugar water and then chewing it during the trial you will greatly enhance your odds of a favorable outcome. Others believe if you chew the root and spit it out, especially in a place where the judge for your case walks through it, you will gain a definite victory.
- **Indian head coins:** An Indian head penny (also simply known as an Indian head coin) is worked with by those who wish to avoid the law. It is believed that the Indian in this case functions as a kind of scout; he will keep a lookout for the individual and warn them if any law enforcement agents are nearby. Indian head pennies are often affixed to property boundaries like walls or fence posts; they can be worn or even sewn on a prayer bag, worn as jewelry, and pasted onto the walls of a home.
- **Mercury dimes:** Mercury is the Roman god of messages, speech, and communication. He is also known to move fast. A Mercury dime is also sometimes referred to as a silver dime. It is worked with to promote clear speech and thoughts in many situations—a court case being one of them.

Special Considerations in Tarot for Court Case Work

The Major Arcana

As usual, we look to the Major Arcana to deliver big, important, and thematic information to us about a case or legal situation. In court and legal work, I find the Major Arcana often delivers useful details about sentencing, which players may be brought over to the querent's side, and the speed at which the legal situation will progress.

The Suits

Coins

Coins deal primarily with financial matters when it comes to court and legal issues—settling for the right amount, not having enough money, settling for a lesser amount, and in some cases the specific world of workers' comp. A number of Coin cards can also indicate the situation is going to drag out for some time or that lots of money will be involved.

Swords

The sword is one of the two tools almost always pictured in images of Justice (the other being the balance). As a tool for justice and legal issues, this sword is used to cut through false testimonies and lies, to clearly illuminate the truth, to implement decisive and wise actions, and to issue sentencing and punishment. The Swords suit, ruled by Air, also deals with speech, can represent the study and profession of law, and can give specific information about witnesses and testimony.

Wands

When it comes to legal issues and court cases, Wands rule over the "hot" emotions (anger, rage, fear). These cards can symbolize situations where new energy and life are breathed into old or stale legal situations, but they can also indicate emotions are running hot, which may impede a fair outcome to the situation. Wands can also be useful in giving a sense of time to the situation. Lots of Wands cards in positive positions mean things are moving and possibly even being rushed. Wands in a challenging position can indicate delays or rescheduled events.

Cups

In court case and legal issues Cups cards can often indicate mental/emotional issues are playing an important and not to be overlooked role in the situation. They also speak to character and the work done to build up or destroy reputation in a court of law. Many Cups cards indicate the querent may need to seek out magical assistance to support them in the midst of their legal issues, and in some cases joining a church, temple, mosque or other kind of house of worship is recommended. A number of Cups cards may also suggest asking for or granting forgiveness can turn a legal situation around quickly.

Now let's turn our attention to individual cards and their meanings with respect to this type of work.

Major Arcana Cards

The Fool. Striking a balance between leading with the heart and listening to the head is essential. This card may indicate victory for the querent even when that seems unlikely. Depending on the context, the Fool could also be advising the querent to listen to the counsel others are giving them. Sometimes, the Fool suggests that someone involved in illegal activities is going to get caught. In a challenging or reversed position it can represent a person who has made bad choices that they may be held legally accountable for or loss of a legal battle. Upstanding members of society who can speak well on the person's behalf, especially clergy, will be helpful.

Magical Techniques: candles/oil lamps, magical words/prayers/petitions, and physical manipulation

Intentions: clarity/wisdom, success/mastery, victory, blessing, protection, healing, gain/increase, beginning, and cleansing

The Magician. This card speaks to working with magic to achieve a victory in the court case or legal situation, blessing lawyers to present the case in the correct way, and sometimes finding a "hidden" witness or testimony that can make all the difference. When well-positioned within a reading, the Magician indicates the querent has the resources needed to obtain victory. When reversed or in a challenging position, this card indicates the querent may be dealing with hidden motivations or lacking something fundamental that would help them triumph.

Magical Techniques: sacred vessels, lodestones, candles/oil lamps, magical words/prayers/petitions, physical manipulation, spraying/washing/spitting/asperging, textile magic, and spirit work

Intentions: clarity/wisdom, success/mastery, victory, attraction, road opening, blessing, protection, gain/increase, beginning, mental/psychic/dream influence, and cleansing

The High Priestess. A gifted female lawyer or judge who may be worked with for success (or in some cases who needs to be avoided depending on the position of the card within the reading), restoring liberty, and finding resolution and healing through a legal situation are all possible indications from the High Priestess. This card also suggests that having a minister, religious leader, or academic specialist assist the querent in some manner is a good idea. When it is reversed, the High Priestess tells us that the querent may not have the right helper on their side or they may not be clear in what they hope to accomplish.

Magical Techniques: sacred vessels, magical words/prayers/petitions, spraying/washing/spitting/asperging, textile magic, and spirit work

Intentions: clarity/wisdom, success/mastery, blessing, protection, healing, stability, mental/psychic/dream influence, and cleansing

The Empress. This card often represents the judge if they are a woman or a good attorney. It can also speak to a key witness involved. The Empress may also point to current or past lovers having a role to the play in the legal situation. In issues of divorce or custody, typically this card indicates that the woman in the situation is favored to win. When well-positioned in a reading, this card points to the role of this person being directly tied to a positive outcome for the querent. If the Empress is negatively positioned or reversed, then this is a person who could be a potential enemy or have a devastating effect on the situation.

Magical Techniques: sacred vessels and lodestones

Intentions: success/mastery, victory, attraction, blessing, gain/increase, and stability

The Emperor. Like the Empress, this card can represent the judge, an attorney, or an essential witness. The Emperor may also suggest that the querent's boss, supervisor, or other professional colleagues will have an important role to play in the unfolding situation. Context is key here. When the Emperor is well-positioned, there is an indication the querent can "strike a deal" and in so doing get a better outcome for themselves. When the Emperor is in a challenging position or reversed, one indication is that a man or men in positions of power are not on the side of the querent; another is that the querent is not standing in their own sense of authority and sovereignty.

Magical Techniques: sacred vessels, lodestones, and physical manipulation

Intentions: clarity/wisdom, success/mastery, victory, blessing, protection, gain/increase, and stability

The Hierophant. This may mean a clergyperson who can testify on behalf of or influence things for the querent. Sometimes the Hierophant can indicate nonprofit legal aid or support. This card emphasizes the roles that community, spiritual/religious traditions, and service to others play in the legal situation. This Hierophant may also identify the judge or mediator. If in a negative/reversed position, this is a figure who will not help the case go in the querent's direction, and/or it can signify the querent is truly guilty of whatever they have been accused of and must pay the price accordingly.

Magical Techniques: candles/oil lamps, magical words/prayers/petitions, and spirit work

Intentions: clarity/wisdom, success/mastery, road opening, blessing, protection, healing, stability, mental/psychic/dream influence, and cleansing

The Lovers. This card can mean romantic or ex-romantic partners will be involved in court case situations, a divorce may be able to be averted, or useful partnerships are forming in or around a case. One situation that happens more than we might like to admit, which needs to be watched carefully, is lawyers and the clients they represent getting romantically involved. The Lovers can also indicate the querent is going to need to make a serious and significant decision. When reversed, the main message is one of acrimony, vacillating on making important decisions, and the querent being in a disharmonious relationship with the people around them.

Magical Techniques: sacred vessels, lodestones, candles/oil lamps, magical words/prayers/petitions, and physical manipulation

Intentions: clarity/wisdom, success/mastery, victory, attraction, road opening, blessing, protection, and stability

The Chariot. This card can mean success and victory in the face of difficult circumstances. Sometimes travel is required, and often an entire legal team has to get involved in the case. Working with astrology-based magic is recommended. There is also a sense with this card that whatever situation the querent finds himself in will not be easily decided and it may be a bit of a roller coaster requiring skill to maneuver. When reversed, the Chariot indicates things will fall apart and victory will be elusive. Sometimes in a reversed position the Chariot suggests that there is a "flight risk" concern in the case.

Magical Techniques: candles/oil lamps, magical words/prayers/petitions, physical manipulation, and textile magic

Intentions: clarity/wisdom, success/mastery, victory, road opening, and stability

Strength. Domestic abuse may well play a role in the case. Often the situation involves sexual harassment or gender discrimination. Another interpretation is to proceed with one foot in front of the other calmly and to trust the process. This card usually indicates the querent is in for a long haul, so they need to be sure to adjust their expectations and also practice self-care throughout the process. In a challenging or reversed position, Strength can indicate the querent is lacking the support and endurance to go through the legal process and/or they may be overpowered.

Magical Techniques: lodestones, candles/oil lamps, magical words/prayers/petitions, and physical manipulation

Intentions: clarity/wisdom, success/mastery, victory, attraction, cursing/reversing, gain/increase, loss/removal, stability, and mental/psychic/dream influence

The Hermit. Silence will play a role here—as in a witness who refuses to testify, a querent not admitting innocence or guilt or pleading the Fifth, or the need to keep others silent. Contrarily, the Hermit can indicate a mentor, teacher, or guide may show up for the individual and assist them with their legal situation. In some readings the Hermit can signify that the querent might want to consider going into the legal profession themselves. When in a challenging position, the indication is the querent has gone into hiding and doesn't want to deal with what is happening . . . this is not an effective approach.

Magical Techniques: sacred vessels, candles/oil lamps, and spirit work

Intentions: clarity/wisdom, blessing, protection, stability, banishing, and mental/psychic/dream influence

Wheel of Fortune. This card can mean surprise—a surprise witness, surprise testimony, surprise evidence. When the Wheel of Fortune shows up, there is an element of change afoot. If things have been going well, then they may start to slow down and there may be some delays. If the situation has been difficult and blocked, then expect roads to open and ways to clear. When reversed, the card indicates a standstill. Depending on the context this could be a positive stabilizing of the situation or a negative stagnation. In all cases the querent should prioritize what is most important and focus on that.

Magical Technique: spirit work

Intentions: clarity/wisdom, success/mastery, victory, blessing, protection, healing, cursing/reversing, gain/increase, loss/removal, stability, and banishing

Justice. This card indicates a fair outcome, the case will go to trial, good lawyers, a fair judge, or the legal system working properly. It is also a good card for the querent to meditate on whenever there is a court case or legal issue. If the card shows up in a challenging or negative position, it can signal justice will not be served, the outcome will not be fair, and the querent may have to get aggressive in their approach to the situation.

Magical Techniques: sacred vessels, candles/oil lamps, magical words/prayers/petitions, physical manipulation, and spirit work

Intentions: clarity/wisdom, success/mastery, victory, attraction, road opening, blessing, protection, gain/increase, loss/removal, and stability

The Hanged Man. This card can mean being framed, set up, left to hang, lawyers or supporters getting hung up on small details. It might suggest losing sight of the big picture. It can also indicate sacrificing yourself for someone else. In some cases, it may suggest capital punishment. The Hanged Man can tell us that there is a new piece of information with the ability to turn the entire situation upside down. When in a reversed position, the Hanged Man advises a moderate approach to the situation and reminds the querent they do not need to sacrifice themselves.

Magical Techniques: sacred vessels, lodestones, candles/oil lamps, magical words/prayers/petitions, physical manipulation, textile magic, and spirit work

Intentions: clarity/wisdom, success/mastery, victory, attraction, blessing, protection, healing, cursing/reversing, gain/increase, ending, loss/removal, and banishing

Death. Death speaks to capital punishment, situations involving homicide, also sometimes the death of someone directly involved in the situation. If the situation the querent finds themselves in is not so dire as all of that, then the Death card is usually a good one to see when it comes to legal situations because it indicates there is a good possibility that whatever the legal hang-up is, it will soon go away. This card can also express a positive outlook for a win and/or settlement, especially if a good amount of money is involved. When reversed, the Death card signals there is energy for something new, a new beginning, a new possibility. Acquittal or appeals may be good choices. Sometimes it can also indicate a financial loss.

Magical Techniques: sacred vessels, lodestones, candles/oil lamps, magical words/prayers/petitions, physical manipulation, and spirit work

Intentions: clarity/wisdom, success/mastery, victory, protection, healing, cursing/reversing, ending, loss/removal, banishing, and cleansing

Temperance. Patience, leniency, reprieve, appeals, and mistrials are all possibilities brought up by this card. It can mean blessing and protection, especially from the Archangel Metatron, or a sacred pause. Often Temperance indicates a last-minute saving grace kind of situation. The querent also should be aware that they need to exist in both worlds at the same time when they receive this card—the world of their legal issues and the real world where their work and families reside. When reversed, the Temperance card tell us there is not a lot of leniency or balance in the situation. People in charge may be biased or the querent is not standing on equal ground.

Magical Techniques: sacred vessels, spraying/washing/spitting/asperging, and spirit work

Intentions: clarity/wisdom, success/mastery, victory, blessing, protection, healing, stability, banishing, mental/psychic/dream influence, and cleansing

The Devil. Addiction may play an outsized role, as could bad characters, people who want the querent to suffer, biased judges, corrupt lawyers and police officers, etc. This card can also come up when a querent is trying to decide on whether they want to take legal action, and when it does, the information is that it will be a long, drawn-out process, but worth it if the querent sticks to their principles and consistently shows up. The Devil can indicate a prison sentence, but if it is reversed, then it can signal a prison sentence will not be forthcoming and the querent will be able to go free.

Magical Techniques: sacred vessels, candles/oil lamps, magical words/prayers/ petitions, spraying/washing/spitting/asperging, textile magic, and spirit work

Intentions: clarity/wisdom, success/mastery, protection, healing, cursing/reversing, loss/removal, stability, banishing, and mental/psychic/dream influence

The Tower. The Tower tells of a case/legal situation falling apart, a mistrial, or new evidence admitted/old evidence thrown out, usually going against the querent. The foundations of the situation are shifting, and whatever has been built on them is about to fall. However, in some cases the Tower card can indicate last-minute evidence or testimony will be found that is absolutely golden for the querent. In a challenging or reversed position this card signifies things are not breaking in the querent's direction and a new approach is needed after a deep cleansing.

Magical Techniques: candles/oil lamps, magical words/prayers/petitions, physical manipulation, spraying/washing/spitting/asperging, textile magic, and spirit work

Intentions: clarity/wisdom, protection, healing, cursing/reversing, ending, loss/removal, banishing, and cleansing

The Star. Clemency, delays in proceedings, a chance to regroup and approach from a new angle, the opportunity to come clean, parole, and freedom are all indications for this card. The Star also, as always, points to consulting the querent's natal chart for information. The Star serves as a reminder to the querent that there is reason and purpose behind their experiences and they need to maintain a position of balance and equilibrium in the face of everything that is happening. When reversed, this card tells us the querent has become muddled, confused, and isn't sure why they are doing what they are doing—clarity is needed in this situation.

Magical Techniques: sacred vessels, lodestones, magical words/prayers/petitions, physical manipulation, and spraying/washing/spitting/asperging

Intentions: clarity/wisdom, attraction, road opening, blessing, protection, healing, mental/psychic/dream influence, and cleansing

The Moon. There are blocks and delays regarding the situation; parenting and childhood history may come into play; emotional trauma or wounds may also affect the situation. This card can indicate the querent has a bad lawyer, usually one that is female or identifies as female. There may be family drama in and around legal issues causing upset and strife for the querent. Another potential meaning of this card is the querent needs to listen to their intuition and emotional intelligence on legal issues. In a challenging or reversed position, the Moon tells us the querent has unrealistic expectations concerning the outcomes of their situation.

Magical Techniques: sacred vessels, spraying/washing/spitting/asperging, and spirit work

Intentions: clarity/wisdom, blessing, protection, healing, gain/increase, loss/removal, and mental/psychic/dream influence

The Sun. The Sun announces success, victory, and liberation from prison/locked institutions. The truth will come to light. If the querent suffered from a situation since they were young, this will finally be removed from their records. If the querent has been kept away from their children or grandchildren due to a legal issue, that order may finally be removed. When in a reversed position, the Sun indicates there may not be victory for the querent, an old sentence or accusation is not being allowed to die/be forgotten, and/or there may be a nasty custody battle ahead.

Magical Techniques: candles/oil lamps and spirit work

Intentions: clarity/wisdom, success/mastery, victory, attraction, road opening, blessing, and protection

Judgement. This card tells of judgments rendered, a good judge, a trial coming to an end, or a case going to court—or, if in a negative position, the opposite. This card can also indicate that doing magical work on people who are in positions of judgment can be effective for the querent at this time. When in a reversed position, this card may tell us the judge/sentencing is not fair or smart. In some cases, it may indicate the querent is likely to be found guilty and so settling out of court is a smart move if possible.

Magical Techniques: sacred vessels, candles/oil lamps, magical words/prayers/petitions, spraying/washing/spitting/asperging, textile magic, and spirit work

Intentions: clarity/wisdom, success/mastery, victory, blessing, and cleansing

The World. The World speaks to victory, success, good settlement amounts, the querent finally being seen for who they really are, repair to a damaged reputation, victory in libel or slander lawsuits. When in a challenging position, the World can indicate the querent's situation is not stable, slander/libel against them will be allowed to stand, or in some cases they may need to go into hiding/change their identity.

Magical Techniques: sacred vessels, lodestones, candles/oil lamps, magical words/prayers/petitions, physical manipulation, spraying/washing/spitting/asperging, textile magic, and spirit work

Intentions: success/mastery, victory, attraction, blessing, gain/increase, beginning, ending, loss/removal, and stability

Court Cards

King and Queen of Coins. These cards stand for judges, lawyers, mediators, and other players in cases and situations that involve money, work, or real estate. The King of Coins, when in a strong position, can indicate the querent is going to gain money, stability, or some other value from their experience.

The Queen of Coins reveals that paying people off, being generous, and owing people favors are a good way to navigate the situation. When in challenging positions, the King of Coins can express pertinent information is being hidden or lied about, and the Queen of Coins can indicate issues around debt and financial troubles.

Magical Techniques: sacred vessels, lodestones, and physical manipulation

Intentions: success/mastery, victory, attraction, blessing, protection, gain/increase, and stability

Knight of Coins. Slow the situation down. Look for supporting evidence, or search out evidence or testimony that is hidden. Take your time and be thorough. This card can also give us the rate at which a legal situation will proceed . . . it may tell us it is going to move slowly or to expect delays. When in a reversed position, the Knight of Coins indicates a feeling of being stuck and stagnant.

Magical Techniques: sacred vessels and lodestones

Intentions: clarity/wisdom, success/mastery, protection, and stability

Page of Coins. The Page of Coins shows searching out the money, hoping for a good settlement but possibly not getting as high of a number as originally hoped for. The Page of Coins is a seeker as all of the Pages are, and he is seeking a more solid foundation, a plan of action, a way to manifest his desires. When in a reversed position, the Page of Coins indicates the querent has not found what they are looking for and calm and stability are not yet available to them.

Magical Techniques: sacred vessels and lodestones

Intentions: clarity/wisdom, success/mastery, blessing, protection, gain/increase, and stability

King and Queen of Swords. These two usually indicate lawyers and/or judges—in some cases, law enforcement agents as well. They signal developing an excellent strategy to engage the legal situation. The King and Queen of Swords are both power players in the legal realm, so when they show up in a positive position, it's good news for the querent's situation. However, when they show up in a reversed position, it can indicate serious challenges ahead, especially from a personnel perspective.

Magical Techniques: magical words/prayers/petitions and spirit work

Intentions: clarity/wisdom, success/mastery, victory, protection, and mental/psychic/dream influence

Knight of Swords. This Knight tells of swift changes in plans, or a change of attack or direction in pursuing justice. Now is the time to act, but the querent should look before leaping. In a reversed position the Knight of Swords tells us the querent is moving too fast, making rash and impulsive decisions, and not exercising self-control. They may also be speaking too much or too freely about details of their situation.

Magical Techniques: candles/oil lamps and magical words/prayers/petitions

Intentions: clarity/wisdom, success/mastery, victory, road opening, protection, and mental/psychic/dream influence

Page of Swords. The querent needs to find a new lawyer or representative. There is a paper chase and making sure documents are going where they need to is imperative. Court dates, important filings, ascertaining the right documents . . . all of these should be emphasized now. Sometimes, this card signifies playing the waiting game. In a reversed position the Page of Swords tells us the querent's thoughts are scattered, unclear, and lack focus and as a result their victory is unlikely.

Magical Techniques: candles/oil lamps and magical words/prayers/petitions

Intentions: clarity/wisdom, success/mastery, protection, and mental/psychic/dream influence

King and Queen of Wands. Both the King and Queen of Wands represent secondary players in legal issues as well as law enforcement agents involved. Depending on the context, these may be helpful figures, or they may have their own motives within the situation. When in a beneficial position, these two are powerful forces of protection and transformation for the querent. When reversed, both cards can indicate high emotions and relay the message that anger and vendetta will work against the querent's favor. The situation may be combustible and those involved may have hot tempers, so cooling work that has justice prevailing as its aim is always a good idea.

Magical Techniques: candles/oil lamps and spraying/washing/spitting/asperging

Intentions: clarity/wisdom, success/mastery, victory, attraction, blessing, and protection

Knight of Wands. This card speaks to stops and starts, delays, mistrials, evidence/testimony thrown out, and depositions. Overall, there is a sense of forward momentum, but it is momentum that gets stalled out from time to time. In a challenging position the indication is impatience and anger can get the best of the querent, so especially if they are working with a mediator or giving testimony, they need to watch their temper.

Magical Techniques: candles/oil lamps and spraying/washing/spitting/asperging

Intentions: clarity/wisdom, success/mastery, road opening, and stability

Page of Wands. This card signals searching for justice or searching for the right person to articulate the querent's case in a more meaningful way, needing a new lawyer or an entirely different view of the situation, starting from scratch, reevaluating the situation from a new perspective. In a reversed position this card indicates confusion, scattered energy, and short tempers that do the querent no favors.

Magical Techniques: candles/oil lamps and spraying/washing/spitting/asperging

Intentions: clarity/wisdom, success/mastery, attraction, and road opening

King and Queen of Cups. Usually these cards represent unbiased, expert witnesses. Occasionally they can indicate emotional issues and past traumas that are playing an active role in the legal situation. Their presence also tells us an emotional or character appeal will work in the querent's favor as will any initiatives around service and/or spirituality. These two can also mean ecclesiastical witnesses who provide testimony to the querent's character or in some cases different options for rehabilitation. In reversed position these cards may reveal that the querent is too emotional about the situation and making poor decisions. They may also suggest the querent does not have the goodwill of any mediating institution (like a church or nonprofit) working for them and this absence is noted and problematic.

Magical Techniques: sacred vessels and spraying/washing/spitting/asperging

Intentions: clarity/wisdom, success/mastery, blessing, healing, mental/psychic/dream influence, and cleansing

Knight of Cups. Magical help is recommended for the case, especially work that seeks to create favorable conditions and bless the querent. Having someone come in and make statements about the character of the querent can also be indicated as useful when this card shows up. The pacing of the case is perhaps not as fast as the querent would like, but "haste makes waste" is absolutely true now and things should not be rushed. In a reversed position the Knight of Cups can denote that the querent is refusing to seek or accept help or the situation feels stuck and like it is not moving at all.

Magical Techniques: sacred vessels and spraying/washing/spitting/asperging

Intentions: clarity/wisdom, success/mastery, victory, blessing, healing, and cleansing

Page of Cups. This card suggests searching for good unbiased witnesses as well as spiritual people who can attest to character or lend support in other ways. Watch what is being said in situations when the Page of Cups comes up. Now is not the time for the querent to rely on their intuition and instead they should be logical and analytical in their approach. In a challenging position the card can indicate people are running off at the mouth and need to hush and/or the querent is making decisions based on emotion and this is not working out well for them.

Magical Techniques: sacred vessels and spraying/washing/spitting/asperging

Intentions: clarity/wisdom, success/mastery, blessing, healing, mental/psychic/dream and cleansing

Pip Cards

Aces

Coins: Money won, settlement achieved, section over and new beginning

Swords: Victory and success—one of the most decisive cards indicating these attributes

Wands: New energy, new shift in a case; also victory and triumph, sometimes a case getting thrown out

Cups: Expert witnesses coming on the team, information around character exerting a positive influence, religious realizations

Intentions: clarity/wisdom, success/mastery, victory, attraction, road opening, blessing, protection, healing, gain/increase, and beginning

Twos

Coins: The likelihood of getting all the querent wants in settlement is unlikely; compromises may have to be made.

Swords: Obstacles are emerging. Surprise evidence or witnesses that have an unclear influence on the case show up.

Wands: Past event coming into play in the current situation

Cups: Good partnership, lawyers working well, legal team getting along

Intentions: clarity/wisdom, success/mastery, road opening, gain/increase, stability, and mental/psychic/dream influence

Threes

Coins: Lawyers, judges, mediators, and all parties reaching a successful resolution though it may not lead to much financial gain . . . at least initially.

Swords: Heartbreak. Divorce will happen and go to court. A trial will not end in the querent's favor. Enemy testimony from an ex-lover or partner, custody battles.

Wands: A long wait is finally rewarded with victory or (more likely) case being thrown out and let go.

Cups: Allies coming forward to testify on the querent's behalf or support the querent in their situation

Intentions: clarity/wisdom, success/mastery, victory, blessing, protection, healing, cursing/reversing, gain/increase, and loss/removal

Fours

Coins: An essential piece of evidence or testimony gone missing, inability to connect with lawyers/judge/mediators/juries, attempting to financially hurt someone (or being financially hurt by someone)

Swords: Ending of a trial or legal situation, often with a neutral outcome. In rare cases it can mean the death of a person involved in the situation.

Wands: Support from community, family rallying together

Cups: Unclear evidence, hung juries, indecisive outcomes, and a question of what approach is best to take to the legal situation

Intentions: success/mastery, attraction, blessing, protection, gain/increase, and stability

Fives

Coins: Light to medium prison sentence and/or having to pay out a chunk of money for settlement. Querent feels like there are no resources to support them.

Swords: Surprise evidence or witness that will weigh against the querent, lies being told, false testimony, and past events that look bad. Also can indicate sabotage from an external source.

Wands: Anger and disruption in the courtroom, sometimes grounds for case dismissal or reassignment

Cups: Melancholy, regret, sometimes a light prison sentence

Intentions: clarity/wisdom, blessing, protection, healing, cursing/reversing, loss/removal, and cleansing

Sixes

Coins: Justice meted out, compromise, and settling out of court

Swords: The situation is blocked, communication mangled; can indicate that any Shut Your Mouth work against others is effective. Depending on the context, this card may indicate that while still challenging, the situation is beginning to slowly improve.

Wands: Victory and success! This is right up there with the Ace of Swords as far as being a decisive victory card. Often this one indicates the querent will win and someone else will lose.

Cups: Someone from the past, sometimes an ex, coming in and cooperating or supporting the querent in their legal situation

Intentions: clarity/wisdom, success/mastery, victory, blessing, protection, gain/increase, and stability

Sevens

Coins: Patience is rewarded; money is awarded; the investment pays off.

Swords: Someone is lying, and their mouth needs to be closed.

Wands: Feeling trapped, a short prison sentence, not having a good option on the table

Cups: Emotional and mental issues may exercise a direct effect on the case.

Intentions: clarity/wisdom, success/mastery, victory, blessing, protection, cursing/reversing, gain/increase, loss/removal, and banishing

Eights

Coins: Slow and steady progress; endurance and strength are important now.

Swords: Surrounded by hostile witnesses, an incompetent lawyer, or a biased judge. The deck is stacked against you, and you need to replace some key personnel.

Wands: New information, vital evidence; the tide is turning in the querent's direction—clear and compelling communication too.

Cups: Settlement that does not go your way, usually not imprisonment but sometimes a steep fine. Relocation may be necessary.

Intentions: clarity/wisdom, success/mastery, victory, attraction, blessing, protection, cursing/reversing, gain/increase, loss/removal, stability, and banishing

Nines

Coins: House arrest, white-collar prisons, walking away with a good amount of money and/or freedom

Swords: Anxiety may affect the case or situation. Staying up late at night, being too obsessive about the legal situation.

Wands: Bad decisions impacting the case or situation, sometimes being physically injured in the process of the situation emerging

Cups: Freedom, getting all key players on your side

Intentions: clarity/wisdom, success/mastery, victory, blessing, protection, healing, cursing/reversing, gain/increase, loss/removal, and stability

Tens

Coins: Huge settlement awards, great money, set up for the rest of your life

Swords: Chronic fatigue. Let the case end; give up. Being betrayed by someone you thought was an ally.

Wands: In it for the long haul. A case will not go away, and it's going to take some time for this to get resolved.

Cups: Divorce avoided, "happily ever after," case resolved, success and victory

Intentions: clarity/wisdom, success/mastery, victory, blessing, protection, healing, cursing/reversing, gain/increase, ending, loss/removal, stability, banishing, and cleansing

---

Suggestions for Further Development

- Which Major Arcana card would you recommend a querent meditate on if they are facing a trial in court and why?
- What plant ally may be used to obtain a merciful sentence and how would you work with it?

Magic-Making

Famous Beef Tongue Spell to Make Someone Hush!

You Will Need

Raw beef tongue

A sharp knife

Personal concerns of your target

Petition paper and writing implement

Ground alum

Red pepper

Black poppy seeds

Stop Gossip/Shut Your Mouth anointing oil (optional)

Black thread

Needle

Process

1. Take the beef tongue and split it down the middle with a sharp knife.

2. In the cut, place the personal concerns of the target, the petition that they stop gossiping/lying/slandering, the ground alum, red pepper, and black poppy seeds.

3. Anoint the black thread with anointing oil if you are working with that and thread the needle.

4. Speaking over the tongue as you sew it closed with the thread, give it the name of the individual, and then command them to shut their mouths and stop gossiping/lying/slandering, etc.

5. Once you have built up the energy by doing this, you may either throw the tongue into a fire or place it in a freezer so that they keep their mouths closed!

Court Case Victory Sacred Vessel Honey Jar

This is magic to bring victory in legal situations.

You Will Need

Petition paper

Pencil and pen

Ritual oil for court case success/legal protection

A miniature jar full of honey

Solomon's seal root

3 small pieces of galangal (Thai ginger, also known as court case root)

A pinch of grains of paradise

A white or brown candle

Process

1. Begin your petition paper by writing down the names of everyone involved in the legal situation—those on your side, as well as those who are not on your side—in pencil, turning the paper 90 degrees and writing your name in pen over their names. Repeat your name as many times as you need to so that it completely covers their names.

2. Then write in pen a petition for victory and success. Something like: victory, success, protection. Repeat these words again and again in a circle around all of the names.

3. Anoint the paper in a five-spot pattern with a ritual oil for court case success/legal protection.

4. Fold the paper toward you; turn it 90 degrees and fold it again. Continue this process until you can place it inside the honey jar.

5. Add the plant allies, and as you do, hold in your heart prayers that you are successful in your legal situation.

6. Light a white or brown candle on the honey jar on Thursdays with the prayerful intention that the legal situation/case is resolved in your favor.

Chapter Seven

When Are You Expecting?

Fertility, Pregnancy, and the Work of Manifesting

When we talk about fertility and pregnancy, we are speaking both literally and metaphorically. Literally, the desire to have a baby and the experience of carrying a child are areas where magic has been consulted for a long time, as have oracles and diviners. Metaphorically working with fertility, pregnancy, and birth is a newer concept, but one that resonates with both women (whether they have actual children or not) as well as many men. First, let's break the three categories up a bit:

- **Fertility:** Fertility is a sense of fecundity, the ability to get pregnant in the first place, and a feeling of abundance, freedom, and ease. From my own experience I can tell you that if you read for others long enough, you will get the woman who wants to know why she cannot get pregnant. It happens; it's a real thing. This is an issue of fertility as much as talking to the artist who is out of images, the writer who cannot find the words, or the entrepreneur who is searching for their next business idea. In each case we are dealing with someone who feels that they are lacking fertility and is experiencing the opposite of freedom and ease. Whether you are speaking with someone who wants to get pregnant and cannot or someone who is searching for the touch of the muse and coming up empty-handed, the quest for fertility begins with assisting the querent in creating freedom and ease around their situation and making sure the creative act is happening. In the case of a woman who wants to get pregnant, who is "trying," the first thing to do is make sure she is in a place where having a baby actually makes sense. Can she provide for the child financially, emotionally, spiritually, and educationally? Does she have help and support? Is she really ready? Obviously, these are conclusions you come to through conversing with her and in some cases her partner, too. The second thing to ascertain is, are medical doctors involved in the situation? Is there a biological reason why she is having so much difficulty getting pregnant? Is she experiencing signs of pre/peri-menopause and hoping against hope she might still get pregnant? In other words, are there external conditions that speak strongly against her ability to get pregnant? If such conditions are in place, it doesn't mean you can't help the querent through divination and magic, but it does mean you need to be honest and realistic with her. Finally—and this may seem obvious but I am here to tell you it is not always clear—is sex happening? Obviously, no sex, no baby! What is interesting to note is that the exact same principles hold for anyone who is having an issue with fertility in a more metaphorical sense. To recap, the initial questions you want to ask and ideas you want querents to consider are:

- Is it the right time/am I in the right place for this?
- Are there real and overwhelming factors working against me that I need to call out honestly?
- Is the "sex" happening?

Now obviously when we are talking about metaphorical fertility, we are also talking about metaphorical sex. For a writer that is the act of actually sitting down to write; for a teacher it's the act of teaching; for a dressmaker it's carving out the time to design and stitch a pattern. Those pieces must be in place before the "idea baby" is ready to arrive.

- **Pregnancy:** Whether we are talking about the nine plus months a woman carries a child or the period of time it takes to gestate your big idea/work of art/book/merger/etc., the main concern during this time centers around safety and tranquility. We want our baby to be safe and the person carrying the child to be safe, and we realize this means there needs to be low stress and smooth as glass sailing for the period of time the gestation lasts. Support is also essential. When a woman is physically pregnant, she recognizes, and the people around her recognize, that her needs and conditions are changing rapidly. She will require new clothes, possibly a body pillow to sleep comfortably, healthy food, and to be relaxed. When we are gestating something less literal than a kiddo, however, it's easy to forget about these things: the need to relax, to be supported, the fact that during any time you are intensely working on something you are going through physical changes, too. Those changes demand acknowledgment and accommodation.

- **Birth:** Birth is a threshold time and a threshold space. This again is true whether you are birthing an actual child or a project, masterpiece, or business. There is risk involved, and there is the potential, even in our age of modern medicine, for death. There is also the possibility of great victory, success, and love and devotion for something that fills every fiber of your being. The act of birthing is magical, numinous, and bloody intense, which is probably why it's called labor. During birth, the focus is on safety but also on endurance, clarity, and faith. Timing is an essential component of successful birthing, as is having the right team in place.

Special Magical Considerations for Fertility Work

Working from the foundation we have established, there are three broad areas of magic correlating to fertility, pregnancy, and birth. The first is paired with fertility and may be called **fertility magic.** I say this about a lot of different types of magic, but fertility magic is some really ancient stuff. Gods, goddesses, seasonal cycles and celebrations, and even many modern-day religious celebrations all turn around the fulcrum of fertility and its associated cycles of growth, maturation, sex, harvesting/death, and (re)birth. The second is often paired with both pregnancy and birth, and that's **road opening magic.** We want to clear the way so that the child/seed/impulse/idea has an easy path to travel. A third form of magic that often comes up is **cleansing and blessing work.** The cleansing work is primarily to remove any obstacles, fears, or anxieties that stand in the way of success, and the blessing work is to strengthen and empower the person or the couple so that their efforts result in generation. If, in our divination, we discover the querent wants to get physically pregnant and is not having regular sex, we may also be called upon to do some sex magic. If, on the other hand, we are reading for a querent who needs to become metaphorically pregnant and they are not taking the time and making the space for the "sex" to happen, then we may be called to do clarity/wisdom work so that the querent can start making that space and that time. If you are talking to someone who is already pregnant, in whatever form, then the focus of magical work changes to making sure that they are safe, protected, empowered, and tranquil in body, mind, and spirit. Finally, it is time to have the baby! Of course, ultimately, we want to bless the baby too!

Special Considerations in Tarot for Fertility Work

The Major Arcana

When it comes to fertility work and all that follows in its wake, the Major Arcana cards alert us to significant blessings, obstacles, challenges, and opportunities as well as some key players that can make a big difference in the querent's overall experience.

The Suits

Coins

Coins deal especially with the birthing part of our triumvirate . . . they are all about manifesting your work, idea, or child into the physical plane. It's time to birth that baby and let them take on a being and nature all their own! These cards will indicate practical concerns as well as material blessings and can illuminate areas where the querent might otherwise become stuck. Many Coins coming up for the areas of fertility, pregnancy, and birth suggests the use of physical magic like prayer bags, talismans, and altar-building and a focus on securing practical resources and manifesting your baby! In challenging or reversed positions, Coins may signal there are financial constraints needing to be addressed, a lack of planning will have negative repercussions, and/or a general avoidance of practicalities that will not serve the querent well.

Swords

As we have seen, the suit of Swords is complicated. Sometimes it can be quite positive, and other times it's really difficult to deal with. When it comes to fertility, pregnancy, and birth, Swords are usually not the cards you want to see. In a few instances, they can indicate supporting figures, but often they represent challenges and obstacles that must be overcome. Because these cards are connected to the element of Air, they can also express issues in the situation with too much thinking, and in some cases too much critical analysis. In some cases, Swords will signal a need for strong protection and also a couple of supporting people who should be attracted to the querent's side during this time. When a number of Swords show up in reversed position, we see that there is a lack of planning, strategy, and clarity in the situation and that is going to make manifesting anything much more difficult.

Wands

Symbolic of vitality, sex, lust, and enthusiasm, a number of Wands are usually a good omen—though in a few cases they can indicate some obstacles or heavy labor that needs to be magically dealt with. Wands speak to transformation, and the experience of pregnancy and birth is, of course, deeply transformational. In less auspicious contexts, Wands can suggest some physical issues the querent might need to be aware of, including but not limited to challenges around cardio health, inflammation, bleeding, and high blood pressure. Reversed Wand cards may also indicate there is an excess of the "hot" emotions in the situation, which lends itself to a lack of reliable stability.

Cups

Cups are the suit we really want to deal with in fertility, pregnancy, and birth work. Ruled by the element of Water, Cups have a strong association with the womb and the ability to contain precious ideas and/or beings and carry them safely to term. A number of these cards usually indicate there is wonderful energy around the querent right now when it comes to fertility, pregnancy, and birth. In some cases, there may also be some issues that need to be worked through in the time-honored magical traditions associated with Water, including cleansing, magical bathing, floor washes, and sacred sprays and waters. The focus is on blessings, personal empowerment, and sensual enjoyment! Cups cards in challenging positions can signify issues with the actual pregnancy, including potential loss or miscarriage, and they may also point to postnatal depression.

Major Arcana Cards

The Fool. Here the Fool does indicate new beginnings and a new possibility. The Fool can also express that the querent needs to have strong faith in themselves and their ability to conceive and prayer work is recommended. In a reversed position, this card tells us the querent is not seeing the situation clearly and may have some unrealistic expectations. The Fool can also come up to announce a surprise pregnancy.

Magical Techniques: candles/oil lamps and magical words/prayers/petitions
Intentions: clarity/wisdom, success/mastery, road opening, blessing, gain/increase, and beginning

The Magician. All the resources are before the querent, whether they want to get pregnant, have a blessed pregnancy, or give birth in a specific way. The road is open; the way is clear; and magic is a good idea! However, if the Magician shows up in a compromised position, it can indicate an essential ingredient is missing or the querent is suffering from illusions around this situation that need to be dispelled. In some cases, the Magician in a challenging position may also show someone is working against the querent and trying to prevent them from getting pregnant or carrying to full term.

Magical Techniques: sacred vessels, lodestones, candles/oil lamps, magical words/prayers/petitions, physical manipulation, spraying/washing/spitting/asperging, textile magic, and spirit work

Intentions: clarity/wisdom, success/mastery, victory, attraction, road opening, blessing, protection, healing, gain/increase, and mental/psychic/dream influence

The High Priestess. This card can indicate the woman will have a difficult time becoming physically pregnant and/or she might have to experience the pregnancy alone. Because the High Priestess is traditionally viewed as a scholar, magic-maker, and creative, it is a wonderful card to get for those working on an intellectual or creative pregnancy, however. In a reversed position the High Priestess warns against having a baby/starting a new endeavor as a way to try to fix something that is not working.

Magical Techniques: sacred vessels, magical words/prayers/petitions, and spraying/washing/spitting/asperging

Intentions: clarity/wisdom, success/mastery, blessing, protection, healing, gain/increase, loss/removal, mental/psychic/dream influence, and cleansing

The Empress. This is the "mom" card par excellence of the tarot. This lady is all about manifesting! For a literal conception/pregnancy and delivery, the Empress reveals that all signs point to yes, and I often have pregnant querents (or those interested in manifesting) focus on and contemplate this card. For those who are less literal, she is about the pregnancy process: letting the work gestate and the reaping of what you have sown. In a reversed position, the Empress can indicate the roads to fertility and pregnancy are currently closed. She might also tell us that if the querent is pregnant, they need to watch out for excessive weight gain/indulgence/being too sedentary.

Magical Techniques: sacred vessels, lodestones, physical manipulation, and textile magic

Intentions: success/mastery, victory, attraction, blessing, gain/increase, and stability

The Emperor. The Emperor is a protective force when it comes to fertility and pregnancy. He is the person(s) in the querent's life (as well as part of the querent themselves) that makes sure things are stable, safe, and protected. He often points to someone who provides financial stability and abundance. When he shows up in a strong position, he indicates everything is safe and stable . . . ripe conditions for fertility and pregnancy. In a challenging position, he asks if the querent is being too rigid in the way they are thinking about fertility, pregnancy, and birth. Are they trying to make too many rules and put too many parameters around the process? Is there enough room for flow? In some cases, do we have "daddy" or paternity issues that need to get sorted out? Is the current situation unsafe?

Magical Techniques: sacred vessels, lodestones, physical manipulation, and textile magic

Intentions: success/mastery, victory, attraction, protection, blessing, and gain/increase

The Hierophant. The querent needs to seek blessing before engaging in procreative acts: blessing for pregnancy, blessing for the birth itself. Sometimes this means the querent needs to look for astrological advice or spiritual assistance that will be with them through the whole process. In more metaphorical terms, sometimes this card can indicate the querent will be most successful with creative endeavors if they are in a group setting—such as a writer's group or life drawing class. When in a challenging position, the Hierophant suggests the road is closed currently for fertility and pregnancy and cleansing, prayer, and blessing work are the way to move forward.

Magical Techniques: sacred vessels, candles/oil lamps, magical words/prayers/petitions, spraying/washing/spitting/asperging, and spirit work

Intentions: clarity/wisdom, success/mastery, attraction, blessing, protection, healing, stability, and cleansing

The Lovers. Make love, make time, make space for your love! Engage in the kind of creative alchemy required for rocking the fertility boat! This card can also confirm the querent has the right people on board. It can also indicate some major hot attraction work is called for to make the world love your creation! As always, the Lovers can tell us an important decision needs to be made. When in a reversed position, this card indicates the love/support/passion is not present. It may signal an issue around lovemaking and physical intimacy. It can also point to indecision or an avoidance of making an important (and tough) decision.

Magical Techniques: sacred vessels, lodestones, candles/oil lamps, and physical manipulation

Intentions: success/mastery, attraction, blessing, and gain/increase

The Chariot. The Chariot speaks to overcoming apparent impossibilities to conceive, carrying a pregnancy to full term, giving birth (and in some cases giving birth in a specific way). This card can also mean transcendence over practical concerns and naysayers. Travel may be required for the situation to be ultimately successful. In a reversed position, this card can signal the road is currently closed, usually because there is too much inner tension and conflict at this time. It may also indicate momentum is being thwarted by outside sources.

Magical Techniques: magical words/prayers/petitions, physical manipulation, and spirit work

Intentions: clarity/wisdom, success/mastery, victory, road opening, gain/increase, and stability

Strength. Strength tells of the ability to take care of yourself during the pregnancy especially, to endure and be consistent in your work, and to deliver successfully. It also expresses watching the words you say and the beliefs they can point to. When this card shows up in a less favorable context, it indicates the querent may need assistance to labor and deliver successfully.

Magical Techniques: candles/oil lamps, magical words/prayers/petitions, and physical manipulation

Intentions: clarity/wisdom, success/mastery, victory, blessing, protection, and mental/psychic/dream influence

The Hermit. Going inward is often seen during pregnancy and 100 percent normal and right-on. This card also points to finding truth in silence, friendships and relationships starting to change, or a period of deep creativity and reflection. When this card shows up, it can be a good idea to hire a doula, coach, or other mentor-type figure to support you on your journey! When reversed, the Hermit indicates that the querent is in need of time and space to go inward right now. At the very least they should be winnowing down their external commitments, and they may want to lean in to the Hermit energy and commit to a retreat, staycation, or other restorative practice.

Magical Techniques: sacred vessels, lodestones, candles/oil lamps, and magical words/prayers/petitions

Intentions: clarity/wisdom, blessing, protection, healing, and mental/psychic/dream influence

Wheel of Fortune. The situation is changing. If it has been easy, then prepare for some challenges; if it has been really hard, get ready for the roads to open. Above all, understand that Destiny is playing her hand now. This card can also speak to the legendary ups and downs in emotions we experience when we are pregnant with someone or something. When this card comes up and it feels like that is the likeliest reading, then the querent should fix themselves to what matters most. When reversed, the Wheel of Fortune indicates the roller coaster is actually coming to a halt—things are about to stabilize and settle down.

Magical Technique: spirit work

Intentions: clarity/wisdom, blessing, protection, healing, cursing/reversing, gain/increase, beginning, ending, loss/removal, and stability

Justice. What the querent puts into this situation is what they will be able to get out of it. It's going to take effort but also suggests making time and space for joy and feeling good! This card may express balanced relationships both internally and externally during the entire pregnancy process. Partnership is emphasized by Justice as well. In a reversed position, Justice signals there is a fundamental imbalance and/or lack of reciprocity causing issues with fertility/pregnancy.

Magical Techniques: lodestones, magical words/prayers/petitions, and physical manipulation

Intentions: clarity/wisdom, attraction, blessing, gain/increase, loss/removal, and stability

The Hanged Man. It's time to change up perspective; what has been tried is not working, so shift gears and move into a new mode of doing/trying/being with the situation. The Hanged Man can also indicate that in order to get pregnant, carry the baby successfully, and/or give birth victoriously, something of the querent's current life/situation may need to be sacrificed. In difficult physical birthing situations, the Hanged Man may be taken literally and recommend the mom try inverted poses or working with tension bands/ropes (under medical supervision of course). When the Hanged Man appears reversed, the indication is the querent does not need to make sacrifices in order to experience an easy pregnancy/birth.

Magical Techniques: magical words/prayers/petitions, physical manipulation, textile magic, and spirit work

Intentions: clarity/wisdom, success/mastery, victory, blessing, protection, healing, cursing/reversing, ending, loss/removal, banishing, and cleansing

Death. Death can indicate the ability to get physically pregnant is simply not present, there will be problems carrying the child or idea full term, and/or physical death will affect the situation in some manner. But it can also signify the death of obstacles that have been standing in your way. In a metaphorical sense the Death card suggests the creative work that seems to be happening is actually not happening and a different approach needs to be taken. Death can also indicate the child will be born with some significant health issues requiring medical intervention and treatment. Reassure the querent if this is the case: kids are born all of the time who beat the odds and survive. I should know—I'm one of them! This card can also signify a need to eliminate a pregnancy. When the Death card shows up reversed in this context, it can indicate that there has been a near miss and baby and family will be healthy and just fine. Death reversed is life, and life is what this chapter is all about!

Magical Techniques: candles/oil lamps, magical words/prayers/petitions, spraying/washing/spitting/asperging, and spirit work

Intentions: clarity/wisdom, blessing, protection, healing, cursing/reversing, ending, loss/removal, banishing, and cleansing

Temperance. Because the angel pictured in the RWS deck is often taken to be Gabriel (in other cases it is seen as Metatron), the Temperance card is often a strong indicator a woman is or will shortly become pregnant—even if it's against the odds. This is because Gabriel is the messenger angel showing up throughout the Bible to tell women they are pregnant, but also because evidence exists pointing to the figure of Gabriel as a Canaanite fertility goddess. So aside from its usual meaning of being patient and moderate in actions and behavior, this card has a special role for those wishing to become pregnant and especially shows up (or is good to contemplate) when faith is flagging. In a reversed position, Temperance expresses obstacles at work against fertility and pregnancy. Cleansing and road opening work is the best way forward.

Magical Techniques: sacred vessels, spraying/washing/spitting/asperging, and spirit work

Intentions: clarity/wisdom, road opening, blessing, protection, healing, gain/increase, stability, and cleansing

The Devil. A situation needs to be addressed/released before safe fertility/pregnancy can ensue. Bad habits, ideas, relationships are keeping someone from having a successful pregnancy and/or birth. The advice here is not to give up, but to know this is going to be a marathon and endurance is key. In challenging or reversed positions, the Devil can indicate negativity or cursing work done around the individual(s) who are trying to conceive that will need to be removed and cleansed before there is success.

Magical Techniques: sacred vessels, magical words/prayers/petitions, spraying/washing/spitting/asperging, textile magic, and spirit work

Intentions: clarity/wisdom, victory, blessing, protection, healing, cursing/reversing, loss/removal, banishing, mental/psychic/dream influence, and cleansing

The Tower. Severe trauma is in the cards—not necessarily physical but it could be. A rug is getting pulled out from under you, or sometimes this is getting pregnant without expecting it. This card can also indicate that once a child (literal or metaphorical) comes into the world, the querent's entire life changes in a radical and, at least initially, difficult manner. The Tower can speak to the (usually sudden) loss of a pregnancy or setback of a creative endeavor. When reversed, the Tower can express the querent or the people around them are stressing out about and stabbing at phantoms . . . although things may feel really overwhelming and difficult, there is actually a lot of room to maneuver.

Magical Techniques: sacred vessels, magical words/prayers/petitions, physical manipulation, spraying/washing/spitting/asperging, textile magic, and spirit work

Intentions: clarity/wisdom, protection, healing, cursing/reversing, ending, loss/removal, stability, banishing, and cleansing

The Star. This card brings soul alignment and blessings. It suggests the successful removal of obstacles that have been standing in the way of getting pregnant or carrying a child safely. Consulting one's natal chart for fertility and inspiration is called for, as well as timing conception and birth to astrological phenomena. For nonliteral pregnancies the Star marks that threshold moment when the idea or dream you are holding is starting to take shape in reality but is not quite there yet. In reversed position, the Star can reveal obstacles are creating difficulties either in getting pregnant or carrying a child to term. It may also signal that the querent's sleep and dream life is disturbed and they need rest.

Magical Techniques: sacred vessels, spraying/washing/spitting/asperging, and spirit work

Intentions: clarity/wisdom, road opening, blessing, protection, healing, stability, banishing, and cleansing

The Moon. Obstacles and difficulties are in the way of getting pregnant and/or carrying the child. If someone is pregnant, it can especially mean difficulties with hormones and emotions. Sometimes the Moon indicates the challenge is for an individual who was on medication prior to pregnancy and now during pregnancy cannot use that medication. In other cases, financial difficulties are causing stress. The general rule of this card is that there are both practical and instinctual responses the querent needs to be aware of. However, if shown in a positive position, then the Moon can demonstrate that pregnancy is quite likely and beneficial. When reversed, the Moon suggests there are illusions/delusions around fertility, pregnancy, and birth that are not serving the best interest of the querent.

Magical Techniques: sacred vessels, physical manipulation, spraying/washing/spitting/asperging, and spirit work

Intentions: clarity/wisdom, success/mastery, road opening, blessing, protection, healing, gain/increase, beginning, ending, loss/removal, and mental/psychic/dream influence

The Sun. Pregnancy! The baby arrives safely! Fertility in all respects is expressed, especially in cases where couple is judged "too old" to have child. I remember reading for my best friend and she got this card. I told her it could mean pregnancy, and she said, "Like metaphorical, right?" And I said, "Mmm . . . could be but also an actual, real-deal baby." Turns out she was pregnant when we were doing the reading—she just didn't know it! Whenever the Sun comes up, be sure to let your querent know it signals a highly fertile time so that they can take precautions if they do not wish to have a child right now. In a challenging position the Sun can indicate a difficulty in getting pregnant or the loss of a pregnancy or child.

Magical Techniques: candles/oil lamps, magical words/prayers/petitions, and spirit work

Intentions: clarity/wisdom, success/mastery, victory, attraction, road opening, blessing, protection, healing, gain/increase, beginning, ending, and stability

Judgement. This card speaks to issues around feeling judged for having children/not having children and/or what your creative work is and where it is—generally catching the querent up on what other people think about them that is keeping them from doing their work. Judgement can sometimes indicate the desire to conceive needs to be examined more closely.... Is this really what the querent wants (or in some cases, doesn't want)? Encourage them to be honest with themselves about where they feel clear and where they do not. In a challenging position, this card suggests the querent is allowing the opinions of others to override what they themselves want.

Magical Techniques: sacred vessels, candles/oil lamps, magical words/prayers/petitions, physical manipulation, spraying/washing/spitting/asperging, textile magic, and spirit work

Intentions: clarity/wisdom, success/mastery, victory, attraction, road opening, blessing, protection, healing, cursing/reversing, and cleansing

The World. Success, victory, and a wide-open road for joy! Pregnancy and birthing in whatever form the querent might be considering is given a big green light. The querent is standing in their sovereignty and has a good support team around them to help them bring new life into the world. This card can also indicate the completion of a cycle, so if the querent is asking about having more children, the World may be saying they have had or are going to have their last. In a challenging position the World tells us the querent doesn't have the kind of foundation and sense of self or support at this time that they need in order to have a successful pregnancy.

Magical Techniques: sacred vessels, lodestones, candles/oil lamps, magical words/prayers/petitions, physical manipulation, spraying/washing/spitting/asperging, textile magic, and spirit work

Intentions: clarity/wisdom, success/mastery, victory, attraction, road opening, blessing, protection, healing, cursing/reversing, gain/increase, beginning, ending, loss/removal, stability, banishing, mental/psychic/dream influence, and cleansing

Court Cards

King and Queen of Coins. Fertility and the ability to get pregnant are in place, but it may be a slow process. Patience is imperative in the situation. Also these cards may indicate financial concerns or blessings, depending on what other cards provide context. When these cards are reversed or negatively positioned, they may speak to challenges around fertility and/or practical or financial concerns needing to be addressed before there is a successful resolution. They also advise that the querent watch out for excessive weight gain and/or poor choices concerning diet and exercise.

Magical Techniques: sacred vessels, lodestones, and physical manipulation

Intentions: clarity/wisdom, success/mastery, blessing, protection, gain/increase, beginning, and stability

Knight of Coins. Slowing the situation down, hitting the "pause" button, refusing to be rushed, taking one's time are all potential meanings here. Depending on context, this card may also indicate the querent needs to seek out help with either fertility or finances before they are ready. When reversed, the Knight of Coins can express intelligent hesitation has turned into stagnant waiting and the time is now to take action and move forward.

Magical Techniques: sacred vessels, lodestones, and physical manipulation

Intentions: clarity/wisdom, success/mastery, victory, road opening, blessing, protection, gain/increase, and stability

Page of Coins. The Page of Coins reveals searching for the right idea or opportunity, perhaps searching for the technology that will allow querent to get pregnant. There is a need to find stability and security around these issues. When reversed, the Page of Coins signals a lack of certainty and stability and the querent might need to take a step back and reassess the situation with a new perspective.

Magical Techniques: sacred vessels and lodestones

Intentions: clarity/wisdom, success/mastery, attraction, road opening, blessing, protection, gain/increase and stability

King and Queen of Swords. These two cards can sometimes signal a lack of fertility or that road opening work needs to be performed. Medical support and intervention may be required in order for successful conception and/or delivery, and generally speaking, the querent should listen to the professionals.

Clarity, communication, and logical thinking are all needed. When either of these cards show up reversed, the querent may be too much "in their heads" and/or too reliant on expert opinion and not listening to their own inner knowing and wisdom.

Magical Techniques: candles/oil lamps, magical words/prayers/petitions, and spirit work

Intentions: clarity/wisdom, success/mastery, victory, attraction, road opening, blessing, protection, healing, cursing/reversing, loss/removal, banishing, and mental/psychic/dream influence

Knight of Swords. This card reveals the need of a helper figure, usually someone connected to medicine. In some cases, advanced fertility procedures or placing oneself amid good and inspiring teachers is required. When reversed, the Knight of Swords indicates the querent is rushing into a situation or decision too quickly and should stop, take a breath, and reassess their circumstances. Sometimes in a challenging position this card also draws attention to the querent's desire to focus on what could be, instead of what is.

Magical Techniques: candles/oil lamps, magical words/prayers/petitions, and spirit work

Intentions: clarity/wisdom, success/mastery, victory, road opening, blessing, protection, healing, cursing/reversing, loss/removal, banishing, and mental/psychic/dream influence

Page of Swords. Not seeing clearly or immaturity is a serious factor in the situation, and there is a need to reassess what is going on. This card indicates it may not be the right time to actually get pregnant, but planning now for future pregnancies could make sense. When reversed, the Page of Swords can signify the querent is in an unstable situation and will need extra support and possibly medical intervention.

Magical Techniques: magical words/prayers/petitions and spirit work

Intentions: clarity/wisdom, road opening, and stability

King and Queen of Wands. These cards suggest a pregnant couple—often an older pregnant couple—great joy and blessings, and alchemy at work. Sometimes the King and Queen of Wands can indicate an unexpected pregnancy that is joyfully received or even a surrogate situation. Remember that pregnancy can be a potent metaphor, and this is especially true with these two as they also speak to creative success and overflow.

Magical Techniques: candles/oil lamps and spirit work
Intentions: success/mastery, victory, attraction, road opening, blessing, and protection

Knight of Wands. There is movement forward and then backtracking, second-guessing oneself around pregnancy issues. (These can be literal or metaphorical.) The querent is caught in a situation causing low-grade stress. This card may also speak to the physical and energetic ups and downs of carrying anything—a child or a creative endeavor—to completion. When in a reversed position, the indication is the querent needs to do whatever is needed to bring stability and clarity to the situation.
Magical Techniques: candles/oil lamps and spirit work
Intentions: clarity/wisdom, road opening, blessing, protection, and cleansing

Page of Wands. This card often marks the moment before conception. It may feel like there is nothing, like you are staring at a blank page or even a series of nos, and then bam—that first spark comes alive and ignites something greater. When this card is drawn, the advice is to be patient . . . to wait, to listen, and to appreciate the pause before the momentum picks up. When reversed, the indication is the querent is exhausting themselves with scattered ideas and scattered energy.
Magical Techniques: candles/oil lamps and spirit work
Intentions: clarity/wisdom, road opening, blessing, protection, and cleansing

King and Queen of Cups. Conditions for a safe pregnancy, fertility, and delivery are perfect. Helpers, angels, guardians, and spirits are present, as are capable supporters. The situation is blessed as are the individuals involved within it. When reversed, either of these cards announce a disruption to flow and fertility. They may also indicate an overabundance of emotions that impede practical thinking and decision-making.
Magical Techniques: sacred vessels, spraying/washing/spitting/asperging, and spirit work
Intentions: clarity/wisdom, success/mastery, blessing, protection, and healing

Knight of Cups. This card tells of a helper figure, usually of a spiritual nature such as a minister, rabbi, or imam, who can help bless the situation, inspire fertility, and in some cases bless the pregnancy. The Knight of Cups may also refer to a medical helper needed to support the querent during this time. The

Knight of Cups can further give us the rate at which something moves—in this case slowly but thoroughly. When reversed, the Knight of Cups indicates help is needed and perhaps either not being found or being refused. A reversal could also point to something being wrong with the speed at which the situation is progressing.

Magical Techniques: sacred vessels, spraying/washing/spitting/asperging, and spirit work

Intentions: clarity/wisdom, success/mastery, victory, road opening, blessing, protection, and healing

Page of Cups. At this point the querent needs to be careful about listening too deeply to their own intuition. They need to consider factors that are real and present, no matter how much they might think they can spiritually or magically overcome them. This card can also indicate the querent is feeling overly emotional and should not make big decisions based on their big feelings. When reversed, the Page of Cups tells us the querent needs to invite reason and logical thinking into the situation now. There may be a danger of being overcome by emotions or intuitions that will lead the querent off on a wild-goose chase while real concerns go unheeded.

Magical Techniques: sacred vessels, candles/oil lamps, spraying/washing/spitting/asperging, and spirit work

Intentions: clarity/wisdom, success/mastery, opening, blessing, protection, healing, and mental/psychic/dream influence

Pips

Aces

Coins: A new and very stable approach to things. Health and strength through the pregnancy process. Pregnancy (metaphorical or literal) coinciding with financial gain or a new financial win.

Swords: Success achieved through the union of opposites and in some cases lovemaking. Occasionally indicating success of a technical procedure like in vitro fertilization. For metaphorical pregnancies this card can point to a new approach that will yield excellent fruit.

Wands: Conception is successful, and the pregnancy is underway. Expect a vigorous baby, often male. This card can also indicate a need for more sex or more of the procreative act.

Cups: A new, healthy, blessed pregnancy and/or delivery. Woman and womb health and blessedness. The beginning of a new family and/or spiritual quest. Sometimes indicates the arrival of a girl.

Intentions: clarity/wisdom, success/mastery, victory, attraction, road opening, blessing, protection, healing, gain/increase, beginning, and cleansing

Twos

Coins: Money issues and stress. A feeling of having to constantly balance between emotional desires and practical concerns. Also the experience of money coming in and then going out due to new expenses.

Swords: The path is blocked, and road opening work is needed; the pregnancy is stressed because the future is uncertain.

Wands: Holding on to the past gets in the way of the present; a past injury or failure is exerting a blockage right now. A decision needs to be made to move forward.

Cups: An excellent partnership is in place providing love and stability to the entire situation.

Intentions: clarity/wisdom, success/mastery, attraction, road opening, blessing, protection, healing, gain/increase, beginning, and stability

Threes

Coins: Adoption, surrogate parenting, and other alternative methods of becoming pregnant/having a baby. In the metaphorical sense this is often a group coming together to create more life . . . like a writer's group!

Swords: Depression, miscarriage, attempting to save a marriage through pregnancy, loss of an idea, loss of a child, someone involved who is spiteful

Wands: A long wait will be rewarded in part through someone else's ingenuity.

Cups: Female friends will come around to support and bless someone so that they may go forth and be fertile.

Intentions: clarity/wisdom, success/mastery, victory, attraction, road opening, blessing, protection, healing, cursing/reversing, and gain/increase

Fours

Coins: Holding back an essential part of oneself from the process of pregnancy and birth, issues of fear around pregnancy and birth, sometimes needing outside financial support

Swords: Accepting things as they are, dealing well with miscarriage or the inability to get pregnant, putting old stories to rest in an attempt to start fresh

Wands: Relationship and community blessed by children/creative work

Cups: Getting hung up on (sometimes tough) decisions; wanting one thing but also not being sure about committing to that vision. Indecision and a lack of commitment.

Intentions: clarity/wisdom, success/mastery, victory, attraction, road opening, blessing, protection, healing, gain/increase, and stability

Fives

Coins: Poverty and lack of financial means to carry a child into world are emphasized now and need to be addressed. The querent needs to get creative and remember the resources they require are actually not that far away.

Swords: Feeling sabotaged, sometimes a surprise pregnancy, a discovery that a friend is pregnant while the querent is not; feelings of competition

Wands: Internal and external conflict, often manifesting as nasty fights and miscommunication with those closes to the querent

Cups: Feelings of loss, regret, depression, and self-blame—potentially postpartum depression and/or depression at inability to conceive or carry child full term

Intentions: clarity/wisdom, success/mastery, blessing, protection, healing, cursing/reversing, loss/removal, stability, banishing, and cleansing

Sixes

Coins: Receiving aid and help, sometimes working with a third party or nonprofit entity. This card can also indicate a religious organization and often refers the querent to adoption or orphanages.

Swords: A difficult situation is starting to slowly improve, and patience is now essential. If the querent has had a difficult time getting pregnant or carrying to full term, then this card indicates it's about to get easier.

Wands: Victory in a situation that has been a long, complicated battle, honors and awards

Cups: A lover, friend, or family member from the querent's past shows up to support and help out in unexpected and appreciated ways. The querent needs to get clear internally about who they are and what they want.

Intentions: clarity/wisdom, success/mastery, victory, attraction, road opening, blessing, protection, healing, gain/increase, and stability

Sevens

Coins: Patience and hard work will bear fruit. Previous investments made will have a return now.

Swords: Hurtful words and/or someone's spite is causing distress, especially during pregnancy itself. Lies and deception are a problematic part of the situation.

Wands: Sense of being trapped, unable to move forward and unable to backpedal either—writer's block or the equivalent.

Cups: Lots of emotional ups and down. It can describe a perfectly normal, albeit quite hormonal, pregnancy or a situation where someone's mental state is getting the better of them and requires medical attention.

Intentions: clarity/wisdom, success/mastery, victory, attraction, blessing, protection, healing, cursing/reversing, gain/increase, loss/removal, stability, and banishing

Eights

Coins: Steady does it and the foundation is being laid down for a beautiful baby!

Swords: Many events are conspiring against the querent; now is not the time to try to conceive or carry a child to term.

Wands: Lots of energy, new information, and a new approach may help the situation.

Cups: The querent feeling that they must relocate and/or let go of their current desire all together

Intentions: clarity/wisdom, success/mastery, victory, attraction, blessing, protection, healing, gain/increase, loss/removal, stability, and banishing

Nines

Coins: The querent is in a good position to mother even if they are by themselves.

Swords: Anxiety, insomnia. The advice is to pay attention to dreams.

Wands: Not thinking clearly, the querent is afraid things are only going to be harder or more difficult even if they are getting better—not seeing self or situation clearly.

Cups: Supportive spouse/partner, self-care, the querent allowing themselves to be taken care of. Sometimes this card can indicate a need for bed rest.

Intentions: clarity/wisdom, success/mastery, victory, attraction, blessing, protection, healing, gain/increase, and stability

Tens

Coins: Creating legacy, solid foundation, family blessings

Swords: Miscarriage, loss of child/opportunity/feeling drained, chronic health issues or high-risk situations that need to be treated as such

Wands: Lots of effort being required to ultimately achieve one's desire, labor may take a long time.

Cups: Happy and blessed family, outlook great for pregnancy/birth

Intentions: clarity/wisdom, success/mastery, victory, attraction, blessing, protection, healing, ending, stability, mental/psychic/dream influence, and cleansing

---

Suggestions for Further Development

- List three examples of a metaphorical or figurative pregnancy.
- What are the three components of fertility magic?

Magic-Making

A Sacred Bath + Lodestone Enchantment for Fertility

You Will Need

For the bath:

A cup of sugar

A handful of dried pine needles

9 pomegranate seeds

Dried pink rose petals

For the lodestone:

A lodestone

Some bathwater from the spiritual bath (collected after you take it)

Ritual anointing oil for attraction/fertility or olive oil (optional)

A petition articulating your desire to get pregnant

A china plate

Magnetic sand or magnetic filings

Process

1. First prepare the sacred bath by combining the sugar, pine needles, pomegranate seeds, and rose petals together and bathing with them.

2. Collect some of the bathwater and pour it into your front yard, holding the prayer as you do so that you become pregnant.

3. Collect a little more of the bathwater and reserve it for the lodestone.

4. Hold the lodestone in your hand and ask it if it is willing to work with you to attract fertility in whatever way you mean.

5. If you receive a yes, then ask the lodestone what its name is.

6. Once you receive the name, wash the lodestone down with the water from the sacred bath, calling it by name and thanking it for its assistance.

7. Anoint the lodestone in a five-spot pattern with the ritual anointing oil if you are working with that. You may also work with regular olive oil to do this.

8. Take your petition and fold the paper once toward you; turn it clockwise 90 degrees and fold it toward you again. Repeat this until the paper is about the size of a Post-it note.

9. Set the paper in the center of the china plate and set the lodestone on top of the paper. Feed the lodestone a little magnetic sand, and then pray over it for the right person to come into your life.

10. Once the pregnancy has been successfully carried to term, bury the plate, petition, and lodestone in your backyard.

Chapter Eight

Fifty Shades of Black:

Baneful Work

WARNING: THIS IS A DELICATE subject that brings the issue of morality front and center. Please keep in mind that some of the material covered in this section comes out of social and religious frameworks other than what you may be used to. Developing and then trusting your own moral compass and discernment when it comes to destructive or baneful magical practices is of the utmost import. If you are unsure about your own personal code of ethics, have not yet developed one, or are in the process of doing so, then my recommendation is that you treat the information in this chapter as just that: information only, and you do not perform any of the magical work described herein.

WHAT IS BANEFUL MAGIC?

Baneful magic is a subset of magic called upon when the practitioner (or the querent on whose behalf the practitioner is working) has suffered an injustice or wants to create a destructive, harmful, negative, and/or combustible situation. In correlation to this, destructive and baneful magics are also the forms of magic employed in psychic attacks, cursing, or hexing spells that a querent may be suffering from and seeking assistance in mediating.

In most magical traditions there is some way of differentiating between proper and correctly aligned magical intention as opposed to intention that springs from a baser impulse, and this is especially crucial when we discuss baneful magic. A tried-and-true example of justly working baneful magic against someone would be binding a rapist so that he cannot harm any other man, woman, or child. An example of working from a less wholesome angle can be found in the querent who wishes to break apart a marriage so that she may have the husband for herself.

If you spend any time researching the history of magic, you will discover that cursing/reversing and hexing make up quite a bit of the primary source material, independent of time, culture, and dominant religious practices. Why is this? I believe the answer is simple and unexciting: there has always been the impulse to have power over others and baneful magic has always been viewed as an easy road to accomplish this.

On the other hand, there has also always been the desire to right wrongs, protect ourselves, and see justice served, and baneful magic can assist with those areas, too. I will sometimes refer to this type of work as "justified." I was taught I should never engage in this type of work unless I could stand before my God and justify my actions. This is an essential component of this kind of work to understand. There are times when baneful magic is an appropriate and aligned response to a given situation; however, before taking on this kind of magic, you should be ready and willing to stand before your understanding of the Creator in perfect alignment with your choice to work such magic. For this reason, in most cases my recommendation to clients is that they have an experienced professional perform baneful magic on their behalf. A seasoned worker will be far more objective than the individual involved directly in the situation, and they will also be more likely to take calm, justified, and effective action.

So why even study it? Most of us will not engage in magical work that is malevolent or baneful, so why bring it up? First, I believe that among magical workers today there is an unwillingness to square up to and face the less lovable parts of our history and body of knowledge. Curse tablets may be as far from "light work" as you can get, but they are a part of the magical corpus. As a Sacred Artist who engages in magical work either for yourself or on behalf of others, you should understand the role baneful magic plays. Second and more importantly, if you do work in a professional capacity for clients or even if you only work for friends, you will find that eventually someone will come to you who feels they have suffered from a curse of some kind. As a magical practitioner you need to understand the root causes of such conditions. There is an old adage in magic that says: "If you cannot hex, you cannot heal." So, if you are not familiar with cursing kinds of magic, then you are also not going to be familiar with how to break curses. I see a basic understanding of baneful magic as required knowledge for practitioners.

Special Magical Considerations for Baneful Work

Any kind of magical technique can be attuned to a baneful intention by incorporating specific ingredients, invoking the aid of particular Holy Helpers, and aligning with the destructive forms of the four elements. However, there are a few magical techniques that have been created expressly for this type of work.

- **Bindings:** This involves binding a person to your will, to another person, or binding them so that they have very little freedom and ability to act under their own free will.
- **Burial and working in the graveyard:** Sacred Artists have long worked with graveyard spirits for a variety of purposes, only one of which is baneful work. Graveyards are threshold spaces where the living meet with the dead. There are two primary ways to work with and in a graveyard. The first is through burial. The graveyard is where you might go to bury something like a sacred vessel or destructive box if you either wanted help from the graveyard spirits in manifesting your desire or wanted to "bury" a person, group, or situation. The second is through working with graveyard dirt. This is dirt that has been collected from a specific grave, in a particular manner, with a singular goal in mind. The particularities of graveyard dirt collection go beyond this book but for our purposes, the graveyard dirt would be worked with as a baneful magical material.
- **Combustible confusion:** Working with a candle, a doll baby, a box, or a beef tongue can intentionally create miscommunication and fights between two or more people. Adding poppy seeds creates confusion, and adding dog and cat hair, hot peppers, sulfur, and/or a bit of gunpowder makes the situation combustible.
- **Destructive box magic:** This entails working with an unlined box or one lined with mirrors, a doll baby representing the person or situation you wish to destroy, and/or a photograph or personal concerns, and then filling the box with all manner of harmful ingredients like red pepper, black pepper, dead insects, sulfur, thorns, pins, needles, barbed wire, broken glass, War Water, urine, feces, poppy seeds, and baneful herbs. Depending on how the box is disposed of, the ritual can be intended to harm or kill a person/situation/event.

- **Divorce and breakups:** A divorce/breakup candle, two candles, a box, two doll babies, and/or two petitions can separate two people and cause them to part ways and/or divorce.
- **Poisoning through sacred waters:** This is not literally poisoning someone but placing harmful items into something that someone is eating and drinking so that they are harmed and/or lose their free will and become ill and easy to manipulate.
- **Psychic warfare:** This can mean invading someone's dreams, causing them nightmares or night terrors, and otherwise causing psychic damage. An ancient and eloquent example of this is the Eummenides' (or the Furies) haunting of Orestes after he killed his mother.
- **Shutting up and stopping up:** Sewing up a beef tongue, working with a doll baby and sewing up its mouth, working with a candle dusted with alum, or even giving an enemy a mojo bag filled with alum and/or a vial of vinegar, lemon, and red pepper (but passing it off as a blessing charm of course) are magical techniques carried out to prevent someone from speaking out. Typically, this type of work is employed when someone is speaking against you, gossiping about you, and in legal cases testifying against you. Stopping Up magical techniques are a bit different but similar in intent. Their goal is to target an individual's digestive and/or reproductive system so that (in the former case) waste from the body cannot be properly eliminated and (in the latter case) sexual satisfaction and/or fertility is impaired in an individual. This is usually done with an eye to taking away a person's vitality and lowering their quality of life. In some extreme circumstances it is performed as killing work.
- **Sour sacred vessels:** One of the most common types of malevolent magical techniques is the sour jar or vinegar jar. These can be designed to achieve a number of things from generally souring someone's life to withering away someone's physical health or causing divorce/separation.

Protection from Baneful Work

Anytime we look at cursing, crossing, jinxing, reversing, and/or revenge magic we also must consider how to protect ourselves from such work. You may read for people who come across as having been cursed, in which case you will want to have some ideas about how to help them. And while it is unlikely you will be on the receiving end of any negative magic, in many cultures strong emotions like envy or jealousy carry their own negativity and can create issues in people's lives. This phenomena is sometimes called the evil eye. As in so many cases, the best offense is a good defense. Regular spiritual cleansing of your home, sacred bathing of yourself, and then setting up spiritual protection are the best way to keep yourself and your loved ones safe from any kind of intentional or unintentional spiritual attack. Methods of protection vary so widely and change across time and place so frequently they deserve (and have) their own books! But there are some standout methods of protection that should be familiar. These include acts like wearing talismans such as Archangel Michael pendants, apotropaic charms against the evil eye such as blue glass evil eye bracelets, wearing/carrying certain minerals like black tourmaline, or even wearing specific colors such as red, black, or white. Another favorite trick comes out of the United Kingdom's faerie tradition: if you feel that you have been targeted by malicious magic, take off your clothes and put them on again inside out. When considering protective magic, I do recommend you take note of the cross-cultural belief that our heads, hands, and feet, are typically the most vulnerable and powerful parts of our bodies and so are in need of extra support and protection.

Special Considerations for Baneful Work in the Tarot

The Major Arcana

The Major Arcana always gives us information about large themes or universal principles at play in our life. We especially want to pay attention to this kind of information when we are thinking about doing intentionally negative or malevolent work against another person, group of people, or situation and it shows up. The Major Arcana cards will often signal proceeding with baneful work is not a wise choice on behalf of the practitioner or querent. In a very few cases, however, the Major Arcana cards may reveal baneful magical work is appropriate and, if so, what magical allies may be called upon so that the work is delivered swiftly and with justice. Note: with all card interpretations offered in this section, it is important to realize the cards are being interpreted with an eye to baneful work the querent might perform on another person(s)/situation and/or baneful work that is creating issues in the querent's life.

The Suits

Coins

Coins deal with the element of Earth. Acts like sacred vessel enchantments, burial and working in graveyards, and creating disharmony in someone's life by attacking their finances and sense of security are what these cards recommend.

Swords

Swords are most directly associated with malevolent or negative work according to tarot tradition. Because they are weapons and as such can be used to harm or to protect, Swords can indicate taking either an offensive or defensive position. Swords are ruled by the element of Air, so using speech, words, ideas, and thoughts to baneful ends is one method of working with these cards and their core element.

Wands

Ruled by the element of Fire, in malevolent work Wands focus on anger, rage, tense situations, inflaming, and the ways we might use those feelings and that kind of energy to our advantage. The focus is on the destructive aspects of the element of Fire and one's ability to "burn it all down."

Cups

Cups deal with our emotional selves as well as our intuitive and psychic senses. They can tell us when someone is attacking, but they can also point out that now is a really good time to attack, especially on a psychic level. On the other hand, a number of Cups cards may indicate cleansing and magical restoration are required.

Major Arcana Cards

The Fool. Success is achieved by attacking an enemy or situation by creating confusion, negative mental influences, and miscommunications. If the querent wants to curse, then these approaches are the way to do it. If the querent feels like they have been worked against, then these methods are most likely how they have been crossed up. When reversed, the Fool indicates the querent is not justified in the work they want to do and there may be a better alternative to get from point A to point B. A reversed Fool may also sometimes announce that a person or group of people did not intentionally mean to cross or harm the querent; they simply made a foolish mistake.

Magical Techniques: magical words/prayers/petitions, physical manipulation, and spirit work

Intentions: clarity/wisdom, blessing, protection, cursing/reversing, gain/increase, beginning, banishing, and mental/psychic/dream influence

The Magician. He is a strong indication that working magic for this situation makes sense and is a good direction to go in. The querent is well-positioned to do some magical damage, so make sure their intention is a direct reflection of their will. This card may also express the querent has all of the resources needed to make the work effective. On the other hand, the Magician was once upon a time called the Juggler and in some decks still is. At the time the tarot was first put to use, jugglers were one variety of street performer, and the whole caste of street performers was looked down on in part because they were often seen as liars, thieves, pickpockets, and con artists. This aspect of the Magician can signal the querent is falling into illusion and not all is as it appears to be, so if there is doubt about the basic understanding of the situation, do encourage them to seek a second opinion. When reversed, this card indicates no magic should be employed at this time and what is needed is cleansing and a reset. Another interpretation of the Magician reversed is someone is doing negative magical work on the querent.

Magical Techniques: sacred vessels, lodestones, candles/oil lamps, magical words/prayers/petitions, physical manipulation, spraying/washing/spitting/asperging, textile magic, and spirit work

Intentions: clarity/wisdom, success/mastery, victory, attraction, road opening, blessing, protection, healing, cursing/reversing, gain/increase, loss/removal, banishing, mental/psychic/dream influence, and cleansing

The High Priestess. Disruption of peace, sense of self, connection to the Divine, academic studies, and/or one's spiritual path are all indicated by this card. The High Priestess can also reveal a blockage around healing (on any level). When reversed, this card tells us that if the querent pursues baneful work, they will harm their relationship with the Divine and so should really think carefully about engaging. Reversed, the High Priestess can also express an unethical woman working against the querent.

Magical Techniques: sacred vessels, magical words/prayers/petitions, spraying/washing/spitting/asperging, and spirit work

Intentions: clarity/wisdom, success/mastery, blessing, protection, healing, cursing/reversing, gain/increase, loss/removal, stability, banishing, and mental/psychic/dream influence

The Empress. Baneful work takes the form of creating a variety of physical issues including weight gain, inflammation, infertility, sexual problems, tension in marriage/relationships, and/or divorce. Fundamentally baneful work aims to undercut someone's sense of self and sovereignty (especially that of women). When reversed, the Empress indicates that if the querent is experiencing these symptoms, they need to reverse the negative magic back to the sender. If, on the other hand, the querent is considering working with this type of energy, then they need to safeguard their own physical health and sense of sovereignty.

Magical Techniques: sacred vessels, lodestones, physical manipulation, and textile magic

Intentions: success/mastery, victory, attraction, blessing, protection, healing, cursing/reversing, gain/increase, loss/removal, and stability

The Emperor. This card is similar in style to the Empress except here the target is a man/husband/father instead of the woman/wife/mom. The Emperor indicates attacking a man's ability to make money, sexually satisfy (and be satisfied), and his overall role in the family are all good ways to "bring him down." Its presence can also point to successful targeting of organizational heads. In some cases, the querent may be able to use someone's prominent leadership position to expose their bad or illegal behavior. However, if this card comes up in a reversed position, it indicates the individual(s) the querent has targeted have strong protection and benevolence on their side and baneful work may fall short from its intended goal.

Magical Techniques: sacred vessels, lodestones, and physical manipulation

Intentions: clarity/wisdom, success/mastery, victory blessing, protection, healing, cursing/reversing, gain/increase, loss/removal, and stability

The Hierophant. This card is about attacking an individual's ties to their community, their reputation (especially in important institutions like their church or spiritual group), or their relationship to important nonprofit institutions. The Hierophant in this context can indicate the fall of guru-type figures. It can also tell us that if the querent wants the work to be successful, they need to seek the expertise of someone who professionally does crossing work (and if they do, they should always be very selective about those they ultimately work with). When reversed, this card indicates after negative or malevolent work the querent needs to do deep cleansing and healing work on themselves.

Magical Techniques: candles/oil lamps, magical words/prayers/petitions, spraying/washing/spitting/asperging, and spirit work

Intentions: clarity/wisdom, success/mastery, road opening, blessing, protection, healing, cursing/reversing, gain/increase, loss/removal, stability, and cleansing

The Lovers. A successful attack aims at someone's love life, romantic relationship, business partnership, or friendships. The major idea is to sow dissension, miscommunication, and anger with the ultimate goal of breaking apart the couple or the group. When the Lovers is reversed, the querent may find they need to reassess their target . . . the relationship is likely too strong to break. If the querent feels like they have been targeted, then the Lovers reversed indicates doing some work to protect their primary relationships.

Magical Techniques: sacred vessels, lodestones, candles/oil lamps, and textile magic

Intentions: success/mastery, victory, attraction, blessing, protection, healing, cursing/reversing, gain/increase, ending, loss/removal, stability, and banishing

The Chariot. When the Chariot shows up, it indicates a good place to hit a target is in their traveling. The querent can intend that the travel be uncomfortable, overly delayed, a source of tension at home, or even dangerous. Another angle to work would be blocking the target's ability to get ahead in work and career. When the Chariot is in a challenging or reversed position, it indicates work against someone else is most likely not going to be effective. If the querent is concerned someone is working against them in the manner illustrated by this card, then the reversal of the Chariot advises them to skip upcoming travel and do some deep protection work.

Magical Techniques: candles/oil lamps, magical words/prayers/petitions, and physical manipulation

Intentions: clarity/wisdom, success/mastery, victory, attraction, road opening, blessing, protection, healing, cursing/reversing, gain/increase, loss/removal, and stability

Strength. This card advises that the best approach to baneful work is to weaken one's opponent by magnifying whatever their greatest challenge or fear is. Another approach to take with the Strength card is to silence one's adversary so that they cannot speak and, even when they do, no one will listen to them. If the card shows up in a challenging or reversed position, it signals the target has strong protection around them and will not be easily manipulated.

Magical Techniques: candles/oil lamps, magical words/prayers/petitions, and textile magic

Intentions: clarity/wisdom, success/mastery, victory, blessing, protection, healing, cursing/reversing, gain/increase, loss/removal, and banishing

The Hermit. The Hermit card indicates that in order to strike out at the target effectively the querent needs to move in the shadows and be sly and sneaky. Isolating the target from friends, family members, and their overall community is a smart move. Disrupting their educational goals and/or professional skill development is an effective way to work against them as well. When reversed, the Hermit suggests the querent needs to think long and hard about doing any negative work as it may have deep and long-lasting repercussions in their own life. If the querent believes they have been on the receiving end of such work, then they should consult a spiritual advisor to get next best steps.

Magical Techniques: candles/oil lamps and spirit work

Intentions: clarity/wisdom, success/mastery, blessing, protection, healing, cursing/reversing, gain/increase, loss/removal, stability, and banishing

Wheel of Fortune. The Wheel of Fortune is a symbol of fate. The Wheel promises us that as things go up they will come down and vice versa. Baneful magic that takes the form of attacking someone's good fortune and multiplying their bad fortune is what the card recommends. In a reversed or challenging position, this card is a warning against doing magic, and this is especially the case when it comes up for baneful work.

Magical Technique: spirit work

Intentions: clarity/wisdom, success/mastery, victory, blessing, protection, healing, cursing/reversing, gain/increase, beginning, ending, loss/removal, banishing, and cleansing

Justice. The Justice card can show up to express the negative work the querent has in mind is justified and can be performed with justification. This card signifies baneful work that seeks to destabilize situations, negatively impact relationships, and even get the law involved with a person or situation is the most effective way to accomplish the querent's goal. However, in a challenging or reversed position the Justice card indicates baneful work is not justified or there is more to the story and the querent is lacking vital information.

Magical Techniques: candles/oil lamps, magical words/prayers/petitions, physical manipulation, and spirit work

Intentions: clarity/wisdom, success/mastery, victory, attraction, blessing, protection, healing, cursing/reversing, gain/increase, loss/removal, stability, banishing, mental/psychic/dream influence, and cleansing

The Hanged Man. The Hanged Man traditionally indicates a needed change in perspective and implies the querent should reconsider their perspective on the situation before deciding to do any baneful work. Working to trap or ensnare a target is a good move when this card arises. In certain cases, the Hanged Man can denote that working to permanently get rid of a person or situation is the correct path. When reversed, the Hanged Man is a promise that while the querent may be successful in their magical work, they will also pay a price for it. If the querent feels like they are the one being attacked and the card shows up, it is a green light to do strong reversal work and send the negativity back to its original source.

Magical Techniques: candles/oil lamps, magical words/prayers/petitions, physical manipulation, spraying/washing/spitting/asperging, and textile magic

Intentions: clarity/wisdom, success/mastery, victory, blessing, protection, healing, cursing/reversing, gain/increase, ending, loss/removal, and banishing

Death. In the context of baneful work the Death card most often signifies physical death and/or graveyard work. It can indicate magical work designed to lead to an actual person's death or it can reveal it's time to kill a toxic situation that no longer serves. Death is the great equalizer, so sometimes this card can come up when a terribly unjust situation needs to be met with extreme force. Another interpretation of this card is the querent should work with a Holy Helper familiar with the death process, such as Hekate, Hades, or Santa Muerte. If the Death card shows up in a challenging position, then the indication is often that the querent needs to allow their desire for revenge/retaliation/baneful work to die.

Magical Techniques: sacred vessels, candles/oil lamps, physical manipulation, textile magic, and spirit work

Intentions: clarity/wisdom, victory, blessing, protection, healing, cursing/reversing, gain/increase, ending, loss/removal, stability, banishing, and cleansing

Temperance. Temperance warns the querent now is the time to be patient and consider all the options. Running off to do baneful work is probably not the best decision. If such work has already been done, Temperance indicates a need for cleansing and healing. Another possible interpretation of this card is the querent or their worker should invoke the aid of Archangel Metatron, the angel envisioned in this card. When reversed, Temperance indicates the opposite: now is the time to act and strike. If the querent feels they have been on the receiving end of baneful work, then the Temperance card points to a need for protection, specifically through sacred bathing.

Magical Techniques: sacred vessels, spraying/washing/spitting/asperging, and spirit work

Intentions: clarity/wisdom, victory, blessing, protection, healing, cursing/reversing, gain/increase, loss/removal, stability, banishing, mental/psychic/dream influence, and cleansing

The Devil. This card often signifies finding oneself (or someone else) trapped in an abusive and/or addictive situation. The Devil can indicate it is time to curse, "bedevil" someone, or to bind up a situation, restricting it and cutting off access to freedom and free will. The Devil can also express the querent would be well-served to work with a Lucifarian consciousness if that is something that makes sense given their traditions and proclivities. If the card shows up in a challenging position, it often signals the querent will create more problems for themselves than their target if they proceed with the baneful work as planned.

Magical Techniques: sacred vessels, candles/oil lamps, magical words/prayers/petitions, physical manipulation, and spirit work

Intentions: clarity/wisdom, victory, blessing, protection, healing, cursing/reversing, gain/increase, loss/removal, stability, banishing, mental/psychic/dream influence, and cleansing

The Tower. The Tower card focuses on destruction and annihilation. This card usually does not refer to the complete destruction of an individual, but it does often indicate a relationship or dynamic needs to be taken down to its foundations. Usually with the Tower some of the magical ingredients used will have a combustible component. (Think: hot pepper, sulfur, and gunpowder.) Like the Devil, if the Tower card shows up in a position of challenge, it often indicates the querent will cause more problems in their own life by proceeding as planned with baneful work.

Magical Techniques: sacred vessels, magical words/prayers/petitions, physical manipulation, and spirit work

Intentions: protection, healing, cursing/reversing, gain/increase, loss/removal, stability, banishing, and cleansing

The Star. Attack an individual or situation by going for their sense of purpose, direction, and balance. Call their major goals and dreams into question or destabilize them completely. Work with astrological factors to make life as difficult as possible. When in a reversed position, the Star indicates cursing and vengeance are not the right path for the querent at this time, and some deep cleansing and spiritual reconciliation should be considered instead. If the querent feels they are under attack, then the Star reversed indicates their feeling is accurate, while the card right side up tells us they should consult their natal chart for information on how to best disrupt the negativity.

Magical Techniques: magical words/prayers/petitions, physical manipulation, spraying/washing/spitting/asperging, and spirit work

Intentions: clarity/wisdom, success/mastery, blessing, protection, healing, cursing/reversing, gain/increase, loss/removal, stability, banishing, mental/psychic/dream influence, and cleansing

The Moon. The Moon indicates a situation or person needs to be blocked, emotionally affected (negatively for these purposes), psychically attacked, or that they are prone to nightmares and hauntings by spirits. The Moon can also reveal that a good way to magically attack a targeted person, group, or situation is to wreak havoc in finances (so that they drain out and they never have enough) and/or to impact appetites, so that they are constantly following their baser instincts and thus getting distracted from their real and essential work. When the Moon shows up in a reversed position, it tells the querent any cursing work is going to encounter strong resistance and difficulties.

Magical Techniques: sacred vessels, magical words/prayers/petitions, spraying/washing/spitting/asperging, and spirit work

Intentions: clarity/wisdom, success/mastery, road opening, blessing, protection, healing, cursing/reversing, gain/increase, loss/removal, stability, banishing, and mental/psychic/dream influence

The Sun. The Sun signals the individual the querent wishes to harm is well-protected and their road is open for success. In order to do them harm, the querent will need to shine a bright light on their biggest mistakes and lies so that their true nature is revealed. Think of radiation or a nuclear blast and you have a sense of how the Sun may work in a baneful setting. When reversed, the Sun recommends a slow and steady attack on a person or situation's vitality, energy, health, and (in some cases) fertility. Reversed, this card can also indicate that if the querent continues on with baneful work, they will find they cannot let go of the past and move into the future.

Magical Techniques: candles/oil lamps, magical words/prayers/petitions, and physical manipulation

Intentions: clarity/wisdom, success/mastery, victory, attraction, road opening, blessing, protection, healing, cursing/reversing, gain/increase, loss/removal, stability, and banishing

Judgement. The Judgement card tells us working with a Holy Helper known to bring down judgment is appropriate in this situation or it's time to do some binding with sacred vessels. This card can also come up after baneful work has been performed and gives two radically different interpretations when it does. The first is that the querent was not justified in performing the work and so radical, deep amends need to be made immediately. The second is that the querent's magical approach took care of most but not all of the problems and some of the concerns are continuing to "sprout up." This card can indicate working with Archangel Gabriel is a sound idea. When reversed, the Judgement card signals the querent has demonstrated poor judgment and needs to make amends.

Magical Techniques: sacred vessels, candles/oil lamps, magical words/prayers/petitions, physical manipulation, spraying/washing/spitting/asperging, and spirit work

Intentions: clarity/wisdom, success/mastery, victory, blessing, protection, healing, cursing/reversing, gain/increase, beginning, ending, loss/removal, stability, banishing, and cleansing

The World. When this card comes up, it indicates the best thing to do is strike at someone's visibility as well as the things that make them feel most secure. The rest will come tumbling down. The World can sometimes also signal the takedown of a famous person or someone who is in the spotlight.

If the World shows up in a reversed position, the advice is for the querent to pause in their actions, lest they lose their core sense of self.

Magical Techniques: sacred vessels, lodestones, candles/oil lamps, magical words/prayers/petitions, physical manipulation, and spirit work

Intentions: clarity/wisdom, success/mastery, victory, attraction, blessing, protection, healing, cursing/reversing, gain/increase, ending, loss/removal, stability, banishing, and cleansing

Court Cards

King of Coins/Queen of Coins. In their baneful aspect, the King and Queen of Coins are the Lord and Lady of Death and deeply associated with the element of Earth as it relates to burial rites. The death can be sweet and natural or cruel and forced, but regardless, death is their domain. The King of Coins also sometimes indicates hidden actions, double-dealing, and even making money through illegal or illicit means . . . as well as the ability to draw the eyes of the law to those who do so. Both of these cards can suggest it's time to let something die off and to bury it once and for all. Another way to interpret these cards deals with finances and striking at the heart of someone's finances. When reversed, the King and Queen of Coins indicate the querent may be "buried" by their own malicious actions. If the querent feels they are on the receiving end of malicious magic, then these two cards advise working with a Holy Helper from the graveyard for protection and possibly revenge.

Magical Techniques: sacred vessels, lodestones, physical manipulation, and textile magic

Intentions: success/mastery, attraction, blessing, protection, healing, cursing/reversing, gain/increase, loss/removal, and stability

Knight of Coins. Targeting a person or situation's finances, especially their ability to attract money, abundance, and opportunity, is the smartest way to achieve one's ends. When reversed, the indication is the querent may be the one to lose resources in their endeavor to curse. If the querent is concerned they are crossed up, then this card would advise them to look to any weird patterns in their finances for confirmation.

Magical Techniques: sacred vessels, lodestones, and physical manipulation

Intentions: clarity/wisdom, success/mastery, attraction, blessing, protection, cursing/reversing, gain/increase, loss/removal, and stability

Page of Coins. Here we have a figure who is yearning for security, financial certitude, and a strong sense of future possibility. The querent may work with the energy of this card by creating confusion, financial instability, and insecurity. When reversed, this card indicates something is amiss with the querent's ideas and understanding of the situation and needs to be reevaluated.

Magical Techniques: sacred vessels and lodestones

Intentions: clarity/wisdom, success/mastery, attraction, blessing, protection, healing, cursing/reversing, gain/increase, loss/removal, and stability

King and Queen of Swords. Striking at someone or something's mental health, intellectual ability, communication, and/or professional career is the move indicated by these two figures. The most lethal of the Kings and Queens, the King and Queen of Swords can also express that the querent might do well to get the law involved and work for a satisfactory legal conclusion to the situation. When reversed, the King and Queen of Swords warn the querent to be careful and not do more damage to themselves than they are trying to do to their target.

Magical Techniques: magical words/prayers/petitions, physical manipulation, and spirit work

Intentions: clarity/wisdom, success/mastery, blessing, protection, healing, cursing/reversing, gain/increase, loss/removal, banishing, and mental/psychic/dream influence

Knight of Swords. He often indicates a great injustice has been committed and correcting it requires swift and decisive action. With his weapon brandished, he implies working to cut off, separate, and in some cases, debilitate someone or something acting unfairly. The Knight of Swords can suggest a military or martial graveyard spirit willing to assist you with this type of work. This card may also be interpreted as working against an enemy by encouraging them to rush and be impatient and immoderate in their actions. When reversed, the Knight of Swords advises the querent to stop what they are doing, take a breath, and reconsider.

Magical Techniques: magical words/prayers/petitions and physical manipulation

Intentions: clarity/wisdom, success/mastery, victory, road opening, blessing, protection, cursing/reversing, gain/increase, loss/removal, banishing, and mental/psychic/dream influence

Page of Swords. Striking at an enemy's ability to think rationally, speak and communicate effectively, and process information is the approach recommended by this card. If the enemy has a habit of lying or slandering, then this card indicates now is the time to reveal those tendencies. When reversed, the Page of Swords tells us the querent is less clear about what they want than they think they are.

Magical Technique: magical words/prayers/petitions

Intentions: clarity/wisdom, protection, cursing/reversing, gain/increase, loss/removal, banishing, and mental/psychic/dream influence

King and Queen of Wands. When either of these cards show up, they advise baneful work through attacking someone or something's creativity, energy, verve, and life force. Creating situations where conflict, anger, and rage are unavoidable is a specialty of these two, as is wielding magic in such a way it dries out and disempowers someone or a situation. Creating dissension, disharmony, and distrust among allies is another specialty. When reversed, either of these cards tell the querent that though their magic may succeed, they will pay a price, usually through the explosion of a meaningful relationship. In some cases, either of these cards can also speak to contagious physical diseases.

Magical Techniques: candles/oil lamps, magical words/prayers/petitions, and spirit work

Intentions: clarity/wisdom, success/mastery, victory, blessing, protection, healing, cursing/reversing, gain/increase, loss/removal, and banishing

Knight of Wands: Here the advice is to close off someone's road and create as many obstacles as possible. The work is less about inflicting harm and more about causing infinite delays, frustration, and finally hopeless exhaustion. Think of the hell loop that is the DMV and you have a good taste of this card! When reversed, the Knight of Wands warns the querent their target has strong protection and any baneful magic will have to be particularly potent.

Magical Techniques: candles/oil lamps and magical words/prayers/petitions

Intentions: clarity/wisdom, success/mastery, victory, attraction, road opening, blessing, protection, healing, cursing/reversing, gain/increase, loss/removal, and banishing

Page of Wands. The Page of Wands is running on empty and looking for fuel in all the wrong places. Take a page from his book and encourage the querent to create a situation like this for their enemies. Deprivation, lack of resource/support, and abandonment are all implied by this card, and an especially potent way to hit at a target is to destroy their social group or standing. When reversed, this card may tell us that the magic being performed is not effective and needs to be reevaluated. It may also indicate that the querant is running out of ideas or has misread the situation in a significant manner.

Magical Technique: candles/oil lamps

Intentions: clarity/wisdom, success/mastery, blessing, protection, healing, cursing/reversing, gain/increase, loss/removal, and banishing

King and Queen of Cups. The King and Queen of Cups are attuned to the element of Water, which symbolizes psychic powers, dream work, sacred bathing practices, and in some cases, spirit work. For this reason, the King and Queen of Cups signify the power to create baneful outcomes by working against someone or a situation through dreams or psychic intentions. They can also indicate hitting at someone's emotional center is a surefire way to cause harm. Finally, work may be successful when it aims to harm or destroy someone's sexual health and ability to procreate. When they show up in a reversed position, the King and Queen of Cups remind the querent baneful work performed without justification is spiritually ruinous and confirming the querent is right in their actions is of paramount importance. If the querent feels they are on the receiving end of baneful work, then either of these cards recommend sacred bathing as the first and most effective method to cleanse, purify, and protect.

Magical Techniques: sacred vessels, spraying/washing/spitting/asperging, and spirit work

Intentions: clarity/wisdom, success/mastery, blessing, protection, healing, cursing/reversing, gain/increase, loss/removal, banishing, mental/psychic/dream influence, and cleansing

Knight of Cups. When he shows up, he continues to speak the message from the King and Queen of Cups: psychically effecting a target in a negative manner is a good approach. The Knight of Cups is a healing figure, so disrupting a target's ability to heal at the physical, emotional, or spiritual levels is recommended. As a Knight, the Knight of Cups also reminds us that closing off someone's road so that they cannot move forward is a good idea. Reversed, this card indicates the querent who has already done baneful work is in need of serious cleansing, in which case magical bathing is recommended.

Magical Techniques: sacred vessels, spraying/washing/spitting/asperging, and spirit work

Intentions: clarity/wisdom, success/mastery, victory, road opening, blessing, protection, healing, cursing/reversing, gain/increase, loss/removal, stability, and mental/psychic/dream influence

Page of Cups. The querent will find success by confusing their target's intuition and ability to listen as well as by sowing seeds of gossip and slander. The cultivation of rumor—one of the most potent weapons of all—is highlighted by this card. When reversed, the Page of Cups indicates some of the information that the querent has about the situation is not correct and needs to be reviewed.

Magical Techniques: sacred vessels and spraying/washing/spitting/asperging

Intentions: clarity/wisdom, success/mastery, blessing, protection, healing, cursing/reversing, gain/increase, loss/removal, stability, banishing, and mental/psychic/dream influence

Pips

Aces

Coins: Create a solid foundation for all baneful work by dedicating an altar space to it specifically. Alternatively, attack an enemy's money, or work to take away their good fortune.

Swords: Decisive victory can belong to the querent. Attack by twisting a person's words, making them reveal themselves as a liar, and making their thoughts unclear.

Wands: Work by siphoning off someone's energy, creating inflamed situations around them, and encouraging confusion when it comes to creative work and self-expression.

Cups: Attacking someone's personal life and love relationships is the way to go. Breakup work is recommended.

Intentions: clarity/wisdom, success/mastery, blessing, protection, healing, cursing/reversing, gain/increase, beginning, loss/removal, stability, banishing, and mental/psychic/dream influence

Twos

Coins: The querent needs to weigh practical concerns with emotional desires. If a decision to attack is made, the querent should go for the target's money and financial security.

Swords: Attack by creating anxiety around the future, the target's sense of purpose or mission, and also by isolating targets from each other.

Wands: A person's or group's attachment to a past event is keeping them from fully moving forward. Use that to attack and create problems.

Cups: Work to harm a person or situation by sowing seeds of discord and ending partnerships.

Intentions: clarity/wisdom, success/mastery, attraction, road opening, blessing, protection, healing, cursing/reversing, gain/increase, loss/removal, stability, banishing, and mental/psychic/dream influence

Threes

Coins: Ideal for when a group or organization is the intended target. Create mistrust, miscommunication, confusion, and anger among all members.

Swords: Excellent card for baneful work indicating that working with the themes of heartbreak, separation, and/or divorce is the correct approach.

Wands: Work against the enemy by keeping them stuck in a specific situation, not allowing them to move forward, and closing the road.

Cups: Advises the querent to put a group together to make any baneful work that much more effective. This is an especially potent approach for certain kinds of legal and political magic.

Intentions: clarity/wisdom, attraction, blessing, protection, healing, cursing/reversing, gain/increase, loss/removal, and banishing

Fours

Coins: The place to strike is at the enemy's finances.

Swords: Sacred vessels and burial for things/situations/people that are still causing problems

Wands: A marriage and happy union is on its way. That of course means it's time to do some serious breakup work. Dividing people from one another and causing drama in the community.

Cups: Work to confuse the enemy and encourage indecisiveness, foggy thinking, and uncertainty

Intentions: clarity/wisdom, success/mastery, victory, blessing, protection, healing, cursing/reversing, gain/increase, loss/removal, stability, and banishing

Fives

Coins: Impoverishment. Again, strike at the money or at a person's ability to get promoted.

Swords: Sabotage. Work quickly and attack from the side instead of head-on.

Wands: Anger and conflict across the board. Indicates breakup work can be effective.

Cups: Regret and melancholy. Work to magnify these feelings and cause distress.

Intentions: clarity/wisdom, success/mastery, blessing, protection, healing, cursing/reversing, gain/increase, loss/removal, banishing, and mental/psychic/dream influence

Sixes

Coins: This card speaks to fair or unfair dealings and advises the best attack is to set up a situation where there is discord and possible financial cheating.

Swords: The path is blocked, or creating a blocked path is an excellent idea at this point in time.

Wands: This is a card of victory. Depending on how the situation is being read, it may indicate the querent will have victory or that the person they have targeted is well-protected.

Cups: A past love or companion is coming into the situation. The querent may want to consider doing breakup work.

Intentions: clarity/wisdom, success/mastery, victory, attraction, road opening, blessing, protection, healing, cursing/reversing, gain/increase, loss/removal, stability, banishing, and mental/psychic/dream influence

Sevens

Coins: Waiting for a financial reward. The best approach is to make sure that reward never happens.

Swords: Lies and deceit. This is a good card to tie someone's tongue, shut them up, or catch them in a lie.

Wands: Trap the target in a box or bottle spell.

Cups: Mental disturbance and disequilibrium. This is a good card to negatively influence an enemy's mental state.

Intentions: clarity/wisdom, success/mastery, protection, healing, cursing/reversing, gain/increase, loss/removal, stability, banishing, and mental/psychic/dream influence

Eights

Coins: Slow and steady does it, and attacking the target's finances and/or career path is a good idea.

Swords: Surrounding the target with unsupportive people who gossip and create mischief

Wands: There is a good deal of energy in the situation right now. Use it to turn up the heat and make things uncomfortable for the target.

Cups: Banishing is recommended.

Intentions: clarity/wisdom, success/mastery, blessing, protection, healing, cursing/reversing, gain/increase, beginning, ending, loss/removal, stability, and banishing

Nines

Coins: This indicates the best way to attack the target is by imposing isolation and undermining their financial well-being.

Swords: Dream work, psychic attacks, and nightmares are the preferred method of attack.

Wands: The target is suspicious, and their judgment lacks clarity. The querent may use that against them.

Cups: The target is attacked through means of mental disturbance—especially depression as well as excessive weight gain and the issues that come with it. Cursing with food and drink is also implied by this card.

Intentions: clarity/wisdom, success/mastery, blessing, protection, healing, cursing/reversing, gain/increase, loss/removal, and banishing

Tens

Coins: Solid foundations are underneath the target. The best thing to do is try to attack them financially, but it may be very difficult to do so.

Swords: Ultimate betrayal. One of the best cards for crossing work.

Wands: Major effort required on the part of the querent's target. The querent can make things tougher now.

Cups: This card often indicates a happily ever after and that means the way to attack is through working against the target's familial relationships.

Intentions: clarity/wisdom, success/mastery, blessing, protection, healing, cursing/reversing, gain/increase, ending, loss/removal, stability, banishing, mental/psychic/dream influence, and cleansing

In closing, this is the darkest and most negative section of this book. It may have brought up some uncomfortable feelings for you. If it did, you have my permission to turn the page and never look at it again. I feel this material needs to be presented because it's a time-honored way of working with the cards and part of the tradition of combining magical work with cartomancy. But remember: just because it's traditional doesn't mean that you need to follow it! If you are feeling especially negative after reading this section, I recommend taking a cleansing bath and sending out lots of blessings to your loved ones. You may also smudge your home with some sage or frankincense and myrrh and recite the following chant:

> I banish thee, I banish thee, I send thee out and set thee free! To dwell in wind, water, and stone and never through my house do roam!

Further Development Tasks

Answer the following questions for reflection and to assist you in crafting your own personal code of ethics:

- In what situations would I find baneful magical work to be a valid approach for myself?
- To "justify" my work means . . .
- Pick out one of the Major Arcana cards that particularly confused you in this section. Spend some time looking at its picture and then sit in stillness and silence allowing it to be internalized. How has your understanding of the card and its message changed? What new messages have you received about it?

Magic-Making

Working a Witch's Ladder

The Witch's Ladder is an old piece of Western European folk magic where the target's personal concerns are woven or tied into a long piece of yarn or thread, anointed with cursing oil, and then worked through prayer and cursing. The way to lift the curse? Find and burn the ladder and scatter the ashes in the four directions.

You Will Need

Personal concerns from your targeted individual or group

Yarn or string

Ritual anointing oil for cursing (optional)

Process

1. Weave or tie each personal concern you have into the length of yarn.

2. Hold in your mind your intention to curse or get revenge on the individual(s) you have in mind.

3. Starting at the top of the ladder and working your way to the bottom, anoint it—yarn and personal concerns—with the anointing oil.

4. Work with the ladder on Saturdays by praying over it your ill intentions.

5. Hide the ladder where it cannot be found.

6. Once your enemy has been sufficiently cursed, you may bury the ladder at their threshold.

Cleansing with a Hyssop Bath

This is a bathing recipe found in the Conjure tradition that specifically aims to rid the individual of any negative energy they may have brought on themselves after doing cursing work on someone else. It makes use of one of the greatest magical books of all time—the Bible—and employs the recitation of Psalm 51.

You Will Need

Kosher salt

Olive oil

A handful of dried hyssop

Psalm 51

Blessing or protection oil (optional)

Process

1. Prepare your sacred bath by combining the salt, oil, and hyssop.

2. Bathe as you normally would, beginning with your head and moving down toward your feet. Be sure to reserve some of the bathwater for ritual disposal.

3. As you do so, read Psalm 51 out loud over yourself.

4. Allow yourself to air-dry—do not use a towel.

5. Anoint yourself with a blessing/protection oil once you have finished bathing, beginning at the feet and working your way up to your head.

6. Put on clean clothes.

7. Take the reserved bathwater to a three- or four-way crossroads and dispose of it so that any negativity can go out and be transformed.

8. Leave the crossroads by going a different way than you came in, so that you do not have to backtrack over the bathwater.

9. Repeat this process for thirteen days during a waning lunar phase for extreme situations.

◆ *Chapter Nine* ◆

Full of Ourselves:
Safeguarding Vital Energy and Opening to Divine Empowerment and Blessings

You will notice I do a couple of things differently in this chapter. First, throughout the chapter I will talk about the cards more particularly as if you are reading for yourself. I am doing this because some of my students and clients are more interested in learning how to accurately read for themselves than for friends, family members, or paying clients, and when it comes to opening to empowerment, beneficial energy, and amping up your personal mojo whether you take on clients or not, we all benefit from this information.

Empowerment vs. Opening to Empowerment

Whenever I write about empowerment, I use the phrase opening to empowerment. This is not my attempt to be cute or floral in my writing: it is grounded in my understanding that empowerment is a much-misunderstood term that requires some clarification. When we speak about empowerment, we often say things like: that speech was really empowering or I felt so empowered after running the marathon. In these instances, our language points to a thought pattern assuming beneficial power can come from other people, events, places, situations, and of course ourselves. However, in my experience as a Sacred Artist, spiritual advisor, ceremonialist, prayer-maker, and teacher, I have found this is not an accurate portrayal of how power functions. Vital and beneficial power is a gift, much like Grace, that comes straight from the Divine. Another way to say this is the Divine is the sole source of empowerment. When empowerment seems like it is coming to you through another person, place, event, etc., what is really happening is that person/place/event is mediating Divine blessings to you. Therefore, we do not empower ourselves and we do not empower one another, but we can consciously open ourselves to empowerment, blessing, benefit, grace, and all the rest of the divinely inspired and mediated gifts.

The Vital Energetic Body—What Is It?

Throughout this chapter I will use the term vital energetic body, and you may wonder what exactly it is I mean by this. In chapter 5 we looked at healing and how healing occurs on multiple levels at the same time. One component related to and always involved in healing is something we often hear referred to as energy management. However, just as we do not empower ourselves or one another, we do not "manage" our energy. The entire terminology implies we are somehow supervising and bossing around . . . ourselves! Instead, we safeguard our vital energetic body. The vital energetic body is one term used to describe the whole of our field of existence—the physical body and subsequent layers of intellectual, emotional, and magical bodies that contain the physical body much like concentric spheres. I go into much further development of these ideas in Wolves and Stars, one of the courses in my Sacred Arts Academy, including ways of working with these bodies. For right now you simply need to know we are more than our manifest physical body.

The Oxygen Mask Metaphor

This is not a new idea, but I do think that it can be repeated as often as possible as a public service announcement: Think back to the last time you were taking a plane ride and the flight attendant told you that in case of a decrease in cabin pressure an oxygen mask would come down from the ceiling. They specified that if you are traveling with children, put your mask on first and then your child's. This is the best analogy I know of for the critical work of maintaining your own sense of vitality and ability to be open to empowerment, especially if part of your vocation is to be of service—as it is for most folks interested in divination and the Sacred Arts. When you get right down to it, much of our work is dedicated to helping others see their own inherent possibility and potential. To do this effectively and honestly, we must be good stewards of our own energy and maintain a keen sense of what does and does not assist us in opening to empowerment and blessing and safeguarding our vitality. Please do not take this to mean you must be "perfect" or always put together, on time, and completely organized; part of opening to empowerment and safeguarding vitality is recognizing we are human and will err as all humans do. This precept of self-care does mean that we each need to have a sense of when our vitality is full or flagging. It also means that as a service provider it is your responsibility to make sure you are energetically in a place where you can provide for and guide the client without depleting your own resources.

Asking the Right Question

Another facet of this chapter that is new is a focus on questions in place of the intentions section. Now I am a fan of questions across the board, and as my Sacred Arts Sessions clients will attest, I ask a lot of questions during a session! Because words like empowerment and energy can be so vague or, as we saw above, incorrectly understood, I think it's essential to ask questions when we are talking about these issues.

Questions help us crack open difficult spaces and allow room and freedom for thought, feeling, sensation, and honest reaction instead of sticking us immediately into a place of judgment and criticism. In my opinion it is a sound idea to ask questions for each one of the tarot cards, but I also think questions can be especially useful in the realm of energy management and opening to empowerment. Likewise, the title of this chapter provides us with a single intention that holds true for all the cards: our intention is to safeguard our vital energy and in so doing open ourselves to divine empowerment and blessings.

Magic for Opening to Empowerment

The magic that we discuss in this chapter is the same as the other chapters. But I would like to say a few words about intention and energy management. I see energy management as the flip side to our ability to truly open to empowerment. Quite simply, if we do not take note of and care for our vital energy, then we are not in a place where we may open ourselves to divine empowerment, and we are certainly not in a place where we might mediate such concentrated forces for other individuals. Everyone and everything has a unique energetic signature. Everyone and everything also has a finite amount of energy for any given activity, day, week, month, or year. Energy is a renewable resource, but it is not an infinite one. Everything that we do, mundane or magical, requires energy. This means we must learn to manage our energy well.

The actual details of right relationship to our vital energies will look different for different people. We are all born with specific strengths and weaknesses both physically and energetically, but it is critical that you discover how they look and feel for you because excellent vital energy management is the key to our ability to open up to and mediate empowerment. Working in the field of divination already requires a big energy investment, but working in the realm of magic calls for even more. This is why I recommend you learn how to replenish your vital energy regularly, early on. You can do this through cultivating calmness and rooting and rising as well as through art, journaling, song, storytelling, physical activities like running/dance/weightlifting/cardio, gardening, or cooking, but you need to find your sources of replenishment and work with them accordingly. Likewise, as you go deeper into your work as a Sacred Artist, you will want to take awareness of your physical health to the next level. Drinking plenty of water, maintaining a proper diet—whatever that means specifically for you—and weaving in various health-supporting elements such as flower essences, necessary prescription drugs, massage, acupuncture, herbal medicine, supplements and vitamins are all essential ingredients to maintaining and supporting your vital energy.

Special Considerations in Tarot for Safeguarding Vital Energy and Opening to Empowerment

The Major Arcana

The key to working with both tarot and magic to increase your ability to open to empowerment is found in the recognition that each card—even the so called negative ones—can actually provide a meaningful message about what themes might be addressed right now as well as what must be considered going forward. Nowhere is this clearer than within the Major Arcana.

The Suits

Coins

Coins deal here as they have in other areas with wealth in all forms, security, solid foundations, and manifesting one's work in the earthly, physical realms. These cards and Wands most often speak to the health of the physical body along with other considerations. Some Coins are tied to longevity, and though it might be nice for all of us to have a long and prosperous life, the longevity that is under discussion here is the legacy we impart to others. Our legacies flow sure and strong when we have successfully allowed ourselves to open to empowerment and to, when appropriate, mediate such empowerment for others. At the same time our ability to open at all and certainly to mediate for others is, as we have already noted, directly tied to our ability to care for our own health and energy. None of these processes can occur if we neglect so-called practical concerns . . . from where we live to how we earn money to what our relationship to our greater community is, the wise Sacred Artist does not ignore the pesky details. Thus, a helpful question when working with the suite of Coin is:

> What practical concerns and necessities do I need to be mindful of?

Swords

By this point you have probably gotten the idea that Swords can be the most ambiguous suit. These cards can indicate high-earning, white-collar professions and players, or they can reveal deception, sabotage, and a blocked or closed road ahead. When it comes to personal empowerment, Swords are associated with clear vision, articulation, and keen understanding. A good general question to meditate on as we develop our relationship to the suit of Swords is:

> What strategies might I put into play now that can assist me in opening to empowerment and protecting my vital energy?

Wands

As in other cases, when Wands show up in the realm of our vitality and ability to open to empowerment, they first and foremost shout out: ENERGY! Whether it's a need to ramp up the energy, to move energy more effectively, or to harness feelings like creative angst, lust, and even anger into working their magic for you, Wands indicate the situation is going to require energy and the courage to embrace rapid alchemical change! Some good questions to ponder as we work with the suit of Wands are:

> Where is my vital energy right now?

> When it is healthy, how I do I experience that energy on physical, intellectual, emotional, and magical levels?

> When it is unhealthy, how do I experience that energy on physical, intellectual, emotional, and magical levels?

Cups

When it comes to our ability to open to empowerment, the suit of Cups turns our attention to our emotions but more essentially to our abilities of donation and reception: giving and receiving. If we are not in proper alignment with being able to both give and receive, then how can we expect to have the capacity to open to empowerment or protect our vital energy? When we are working with the forces of Cups, two useful questions are:

What might I give in this moment and to whom/what?

What might I open myself to receiving and from whom/what?

Major Arcana Cards

The Fool. Initiations, new beginnings, coming full circle, learning about animal allies, taking the leap of faith—the Fool shows us what opening to empowerment really looks like. But he also reminds us to be prudent as we lead with our hearts. In a challenging position he signals we are not paying attention to the messages our physical and vital bodies are sending to us and our energy suffers as a result. Greater awareness is called for. Reversed, the Fool shows us that we are beyond not paying attention and in active denial when it comes to signs and signals that we are receiving. This reversed card can also warn that we have placed our faith in the wrong thing.

What do I need to be aware of in order to fully open to empowerment?

Magical Techniques: candles/oil lamps, magical words/prayers/petitions, physical manipulation, and textile magic

The Magician. It's time to learn about magic and start working with the Sacred Arts to facilitate your ability to open to empowerment and safeguard your vitality. Our modern definitions of magic tend to focus on willing various outcomes to manifest, but if we recollect the idea that "magic is a way of asking the universe for help," we can realize that, actually, much of what we aim to accomplish is an ability to open to that which is Greater. Recognize that all of the materials you need to successfully accomplish your work are right in front of you! Reversed, the Magician indicates trickery or being conned.

How does the intermingling of heaven and earth assist me in safeguarding my vitality?

Magical Techniques: sacred vessels, lodestones, candles/oil lamps, magical words/prayers/petitions, physical manipulation, spraying/washing/spitting/asperging, textile magic, and spirit work

The High Priestess. An especially meaningful card when pulled by a woman or man deeply connected to their feminine nature, the High Priestess often indicates such a person is in a position in life to behold great mystery and meaning. Often this is a period that comes after some severe difficulties and is part of the individual's work of putting their life back together from various pieces often shattered by trauma. Reversed, the High Priestess points to a resistance or refusal to heal.

What requires healing in order for true transformation to occur?

Magical Techniques: spraying/washing/spitting/asperging, textile magic, and spirit work

The Empress. This card also usually indicates a woman or man uniquely related to their feminine nature, typically one whose work is to "mother" in some manner and in some cases also to be mothered. When pulled for creative types, the Empress expresses the work needs to manifest and must begin supporting the entire life. Reversed, the Empress indicates problematic excess and indulgence.

What seeds have I sown in the last six months, in the last year?

What have they yielded?

Magical Techniques: sacred vessels, lodestones, and textile magic

The Emperor. Often this indicates a man but can also indicate a woman who is in a position of authority and power. The challenge is to balance the desire to be active with the desire to sit back and enjoy the fruits of the work already accomplished. The Emperor is one of the few Major Arcana figures who is in a position of actively bestowing blessings on the reader/querent. This is best demonstrated in the position of his hands. As a result, he is a forceful reminder that we do not need to do anything in order to open to the benevolent forces of empowerment, rather we need to embrace a sense of cultivated calmness and stop reaching. Reversed, the Emperor suggests greed and lethargy are playing a problematic role in our lives.

What do I keep seeking out that is already contain within?

Magical Techniques: sacred vessels, lodestones, and physical manipulation

The Hierophant. When the Hierophant emerges in response to our intention of safeguarding vital energy and opening to empowerment, his presence can signify multiple possibilities. One is we have been giving of ourselves (often in a magical or Sacred Arts context) and need to cultivate calmness to allow our vital energy time to rebuild, receiving nourishment and rest. In other cases, this card may indicate the need for a magical mentor or that the time has come for you to put on the mantle of teacher/guide and begin mediating knowledge and understanding of the unseen worlds for others. Reversed, this card signals a refusal to heed the call for greater spiritual work and service.

What needs to be blessed in my life?

How might I be a blessing to others in turn?

Magical Techniques: magical words/prayers/petitions and spirit work

The Lovers. The Lovers card takes on a very different nuance in this section. Instead of signifying, as it normally does, the presence of romance, sex, and emotional connection with other human beings, the Lovers card here indicates an ability to cocreate/walk with your Holy Helpers as a means of opening to empowerment and safeguarding vitality. Individuals who receive this card when focusing on the intentions we have set forth are often gifted in otherworld journeys and might seek to develop their abilities in that direction. Reversed, the Lovers tells us we are closing ourselves off to relationships with Holy Helpers.

What and who are my Holy Helpers in safeguarding my vital energy and opening to empowerment?

Magical Techniques: lodestones, candles/oil lamps, magical words/prayers/petitions, and spirit work

The Chariot. When we receive the Chariot card, it often indicates we are being "cooked" in a crucible of intensity, with various and seemingly diametrically opposed forces working against us, but in reality they are working on us. Our complementary job is to take the dynamism presented here and allow it to give us lift, instead of keeping us tied to the ground. In some cases, the Chariot might also indicate a need to relocate physically in order to safeguard vitality. Reversed, the Chariot tells us the different energetic levels are not in communion with one another and this is creating issues.

What current tensions in my life might be understood as blessings, and how can I work more effectively with them?

Magical Techniques: candles/oil lamps, magical words/prayers/petitions, and textile magic

Strength. The Strength card is often (and accurately) interpreted as an individual, male or female, winning the day not through sheer physical force but rather by strength of mind and will. The "win" is against the parts of ourselves easily moved off-track: the part for instance that wants to get up at 5:30 a.m. every morning to do a twenty-minute prayer cycle but somehow manages to sleep up until a quarter to seven! However, here the Strength card indicates a recognition and striving for right relationship, within our own bodies and between ourselves and all creatures, are essential if we truly wish to open up to empowerment. Reversed, Strength means a lack of self-control is now creating problems.

What does internal right relationship look and feel like for me?

What does right relationship with other beings look and feel like for me?

Magical Techniques: sacred vessels, candles/oil lamps, physical manipulation, and textile magic

The Hermit. The Hermit reminds us there is no power without purification and purification is something attained through practice, dedication, and a discerning eye toward what actions (on all levels) no longer serve. Reversed, this card indicates a desire to intentionally isolate ourselves.

What actions and behaviors require restriction in my life and what actions and behaviors should be embraced more fully?

Magical Technique: candles/oil lamps

Wheel of Fortune. Here the Wheel of Fortune highlights our relationship to the whole of the cosmos—which has classically been conceived of as wheels within wheels. This card also brings up the tension that every Sacred Artist must make their peace with: that of free will and the forces of destiny. Reversed, the Wheel of Fortune indicates we are not as attuned to seasons and cycles as we need to be.

What is the role that free will plays in my life?

What role does destiny play?

Magical Technique: spirit work

Justice. The Justice card is a reemphasis of the theme we find in the Strength and Lover cards: that of right relationship. In the Justice card we come to the idea of balance, and if you are starting to clue in to the fact that when the tarot gives us polar forces to work with, then the work often involves understanding the tensions and then encountering ways to establish equilibrium, you are paying attention! Reversed, the indication is we are out of balance and right relationship and a course correction is called for.

What is the role of effort and reciprocity in my life right now, and how does it relate to my ability to open to empowerment?

Magical Techniques: magical words/prayers/petitions and physical manipulation

The Hanged Man. Some define a miracle as a shift in perspective, and that idea is especially prevalent with the Hanged Man card. Here we find the Hanged Man telling us in no uncertain terms that our energetic needs are changing and we need to take note: what has worked before may no longer be appropriate and what we have had no need of may soon become indispensable. Likewise, to truly open up to empowerment there are things we need to absolutely let go of. Reversed, the Hanged Man indicates a refusal to sacrifice part of oneself for the greater good.

What energetic changes have I experienced in the last year? (In this question is it helpful to be specific and examine all four areas of energetic exchange: physical, intellectual, emotional, and spiritual.)

Magical Techniques: candles/oil lamps, magical words/prayers/petitions, physical manipulation, textile magic, and spirit work

Death. When the Death card emerges under the intention of safeguarding energetic vitality and opening to empowerment, it provides us with two possible interpretations. The first is we are literally running ourselves to death—although usually on a metaphorical level initially—because we are not caring for our vital energy the way we need to. The second interpretation flows from the ground covered by the Hanged Man: a part of ourselves has died off in whatever manner so that something new can come into being. Another way to think about this is with the image of inward or outward directed forces. For a new inward directed force emanating from the stellar, lunar, or solar realms to be brought into our field of existence, an equal and opposite outward force should be departing from us into one of these realms. When reversed, we find an unhealthy fear of Death that ironically keeps us from releasing what is ready to be released.

What is dying back right now and in need of attention?

Magical Techniques: candles/oil lamps, magical words/prayers/petitions, physical manipulation, spraying/washing/spitting/asperging, textile magic, and spirit work

Temperance. Be patient with yourself; focus on reciprocity and balance. This card encourages special attention be paid to what you eat and drink in order to ensure they are truly nourishing. This is especially valid if you work in service to others. Reversed, the Temperance card indicates harmful excess that is creating problems in other areas of life.

What are you giving, and what are you receiving?

Whom do you serve and what do you do, but most importantly, how do you replenish yourself?

Magical Techniques: sacred vessels, magical words/prayers/petitions, and spraying/washing/spitting/asperging

The Devil. Here we have the adversary, challenger, and trickster all rolled into one. The Devil confronts us on whatever it is we say matters most, asking us if it really does and what we are willing to do to protect ourselves and our beloveds. This card also speaks to chains . . . those we find ourselves bound in by external forces, old stories, outmoded ideas or behaviors. The secret is we can free ourselves whenever we are ready to do so. Reversed, the Devil signals we are ensnared by our own actions/attitude.

What or who is holding you back?

What attitudes and beliefs have kept you in chains for way too long?

When will you choose to break them?

Magical Techniques: candles/oil lamps, magical words/prayers/petitions, physical manipulation, and textile magic

The Tower. This card speaks of the dismantling of one dream or way of being so that another can be built. It reminds us that there is treasure in the ruins if only we will take the time to look. Reversed, the Tower card indicates our focus is exclusively on what feels broken to the exclusion of what is—and could be—blessed.

Will we see clearly by the light of a burning bridge, and will we make changes so that the next thing that we build is truly amazing?

Magical Techniques: candles/oil lamps, spraying/washing/spitting/asperging, textile magic, and spirit work

The Star. Alignment is the key idea with this card. The Star reminds us we are best able to open to empowerment when all the parts of ourselves are in communication and relationship. This card can also indicate consulting our natal charts is a smart idea for more insight when it comes to safeguarding our vitality. Reversed, the Star advises us to pause and reorient ourselves with where we are and what we want.

How can we make our actions line up with our thoughts and our thoughts line up with our words?

Magical Techniques: spraying/washing/spitting/asperging and spirit work

The Moon. The Moon celebrates and honors female and goddess–based mysteries. It speaks to cultivating a healthy and wise relationship around fears and understanding the relationship between necessity (herself an ancient goddess) and desire. Reversed, the Moon tells us our emotional body has become imbalanced with everything else and requires a course correction.

What have my fears taught me, and how might I honor them as teachers?

Magical Techniques: sacred vessels, magical words/prayers/petitions, and spraying/washing/spitting/asperging

The Sun. Your time to shine has arrived. Be free and embrace all possibilities and potential and fall into the changes that are occurring on every level. Deep and divine truths are soon to be revealed. A new possibility—perhaps even a new physical child—is about to come into being. Finally, gifts of prophecy often come with this card. Reversed, the Sun expresses we are intentionally ignoring something because looking at it directly is too painful.

What do I need to see?

Magical Techniques: candles/oil lamps, magical words/prayers/petitions, and spirit work

Judgement. Above all else this is a card of resurrection. We go through the Hanged Man, Death, and the Tower, and like a snake we shed, shed, shed, and give much of ourselves away. When we reach the penultimate card in the tarot, the indication is that something within us we previously thought was lost forever has been resurrected and revivified, but like all mysteries it is not what it was when we last encountered it. Reversed, the Judgement card asks us to be more discerning and/or to finally and fully emerge from the psychic underworld.

What has been resurrected for you and integrated into your life in a new and different way?

Magical Technique: spirit work

The World. This is the card that says we have opened ourselves truly to the benevolent, empowering forces of the cosmos. We all do this in slightly different ways, but when the World shows up in an advantageous position, the indication is we are now in right relationship. However, if this card emerges in a reading and is reversed, it may be telling us the concerns of the world are playing too heavy a role in our life and this needs to be reevaluated.

Remember a time in your life when you were sure you were in right relationship: what did that look and feel like, and is there any area where you experience that today?

Magical Techniques: sacred vessels, lodestones, candles/oil lamps, magical words/prayers/petitions, physical manipulation, spraying/washing/spitting/asperging, textile magic, and spirit work

Court Cards

King and Queen of Coins. There is a need to connect to family members, ancestors, and history. Personal history, world history, history of place—any or all of these are relevant now. Roots are the focus and the path through which you will find an ability to open to empowerment and safeguard your vitality. Folkloric forms of all kinds are appropriate here. Reversed, either of these cards indicate a rupture with or in your lineage is poised to cause complications.

What does my past and ancestry teach me about safeguarding what is precious and opening to empowerment?

Magical Techniques: sacred vessels, lodestones, physical manipulation, and textile magic

Knight of Coins. This Knight points to a pregnant pause, catching your breath and celebrating all that you have accomplished. Reversed, he tells us a refusal to pause or take stock is creating issues.

What gifts has my journey brought me thus far?

Magical Techniques: sacred vessels and lodestones

Page of Coins. The key question for this card is: what piece is missing? Specifically, we want to know what is needed so that you feel nurtured, grounded, and centered in the world. Reversed, the Page of Coins tells us there is a refusal to see that something is missing and that is creating an issue.

How might I fully support myself in the work I am doing now?

Magical Technique: lodestones

King and Queen of Swords. Now is the time to get clarity around your work and your vision. Thinking about the future and what kind of a future you want to invoke is essential at this point, as is surrounding yourself with like-minded people who will collaborate with you in a million delicious ways. Reversed, either of these cards reminds us that cutting off our rational thinking from our deep feelings leads to nothing but error.

What is the best strategy for me at this time, and who are my allies?

Magical Techniques: magical words/prayers/petitions and spirit work

Knight of Swords. He shows up to help you cut through the muck and drama and get to whatever is essential. In some cases, the Knight of Swords will also help you get free from the stuff that is holding you down. Reversed, the message is to slow down, look before you leap, and not drain yourself of vitality.

What needs to be freed up?

Magical Technique: magical words/prayers/petitions

Page of Swords. The vision of the future is unclear and foggy. Return to your basic principles, your *telos* (ultimate purpose), so that you can move forward with decisiveness and cohesion. Reversed, the indication is now is the time to make a plan.

What is my fundamental purpose in this work?

Magical Technique: magical words/prayers/petitions

King and Queen of Wands. It's time to get fierce and let your passion unfold! This is the moment to take risks, to lay it all out and know that like-minded supporters have your back if you should trip or fall. Adventure and alchemy unite! Reversed, either of these cards indicate energetic leakages and a loss of vitality.

What do I burn for?

Magical Techniques: candles/oil lamps, magical words/prayers/petitions, and spirit work

Knight of Wands. This card points to dealing with small fears and other leg traps that seek to keep you from going in the direction you need to go and doing the work you need to do. You possess the endurance and courage to carry on even when in doubt. Reversed, this card signals a refusal to nourish your creative impulses is closing a road.

When and why do I hesitate?

Magical Techniques: candles/oil lamps and spirit work

Page of Wands. The Page of Wands suggests looking for creativity/satisfaction/love/fill-in-the blank in all the wrong places. By focusing on the external as opposed to the internal, you are stalling yourself out because you keep competing with some invisible competitor. Reversed, the indication is you are exhausted and need to replenish yourself in every way.

What leaves me feeling dry and devitalized?

Magical Technique: spraying/washing/spitting/asperging

King and Queen of Cups. These monarchs express diving deep, going into the dark and scary places to look for treasure, spiritual intensity, and bringing your magical and intuitive gifts into the world. You knowing you have the blessing and support of like-minded people and spirit work to assist you in your sacred endeavors. Reversed, either of these cards can indicate emotional difficulties or mental disequilibrium.

What is the current state of my intuitive knowing?

Magical Techniques: sacred vessels, spraying/washing/spitting/asperging, and spirit work

Knight of Cups. The Knight of Cups signifies blessing yourself and being blessed, spreading blessings out into the world, being a force of healing. When reversed, this card indicates a need to slow down and allow yourself to heal.

What blessing do I need in this moment?

Magical Techniques: sacred vessels and spraying/washing/spitting/asperging

Page of Cups. Thig card expresses ignoring or working with the inner voice when it starts leading you down a trail of frustration and depression. Reversed, the Page of Cups suggests taking some incorrect intuition as gospel truth.

What illusions or delusions do I need to particularly be on guard for?

Magical Technique: spraying/washing/spitting/asperging

Pips

Aces

Coins: Setting strong foundations for your work so that you have the freedom and space to really experience your power and energy

Where do I find rest?

Swords: A new venture, idea, understanding of opening to empowerment, and sovereignty, often found through combining forces with others

Who is an ally in this work?

Wands: Magic and alchemy are at work. Harness the energy now, and watch energy management, sexuality, passion, and creative fire all begin to speak to you.

What flame needs to be stoked?

Cups: Magical renewal and adventure

Where do I need to journey now?

Twos

Coins: Finding a way to create a conversation around practical concerns and emotional needs

What needs balance?

Swords: Setting boundaries is essential right now.

What do I stand for?

Wands: Ready to take the next step, time to let go of the past

What am I waiting for?

Cups: Working with partners and creating beauty and commitment

Whom do I love?

Threes

Coins: Collaborating with nonprofits, religious institutions, and other service organizations for the greater good

What might we build?

Swords: Heart hurts that must be healed in order for full magic and energy to come through

What wound still bleeds?

Wands: The ships you have sent out are returning to port, and they are loaded with blessings.

What blessed return is happening?

Cups: Sacred community, sisterhood/brotherhood, and support

What needs celebrating?

Fours

Coins: Holding back the heart of your vision and working out of fear. Choose love and let go.

What do I withhold that in turn limits me?

Swords: Acknowledging the past and the role it has played in your life and putting it in its proper resting place

What needs to be forgiven?

Wands: Strong ties to partner and community are a major source of mojo for you.

What ties must be strengthened?

Cups: Indecision is killing your vision and sucking out your life force. Get clear, get cohesive, and go forward.

What will I pursue?

Fives

Coins: Poverty, lack of resources, but also a lack of resourcefulness

What cannot be saved?

Swords: Sabotage, self-sabotage, and also being in an environment that is not supportive

What needs greater support?

Wands: Conflict—inner and outer—and again, not being supported by those around you

What requires clarity, purification, and peace?

Cups: Regrets, wishing things could be other than they are—the need to move energy away from that

What must be accepted?

Sixes

Coins: Equality, sharing, and in some cases sharing wealth with collaborators

What might I share?

Swords: The path is blocked but not so terribly. There just needs to be a slight refinement of vision and connecting to people who will help take you to the next level.

How might I open this road?

Wands: Victory, success, and starting to get recognized

What honors do I seek and why?

Cups: Someone from the past showing up and lending a helping hand

How can I help and be helped?

Sevens

Coins: Time to reap the harvest you have sown!

What is my yield?

Swords: What lies have you told? What lies have you believed?

What is my relationship to deception?

Wands: Feeling trapped—recognizing you can walk away and find freedom whenever you are ready

What trap have I agreed to?

Cups: Emotional highs and lows—accept them, roll with them, and if you need to seek help, do so.

Where do I stand with respect to my emotions?

Eights

Coins: Creating consistent awesomeness and storing up energy to boot!

Where am I consistent?

Swords: Surrounded by negative people and negative ideas to the point where you and your energy have been paralyzed and having a really hard time moving forward

How may I become free of this situation?

Wands: New information, potential, and desire to move. Go! Fly! Do it.

What have I learned?

Cups: You may need to relocate physically and/or metaphorically to free up some energy and really find your power.

Where do I need to go (or return) to?

Nines

Coins: Secure, satisfied, creating beauty and wealth with energy stored up for later too.

What is sovereignty?

Swords: Dreams are getting invaded; feelings of fear and anxiety need to be managed.

Where do I find peace?

Wands: Lack of vision, feeling stuck and not seeing clearly—don't give up!

What wound has been left untended?

Cups: Open, ready for the next big thing, energy and magic are flowing!

What wish do I have?

Tens

Coins: Solid foundations that allow you to leave legacies

What is my legacy?

Swords: Drained and dried up—find beauty, sources of inspiration, and joy now.

How might I best care for my chronic wound?

Wands: Effort is required of you (and possibly skill-building too), but you can do it!

How can I put forth my best effort?

Cups: Joyful family, finding energetic support for yourself and your work on all levels

What is my role within my family?

There are no further development tasks for this chapter—simply answer some or all of the questions posed throughout this section!

Magic-Making

Active Imagination Meditation to Uncover/Recover Your Intuition

The intention for this meditation is to recollect and recover your gift of intuition.

Cultivate Calmness

Feel your own breath—in and out, in and out.

Simply breathe regularly and allow your breath to gradually slow down.

Begin to notice the space between the in and out breath. Allow that space to grow until it surrounds you. All is calm. All is quiet.

Root and Rise

Take in a full and deep breath, and as you do so, see, sense, touch, know, hear, and feel the land underneath you.

See, sense, touch, know, hear, and feel your own body extending out and down, down into the topsoil, down into the bedrock, and the tangled roots of trees, down through the delicate webs of fungi, the layers of geologic time, down through root and stone and bone.

Down through the graves of your ancestors, your Beloved Dead who hold such love and wisdom for you. Root yourself down until you see, sense, touch, know, hear, and feel the presence of the earth's core, pulsing out its life-giving energy and vitality. Affirm and acknowledge that you participate in this energy, that it blesses you and that you, in turn, bless it.

Bring your awareness back to your breathing. On your next exhalation, bless, in gratitude, the earth and specifically the lands where you live and the creatures, seen and unseen, who form it.

As you are ready, on your next exhalation, see, sense, touch, know, hear, and feel that you are now fully rooted in the deep earth and at the same time extending your upper body up and out toward the heavens. Your body's energetic presence rises up, up through the tree branches, up through the clouds, up by the mountains, up through the atmosphere, up through the whispers of your descendants—all people who come after us and who hold a vision of what is possible and what is needed—up into vast space itself where you are surrounded by the very stuff you are made of: stars.

See, sense, touch, know, hear, and feel these stars surrounding you, pouring their light over and through you so that anything that needs to be soothed, healed, or mended is take care of at this time. Exhale a blessing on your future and the future you are dreaming into existence.

You are risen and rooted.

Breathe in a blessing on your blessed body: companion and ally, first altar and beloved friend who travels with you day in and day out. Exhale in gratitude: thank you.

Breathe in a blessing on the land where you live and all of the creatures, seen and unseen, who dwell upon and within it. Exhale in gratitude: thank you.

Breathe in a blessing on your beloveds, those who bring a smile to your face and softness to your heart. Exhale in gratitude: thank you.

Breathe in a blessing on your unique path and all of the many ways you travel it. Exhale in gratitude: thank you.

Go into your sacred space and get into a position that is comfortable for you.

See, sense, touch, know, hear, and feel that it is dusk, a magical and in-between time. The sun is setting but has not completely gone down, and you begin to walk toward the west. As you walk, take note of your surroundings and especially prick up your ears to hear sounds beneath the earth's surface. You may hear the wind through the trees or an owl preparing to hunt for the night.

Continue walking until you hear the sound of an underground river flowing over root, rock, and stone. When you hear this, pause for a moment and notice that wherever you are you are standing in the middle of a four-way crossroads.

Since ancient times the crossroads have been a place of magic and decision-making. This evening your decision is this: will you open up to your inner knowing, your soul-deep wisdom and your ability to see beyond the veils?

Think on the question seriously and do not answer it too quickly. You may not be ready to take the plunge and that's OK. You can come back here. But if you are ready, knowing full well that your life will change and never be the same, take another step to the west.

Looking down, you realize you were standing at the source of the underground river, and you know in your heart and see in your mind that this river is actually your own intuition flowing underneath and through the surface of your life. Now notice what the source of this river looks like.

Is it clogged with rocks or debris?

Has it been dammed up or blocked?

Did someone pour concrete on it?

Are there animals around the source or sacred plants growing nearby?

Are there fish or aquatic creatures in the water?

Take a few moments now to do some cleanup and housekeeping around your source. If it's been clogged or blocked, pull the debris out. If it's been covered in concrete, break that concrete up and move it out. The waters of intuition can only run as deep and pure as your source.

Note how your body feels at this time.

Note how your heart feels: sad, heavy, betrayed, angry?

Breathe it out into the earth all around you.

Once you have done your upkeep around the river source, you see that you have created a beautiful reflecting pond and in your left hand there is a silver chalice.

Dip it into the pool and drink its sweet waters under the moonlight.

Close your eyes.

Take a breath and kiss it up to your crown, then open your eyes.

As you are ready, acknowledge that it is time for this journey to come to an end, but you may return here anytime you wish.

Breathe in a blessing on your unique path and all of the many ways you travel it. Exhale in gratitude: thank you.

Breathe in a blessing on your beloveds, those who bring a smile to your face and softness to your heart. Exhale in gratitude: thank you.

Breathe in a blessing on the land where you live and all of the creatures, seen and unseen, who dwell upon and within it. Exhale in gratitude: thank you.

Breathe in a blessing on your blessed body: companion and ally, first altar and beloved friend who travels with you day in and day out. Exhale in gratitude: thank you.

As you are ready, bring your awareness to the room you are in. Allow your eyes to gently open if they have been closed. Feel the weight of the air on your skin, and allow yourself to stretch and move in any ways that feel good and useful.

Conclusion:
The Magic in Your Hands

Once upon a time, there was sight and there was vision. And there were those who knew the difference.

Throughout this book, we have journeyed together through the landscapes of tarot—not just as images on cardstock, but as doorways to action, transformation, and magic. We began with questions: Will it be OK? How will it be OK? And we have discovered, card by card, that the answers have always resided in the space between seeing and doing.

Remember when we started?

I spoke of blind seers who, lacking physical sight, developed profound vision. I spoke of divination as the telling of a story. And now, as we come to the close of our journey together, I want you to hear this:

You are not just the reader of the story. You are its writer.

This is the magic that our ancestors knew. This is the wisdom that was fractured, hidden, and now reclaimed. Divination was never meant to be a passive acceptance of fate, a grim nodding at inevitable outcomes. It was always meant to be a conversation, a negotiation, an invitation to cocreate with the forces that shape our lives.

The cards remember this. And now, so do you.

When you lay out some cards, you're not just looking at pictures. You're not just nodding at symbols. You're receiving a map, yes, but more importantly, you're being handed tools. The Tower that appears is not just a warning of destruction; it's an invitation to controlled demolition. The Death card is not just an ending; it's a doorway to transformation that you can step through deliberately, with purpose and power.

There is a profound difference between those who merely see the cards and those who vision through them into action, between those who receive readings and those who make magic with what has been revealed.

You now stand among the latter.

Will it be OK?

That depends on what you do next. On the candle you light, the water you bless, the boundary you set, the offering you make, the conversation you have, the silence you keep, the threshold you cross. On whether you remember that magic isn't something you wait for, but something you make.

How will it be OK?

By your hands. By your belief. By your magic.

The ancient connection between divination and practical magic wasn't lost by accident. It was severed intentionally—because people who can both see clearly and act powerfully are not easily controlled. People who understand that fate is just a starting point, not a conclusion, tend to change the world around them.

As you close this book and return to your cards, remember: the images may be traditional, but the magic you make with them is one-of-a-kind. The spreads may be conventional, but the enchantments you cast from them will be uniquely yours. The symbols may be universal, but the actions you take will be singular, personal—perhaps even revolutionary.

There is sight, and there is vision. One shows you what is. The other reveals what could be.

And the magic? The magic is in the distance between the two, in the steps you take to transform one into the other.

That magic is, and really has always been, in your hands.

Go make it.

Well-Resourced:

The Making Tarot Magic Spread, Prayers, and Blessings

The Basic Making Tarot Magic Spread

Once upon a time, there was the question and the ones who asked it—the seekers, the wonderers, the ones standing at crossroads both seen and unseen.

This is a spread for them and for you: for anyone who knows that seeing clearly is only the beginning of magic.

Card 1: The Mirror

This card reflects the current situation as it truly stands.

Sometimes the Mirror confirms what you already know in your bones: yes, this relationship is ending; yes, this opportunity has real potential; yes, this fear is founded.

But sometimes . . . sometimes the Mirror shows you what your eyes have been sliding past: The assumption that isn't true. The information that's been twisted. The story you've been telling yourself that's more comfort than truth.

Look deeply into this card. Does it match what you believe about your situation? If not, pause here. Breathe. There's something you've been missing.

Card 2: The Stone in the Path

Every journey has its obstacles. This card reveals yours.

This is not just any challenge, but the challenge—the one that stands most firmly between you and what you seek, the one that must be faced or navigated around or transformed entirely.

This is the stone in your path. Name it. Know it. Only then can you decide how to move forward.

Card 3: The Horizon

If you continue walking as you are, this is where you'll arrive.

The Horizon shows the natural unfolding of current energies without intervention. This is not fate carved in stone; this is trajectory—the river flowing along its current path.

If the Horizon pleases you, wonderful! If it troubles you, take heart. The next card holds the key to changing course.

Card 4: The Key

This is where magic enters.

The Key reveals both practical actions and magical workings that can shift your trajectory. It might point to candles that need lighting, conversations that need having, boundaries that need setting, or offerings that need making.

This card doesn't just tell you what to do; it reveals the energy that needs addressing. Your own magic and wisdom will tell you how best to work with it.

Remember: the cards don't make magic; you do. They simply show you where to direct your considerable powers.

The cards remember. And so do you.

Prayers and Blessings I Have Found Helpful

All prayers and blessings are written by me unless otherwise noted; feel free to work with them in your own practices so long as credit is given.

To Open Sacred Space

> By the Earth of my body, by the Air of my breath, by the Fire of my spirit, and by the Water of my blood, the circle is cast, allies called, and the work is blessed. As above so below, as within so without, and so it shall be, amen.

To Close Sacred Space

> Go out.
>
> Be blessed.
>
> And be blessings in turn!

Before a Reading or Divinatory Session

Blessed Ones, thank you for the earth beneath our feet, the sky above our heads, the breath running through our bodies, and the blood running through our veins. We ask that you give us eyes to see, ears to hear, and hearts to know the right path to follow with wisdom and discernment. And so it is.

You may say this as an opening prayer before doing a reading for yourself or someone else, but you may also say this as a way to energize any divination tool you work with.

Full-Body Blessing

Blessed be my feet that walk upon Her face.

Blessed be my knees that bow before His grace.

Blessed be my sex/womb origin of creative power.

Blessed by my heart for it is love's bower.

Blessed be my lips may they tell the stories true.

Blessed be my eyes as they perceive what my heart already knew.

Blessed be my mind and the workings there within.

Blessed be my ancestors, may they guide me from here until the end.

May I go in beauty.

May I work in peace.

May I walk in wisdom.

As I will it so shall it be.

When I perform this blessing, I touch each part of the body referenced. If I perform it for someone else, I ask their permission to lightly touch each part of their body that is mentioned, and if I receive it, then I do so. You could also hold your hands over someone else's body without physically touching them if that is more comfortable to you. When it comes to the ancestors, I place my hands about four inches above my head and then bring them to my heart.

For Banishing

I banish thee, I banish thee!

I send thee out and set you free!

To dwell in water, air, and stone.

And never in my house do roam!

You may change house to whatever is appropriate, e.g., car, flat, office.

Acknowledgments

DURING THE WRITING OF THIS book two events occurred that have had a deep impact in my life. The first is that my oldest child went partially blind. So my first bow of gratitude goes to my son Jasper for showing me in the starkest way possible the differences between sight and vision and inspiring me with his immense talent, work ethic, and courage. I love you so much and am so proud of you.

The second event was the death of my maternal grandmother, Nana, who, as a Bible-loving Baptist, knew that there was always a prayer to help improve any situation. She was one of the finest and kindest Sacred Artists I've ever met.

David Saussy, dad, husband, work partner, and teacher extraordinaire.... I haven't quite figured out what you can't do and I love you more every day.

Thanks to Heath Saussy, my little firecracker who knows more about creatures than anyone I have ever met and is the best fellow prayer-maker, altar-creator, and magic-lover to have by my side!

Mom and Dad, thank you for always having my back, babysitting the grandkids, and reminding me to have fun.

To my sister Brittany, thank you for teaching me how to make the hard holy.

Thank you to Lindsey Smith, my agent for handling the dealmaking and logistics, to Alexandra Franzen for introducing me to Lindsey, sending me gorgeous pictures of Hawaii, and being a brilliant friend and sounding board for over a decade! Thanks to Theresa Reed, aka The Tarot Lady, for introducing me to Weiser and being my best business buddy, confidant, and advisor ... and for writing a foreword to this book that had me tearing up. Thank you to Kathryn Sky-Peck for looking at my early scribblings and seeing a book and making it so! Thank you to Amy Lyons for the just-right editorial magic!

cat yronwode, Natalie Goldberg, Dr. Clarissa Pinkola Estes, R.J. Stewart, and Anastacia Nutt have all been generous teachers, and I have learned much from working with each of them—thank you, dear ones.

Thanks to Jordan Delaney, the best fitness buddy and fellow mom sister I could ever ask for.

Thanks to Roxana Zirakzadeh, my sister from another mister, the Persian Sandstorm to my Texas tornado . . . I love you!

Dr. Marion Cook for talking to birds and plants as much as I do and normalizing our completely wild behavior . . . I adore you.

Thanks to Terri Windling for filling the world with gorgeous words and art.

Thanks to Myra Krien for always reminding me to dance!

Thanks to Elizabeth Barrial, for being cool if I disappear for two years and then text about life, work, and kids like not a moment of time passed.

Thanks to Jacquelyn Tierney for art, design, and shooting for the stars brilliance!

Thank you to my students, clients, and community of soulful seekers, many of whom have been with me year in and year out. I love you all and am honored to serve you. This one is very for much for y'all.

Finally, thank you to my ancestors and descendants—those who come before and those who will come after. May I safeguard your wisdom and be inspired by your brilliance.

About the Author

Danielle Cohen

BRIANA SAUSSY is an author, storyteller, teacher, spiritual counselor, and founder of the Sacred Arts Academy, where she teaches magic, divination, ceremony, and other sacred arts for everyday life. She is well-grounded in the world's great religious and intellectual traditions, as well as Western psychological practices. She holds a BA and MA in Eastern and Western classics, philosophy, mathematics, and science and is a student of ancient Greek and Sanskrit. Briana's work has been featured in *The Paris Review, Yoga Journal, Enchanted Living*, and more. Visit her online at *brianasaussy.com*.

To Our Readers

Weiser Books, an imprint of Red Wheel/Weiser, publishes books across the entire spectrum of occult, esoteric, speculative, and New Age subjects. Our mission is to publish quality books that will make a difference in people's lives without advocating any one particular path or field of study. We value the integrity, originality, and depth of knowledge of our authors.

Our readers are our most important resource, and we appreciate your input, suggestions, and ideas about what you would like to see published.

Visit our website at *www.redwheelweiser.com*, where you can learn about our upcoming books and free downloads, and also find links to sign up for our newsletter and exclusive offers.

You can also contact us at *info@rwwbooks.com* or at

Red Wheel/Weiser, LLC
65 Parker Street, Suite 7
Newburyport, MA 01950

Magical Techniques: candles/oil lamps, magical words/prayers/petitions, physical manipulation, textile magic, and spirit work

Intentions: clarity/wisdom, success/mastery, protection, healing, cursing/reversing, ending, loss/removal, stability, and banishing

Death. This card marks the ending of a job or career and the need to look for new work and a new beginning. It could be a physical death that dramatically affects the querent and the workplace. Or, it could be the "death" of jobs in the forms of cuts and layoffs just like the Hanged Man. This card can also, in the right context, indicate the querent is in a position to make a significant amount of money, to "harvest" seeds they have sown long ago. The presence of this card may also remind the querent they need to pay special attention to the other inevitability of life: taxes! When in a reversed position, Death often suggests the querent or those around them are refusing to let something die that needs to go in order for something new to come in.

Magical Techniques: candles/oil lamps, spraying/washing/spitting/asperging, textile magic, and spirit work

Intentions: clarity/wisdom, blessing, protection, healing, cursing/reversing, ending, loss/removal, and banishing

Temperance. Patience, especially when waiting for promotion; work-life balance; boundary-setting; sincere reciprocity among colleagues and supervisors—these are just some of the themes we find in the Temperance card. Depending on the context, this card can indicate the querent would do well to get involved in the food or beverage industry. Sometimes Temperance, like the Sun, can signal fertility/pregnancy will have an outsized effect on career and work. In a challenging or reversed position the card may indicate issues with drugs, alcohol, prescription meds, or other mind- and mood-altering substances are becoming problematic at work, either for the querent or a colleague/supervisor.

Magical Techniques: sacred vessels, spraying/washing/spitting/asperging, textile magic, and spirit work

Intentions: clarity/wisdom, blessing, protection, healing, stability, and cleansing

The Devil. When the Devil shows up, he can indicate the querent feels tied to a bad job or finds themselves in a toxic workplace situation. When it comes to career, this card suggests the querent feels stuck and also not free to make a